C000180713

Body 115

Body 115

The mystery of the last Victim of the King's Cross Fire

PAUL CHAMBERS

WILEY

Published in 2007 by   John Wiley & Sons, Ltd, The Atrium, Southern Gate
Chichester, West Sussex, PO19 8SQ, England
Phone (+44) 1243 779777

Copyright © 2007   Paul Chambers

Email (for orders and customer service enquires): cs-books@wiley.co.uk
Visit our Home Page on www.wiley.co.uk or www.wiley.com

Other Wiley Editorial Offices

John Wiley & Sons, Inc. 111 River Street, Hoboken, NJ 07030, USA

Jossey-Bass, 989 Market Street, San Francisco, CA 94103-1741, USA

Wiley-VCH Verlag GmbH, Pappellaee 3, D-69469 Weinheim, Germany

John Wiley & Sons Australia, Ltd, 33 Park Road, Milton, Queensland, 4064, Australia

John Wiley & Sons (Asia) Pte Ltd, 2 Clementi Loop #02-01, Jin Xing Distripark, Singapore
129809

John Wiley & Sons Canada Ltd, 22 Worcester Road, Etobicoke, Ontario, Canada,
M9W 1L1

Wiley also publishes its books in a variety of electronic formats. Some content that appears
in print may not be available in electronic books.

CIP catalogue records for this book are available from the British Library and the US Library
of Congress

ISBN-13   978-0-470-01808-8 (HB)
ISBN-10   0-470-01808-9 (HB)

Typeset in 10.5/13.5pt Photina by MCS Publishing Services Ltd, Salisbury, Wiltshire.
Printed and bound in Great Britain by T.J. International, Padstow, Cornwall.
This book is printed on acid-free paper responsibly manufactured from sustainable forestry
in which at least two trees are planted for each one used for paper production.
10 9 8 7 6 5 4 3 2

Contents

Acknowledgements

I am deeply indebted to the following people for their assistance during the preparation of this book: Craig Goldman, Tim Haines, Ken Hines, Jasper James, Jim Kennedy, Monika Kosicka, Janet Richardson, Laura Scougall, Chester Stern, Matthew Taylor, Hélène Vantours, Kathy Wilson and Robin Young. I am especially grateful to Detective Chief Superintendent Nick Bracken, Superintendent Philip Trendall and Inspector Ian Wilkinson of the British Transport Police for their help and advice and most especially for agreeing to review a copy of the draft manuscript. Likewise, I am very grateful to Mary and Andrew Leishman and their relations for their help in the latter stages of preparing the manuscript and for their comments on its content. A number of other people also helped but have asked that they remain anonymous; I thank them also.

I am also grateful to the staff at the following institutions and companies who answered all my enquiries with diligence and patience: Addenbrooke's Hospital, British Association for Immediate Care (BASICS), BBC Scotland, Bodleian Library, the British Library, British Newspaper Library, Cambridge University Library, Cruciform Library (University College Hospital), Department for Transport, D.M.S. Watson Science Library (University College London), Eastman Dental Institute (London), Family Records Centre, Grampian Police Headquarters, Hertfordshire Library Services, *Horncastle News*, Impossible Pictures, Institute for Historical Research, ITN Archive, IPM TV Ltd., Lincolnshire Coroner's Office, Nottinghamshire Coroner's Office, Scottish

National Archives, Society of Genealogists, the National Archives: Public Record Office and *The Times* newspaper.

I should like to offer a big thank you to my agent, Sugra Zaman, for her continued sterling efforts on my behalf and to Sally Smith and others at John Wiley and Sons, Kate Santon and MCS Publishing Services for their professionalism, outstanding patience and good humour. This book could not have been written without the moral support of my family, especially my parents and John and Elizabeth Baxter, all of whom selflessly gave up their own time in order to help me. Finally, the biggest thank you of all goes to my wife Rachel and daughter Eleanor who always manage to soothe away the stresses and strains associated with long days in front of a word processor. I love you both, always and forever.

The information contained within this book came from sources that are in the public domain or from interviews given to the author. A draft version of the manuscript was reviewed, commented on and approved by senior police officers associated with the Body 115 investigation and also by immediate members of Alexander Fallon's family.

Introduction

For sixteen years a pauper's grave in a north London cemetery held a mystery that resolutely defied solution. Buried there was an unknown man who had the misfortune to be in London's King's Cross Underground Station on 18 November 1987. That night a fireball swept through the booking hall killing thirty-one people and injuring many others. The unknown man's body was recovered but the intensity of the heat had reduced him to a charred mass; anything that could be used to establish his identity, such as clothes or a wallet, had been destroyed. In the absence of a name, the unknown man became known as Body 115, taken from the number on his mortuary tag. Police officers were quickly able to identify the fire's thirty other victims, but Body 115 remained anonymous.

Set against the backdrop of one of London's worst tragedies, this book tells Body 115's incredible story and that of the small group of people that battled to find his name and next of kin. With only a handful of forensic details and eyewitness statements, a dedicated police team was able to piece together a picture of Body 115's life. Then, using detective skills and the latest scientific techniques, the team set about tracing his identity. It was a prolonged and convoluted investigation that produced moments of revelation and, all too frequently, feelings of despair when promising leads fell to pieces.

The hunt for Body 115's name is a tale with many twists and turns. It showcases the miracles of modern forensic science but also delves into the shadowy world of missing persons and the frustrations of searching for an anonymous man amongst a legion of people who have chosen to distance themselves from main-stream society. The police alone devoted more than 6000 working hours to the mystery, and on a number of occasions believed that they were close to a solution only to have their hopes dashed. At times a variety of other experts became involved, including pathologists, forensic scientists, fingerprint specialists, medical artists, surgeons and many others, but all too often they also found themselves defeated.

Body 115's story offers an insight into a field of police work that the public rarely gets to see. It details the problems that face the authorities in the aftermath of a major disaster and shows how a combination of dogged determination and scientific deduction can be used to overcome an apparently insurmountable problem. It is a detective story for our times.

CHAPTER ONE

Flashover

It began with a thoughtless act. At around 7.25 p.m. on Wednesday 18 November 1987, a day that had hitherto been quite unremarkable, an anonymous passenger using London's King's Cross Underground Station boarded the upward-moving escalator taking people from the Piccadilly Line platforms to the large booking hall area above. On seeing that there were few other people around, the passenger took out a cigarette and put it in his or her mouth. A match was struck and the cigarette lit. The redundant match was dropped to the ground.[1]

Countless numbers of lit matches have been dropped in the London Underground; almost all have fallen to the floor where they harmlessly burned themselves out or were extinguished by the feet of other passengers, but on this occasion the discarded match did not conform to that pattern. By chance, it fell from the hands of its owner and passed through a gap of less than a centimetre between the escalator's moving steps and its side panel. Beneath this narrow gap is the running track, a shallow trench that contains part of the escalator's machinery. The burning match landed in a layer of grease, fluff and litter that had built up around the moving chains, cogs and wheels. The detritus was highly flammable and ignition occurred as soon as the match touched it; a small fire was created and it began to spread further along the running track.

Two minutes later, at around 7.27 p.m., a Northern Line Underground train arrived at King's Cross, bringing with it several dozen passengers. Among them was Philip Squire, a young man from north London who was travelling to meet a girlfriend. Squire walked towards the platform's exit and began to head up towards the surface which involved a short escalator journey to a wide concourse area and, from there, a ride on the much longer Piccadilly Line escalator up to the central booking hall. Squire recalls that everything seemed normal until he was about two-thirds of the way to the top of the Piccadilly Line escalator, at which point he spotted a small wisp of smoke emanating from underneath one of the wooden treads ahead of him.

'It was curving over the top of the step and coming towards me,' recounts Squire. 'At first I thought it was a cigarette, but I looked between the end of the step and the panel on the right-hand side and saw a ball of sparks which was very intense. Within seconds the smoke had increased. On seeing this, I jumped over the three steps ahead of me, and by then I was close to the top.'

A few steps below Squire was Debbie Wren, a young secretary returning home from work. As she travelled upwards her feet seemed unnaturally hot but she initially dismissed the feeling. 'This is crazy,' she thought to herself, 'I must be imagining it.' She looked down and saw what appeared to be a red light under the escalator. As though hypnotised, she watched for several seconds before realising that the glow was being produced by a naked flame. At the same instant she detected the faint but unmistakable smell of smoke. Her brain made the connection, and she knew that there was a fire beneath the escalator.

Debbie remembers that she began to push the person standing in front of her. 'The escalator is on fire,' she said and added, with her voice rising in panic, 'we've got to get off!' Her words had some effect and the orderly queue of people standing on the right of the moving staircase began to push upwards. Within seconds, and to her relief, Debbie found herself in the booking hall area. Ahead of her was Philip Squire who was already making his way to the excess fare window of the booking office. 'Excuse me,' he said to a male clerk, 'but I think that there's a fire starting on the escalator.'

The clerk came out of his office and walked with Squire to the top of the Piccadilly Line escalator which was still disgorging passengers into the booking hall. Debbie watched Squire and the clerk and, satisfied that the situation was in hand, exited through the ticket barrier. Squire remained in the booking hall for a short while as he wanted to make sure that his warning had been taken seriously. A few seconds later he heard somebody shout 'Clear the escalator!' and, happy that the fire was being attended to, he walked through the convoluted, concrete-lined passageway that led into King's Cross train station.[2]

At 7.30 p.m. Derek Newman, the ticket clerk Squire had alerted, found himself standing at the top of the burning escalator trying to spot the flames. He could see nothing out of the ordinary, but as he stood there a passenger stepping off the escalator caught his attention and told him that there was a fire beneath the stairs. Mr Newman walked back to his booth and made a telephone call to the station's safety inspector, a man named Christopher Hayes.

As he did so another passenger, Abdeslam Karmoun, had been alerted to the danger after seeing smoke rising through the escalator slats. Mr Karmoun was concerned enough to press the emergency stop button at the top of the staircase. He shouted to the passengers below that there was a fire and instructed them to get off as soon as possible. Many were less than amused that Karmoun had stopped the escalator and few took any notice of his warning. Even though the escalator was now stationary, passengers continued to join it at the bottom.[3]

One of these, Olive Capes, instantly sensed that something was wrong. She recalls moving forward two or three steps before sensing danger and recoiling backwards. Her unusual behaviour attracted the attention of other passengers: 'I felt foolish as people coming down the far escalator were laughing.' Olive found another way up to the booking hall where she started to warn people about the fire. 'This is going to blow,' she shouted. 'We have got to get out!'[4]

This commotion was ignored by other passengers but it did draw the attention of two members of the British Transport Police, Constables Terry Bebbington and Kenneth Kerbey, who were on duty in the booking hall area. They moved across to the escalator to see what the problem was. There they were joined by Safety Inspector Hayes, who had responded promptly to Newman's phone call, and a further London Underground staff member who had been alerted by the fuss.

For some reason Hayes and the other staff member were under the impression that the fire was not on the Piccadilly Line escalator but was elsewhere in the station and they went off to try and find it. In the meantime, Constable Bebbington took the downward-moving escalator adjacent to the one where the three passengers had reported seeing the fire. He was barely halfway down when he spotted a small stream of white smoke emerging from underneath the steps. As he looked a single flame, about eight centimetres in height, appeared at the far side of the escalator. It flickered and then disappeared again.

Constable Bebbington acted immediately and ran back up to the booking hall. His priority was to alert the emergency services to the fact that there was a fire inside King's Cross Underground Station. Unfortunately his police radio did not work below ground and so he was forced to make the long journey up to street level, wasting precious time. Standing on the steps leading to Euston Road he radioed his headquarters and asked them to alert the London Fire Brigade. The fire was, he said, only a minor one.

The time was 7.32 p.m. and as Bebbington made the call people were pushing past him in an attempt to get to the booking hall. Minutes later some of these same people would emerge again, their clothes and skin burned and blackened. Some would not emerge at all, or at least would not emerge alive.

Inside the station Constable Kerbey stopped the remaining two Piccadilly Line escalators and tried to divert people away from them. His efforts were in vain; even though the smoke from the fire was evident, it did not stop passengers from boarding the halted escalators. A businessman in a suit who had just reached the top of the escalator started shouting down to those below him 'Don't get on this thing. There's a fire on it somewhere. Get back!'

At the bottom a woman also saw the danger. She too started shouting at her fellow passengers. 'Don't go up there!' she cried, 'it's on fire! It's dangerous!' After being ignored, she tugged at people's arms, trying to stop them from boarding the escalator. They shrugged her off and with blank, forward-staring faces continued on their way, seemingly ignorant of the danger. Neither she, nor policeman Kerbey who was nearby, could understand why people were ignoring the blatant danger ahead; one member of staff was even pushed to the ground when trying to stop a businessman from boarding the burning escalator. [5]

Journalist Roger Highfeld was one of those who heard the warnings but nonetheless continued his journey. 'I was unconcerned by the slight smell of smoke,' he said. 'Like other commuters, I was on autopilot, seeking the route of minimum effort on my way home. The escalator on the right was being roped off so we started walking down the central, disabled escalator. It was full of commuters slowly walking down to the Piccadilly Line platforms. Some, like myself, gazed at the wooden escalator to our right and attempted, in vain, to link the smoky smell with fire.'

Like Highfeld, regular users of the London Underground are often so obsessed with getting to their final destination that they become oblivious to official instruction. To them, London Underground staff are often viewed as irritants whose advice and orders can be ignored. That night many passengers probably did not even hear the warnings of fire; they were focused on catching their usual trains home and if the Piccadilly Line escalators were the quickest way of getting there then that was the route that they would take, fire or not.

Constable Bebbington returned to the booking hall. His call to headquarters had alerted other police officers in the mainline train station, many of whom were coming into the Underground to see the scene for themselves. On entering the Tube station some officers remember being aware of light wisps of smoke and a faint smell of burning rubber. This was a sign that the situation was growing more serious.

Station Inspector Hayes, who had initially gone to the wrong part of the station, had found his way to the base of the Piccadilly Line escalators. He opened up the lower machine room that led underneath it but could not see any sign of a fire there. 'It must be in the upper machine room,' he said. On leaving the lower machine room, Hayes was joined by other members of staff and police. One had bought some emergency tape with him and, with some difficulty and protests from passengers, they managed to cordon off the bottom of the escalator. For good measure they dragged a small builder's skip from nearby to act as a barrier. Despite this, people were still boarding the escalators from the top end by the ticket office.

The grumbling passengers on the lower concourse were diverted to the Victoria Line escalators. These could only be reached by walking along a steep and narrow passageway that consisted of five flights of stairs, two right-angled corners and a hairpin bend. It was hardly ideal as an evacuation route, especially for the elderly or those with luggage or young children but, faced with no alternative exit routes, the staff had little choice. The passengers pouring from the Piccadilly and Northern Line platforms began taking the diversion where they joined those people leaving the Victoria Line platforms. All these people were coming out into the main booking hall only a matter of feet from the top of the burning Piccadilly Line staircase.[6]

It was 7.36 p.m. when the London Fire Brigade Station in Soho received a call from the British Transport Police informing them that there was a small fire in King's Cross Underground Station. Within seconds firefighters were scrambling into the duty tender. In the cab was Station Officer Colin Townsley; he activated the tender's siren before pulling into the busy street outside. Other fire engines were also on their way from stations in Clerkenwell and Manchester Square but, being closest, the Soho ones would be on the scene first.

Meanwhile, inside the station, Safety Inspector Hayes had found the seat of the fire. It was in the upper machine room of the Piccadilly Line escalator but the heat had become so intense that he could not get near to it. A railwayman brought Hayes a fire extinguisher but it was useless; the steps of the fifty-year-old escalator were wooden and highly flammable, allowing the flames to spread a considerable distance upwards. Smoke was beginning to billow, accumulating in the ceiling of the stairwell before being carried by the wind into the main ticket hall area.

Hayes abandoned the fire extinguisher and retreated from the machine room. On the surface the fire was now clearly visible. He was convinced that it could only be dealt with by the fire brigade but he was wrong: in the confusion he had forgotten that the escalator was fitted with a water sprinkler system. However, it too was old and could not automatically be triggered by heat or smoke detectors; it had to be operated using a manual switch. If someone had remembered to turn it on, then events that night might have turned out differently.

Hayes informed some of the police in the booking hall that the fire was beyond their control. The decision was taken to clear the station of people but none of those present were aware of the official evacuation procedure and so the plan progressed erratically. The police ordered the booking clerk to stop selling tickets and tried to get those people milling about the ticket barriers to leave via the street level exits. Many ignored the request and descended into the station instead. Even as some people were being forcibly herded towards the exits by the police, others continued to push their way against the flow to get into the station. As the booking hall began to fill with black smoke, a queue of people stood at the automatic ticket machines, still attempting to purchase tickets.

The police at last managed to cordon off the top entrance to the burning escalators, forcing those foolhardy enough to enter the station to use those of the Victoria Line. As a precaution London Transport Headquarters was asked to prevent any further Tube trains from stopping at King's Cross. It was hoped that this would stem the flow of people entering the station via the platforms, but it also meant that anyone stuck below could only exit the station via the booking hall.

At 7.42 p.m. Colin Townsley's fire engine stopped on Euston Road outside the exit to the Tube station. As they went down the steps Townsley and his colleagues were greeted by the sight of people rushing to get out of the station, some of them evidently in a state of agitation. Once inside the booking hall, the firefighters were privilege to a more worrying sight: on the far left, thick black smoke was pouring up from the burning escalator. It was beginning to fill the booking hall and they could feel heat from the blaze, even from several metres away. Passengers were still coming off the Victoria Line escalators, having been directed there by the police in the network of tunnels below.

Townsley and one of his deputies went over to the scene of the fire. From the top of the escalator they could see that the blaze had broken through to the surface. An area of flame about the size of a large cardboard box was licking at the handrails and the burning rubber was producing a pall of dark, toxic smoke.

Both men walked a little way down the adjacent escalator to get a better view. As they did so a Piccadilly Line train pulled into the westbound platform and let out around seventy passengers. Despite the obvious danger and the cordons, some of them attempted to use the burning escalator until they were shouted at by the two firefighters. Townsley recognised that he was dealing with a potentially serious situation. He ordered his colleagues to retire to the fire engine and wait for the arrival of a second vehicle that held their breathing apparatus.

'Radio headquarters,' Townsley said to his departing deputy. 'Tell them to prevent any more trains from stopping here and that we're going to need at least four engines to deal with this one.' As an afterthought he added: 'Tell them to get some ambulances here as well, I think we're going to need them.'

Townsley's firefighters obeyed their instructions and left the booking hall to await the arrival of their safety apparatus. The fire chief himself did not follow them back to the engine. He had apparently become alarmed at the number of people who were still entering the booking hall, both from the Victoria Line escalators and from street level.

The smoke was getting thicker and a smell of burning electrics pervaded the scene. Even the air itself was beginning to get oppressively hot, making it painful to breathe. Townsley could sense that mild panic was beginning to break out, and so he began marshalling people towards the exits while at the same time shouting at those entering the station to return to street level. Incredibly, some ignored him.

At 7.43 p.m., in the deepest level of the station, a Northern Line train pulled alongside the platform, stopped and opened its doors. A number of unsuspecting passengers got out, including Mark Silver, a salesman on his way home to Hertfordshire. 'As soon as I got off the train I could smell burning,' he later recounted, 'and then I saw the smoke coming round the exits. It was curling round the train.'

Other passengers were also aware of the danger but as Mark turned to get back into the carriage, the doors closed. The train did not leave the platform but just stood there, the driver obeying the rules: once the doors are shut and the train is ready to go, do not open them again.

Mark hammered on the doors trying to get the driver to open them again. Along the platform others were doing the same thing but it was hopeless. The signal went from red to green and the train pulled away. A woman screamed in panic and, disregarding the danger presented by the live rail, jumped onto the tracks, chasing the train into the tunnel, swearing at the driver and then shouting 'Let me in! Let me in!'

Those stranded on the platform began to rush towards the exit, vaulting up the steps in an effort to escape. Mark found himself on the lower concourse at the foot of the burning escalator where there was a police officer. He directed Mark towards the narrow diversionary passageway that would take him to the Victoria Line escalators. The smoke was getting thicker and, according to Mark, seemed to be spreading 'like an alien intelligence'.

After a couple of minutes of being squeezed with others in the narrow, winding passageway, Mark arrived at the bottom of the Victoria Line escalators. The overpowering smell of burning was starting to inspire panic and some people began to fight their way up the moving staircases, desperate to reach the street outside. Most of the others, including Mark, stood still, letting the escalator take them upwards to what they believed was the safety of the booking hall.

'As I slowly ascended,' recalled Mark, 'I could feel my legs burning. I looked up and saw the walls and ceiling sizzling but I was amazed to see that people were still descending on the downward track.' An even worse sight awaited him. The booking hall was filling with smoke, making it difficult to see where the exits were. 'There was shouting, screaming, panicking every-where. Yet to my amazement there were these passengers queuing for tickets – they were literally queuing for death! I can still see six of them now. Three were young lads with jeans, two were businessmen in suits and there was a young girl with brown hair.'

Mark was lucky. As a regular King's Cross commuter he knew how to navigate the passageways up to street level. Aware of the increasing levels of heat and smoke, he ploughed his way across the booking hall, through the ticket barriers and went instinctively to the right-hand tunnel that led directly into the mainline station. Panic-stricken, he ran up the steps and into King's Cross train station before collapsing onto the ground, gasping for breath.

Immediately behind Mark was Stephen Holt, a marketing director who remains shocked by his experience. 'It was very hot,' he recalls, 'At the top of the [Victoria Line] escalator, the heat was much thicker and denser. It seemed like burning rubber. It really got into the lungs. I put my jacket over my head and just wanted to get out as soon as possible.' The time was 7.44 p.m.

In the stifling booking hall, fire chief Colin Townsley had placed himself at the top of the Victoria Line escalator. He was shouting at people, directing them away from the fire and towards the exits. Also in the hall was Constable Stephen Hanson, who had been on the lower concourse below the Piccadilly Line escalator when he saw the fire leap upwards and start to burn the ceiling tiles. Alarmed by this, he had taken the Victoria Line escalator and was, like Townsley, trying to hurry people out of the booking hall.

The digital clock on the station wall clicked from 19:44 to 19:45. A few seconds later there came the sound of whooshing air from the direction of the burning escalator. Immediately afterwards a fireball exploded outwards from the staircase sending sheets of flame into the booking hall, causing the already hot air in there to ignite spontaneously. In less than a second the booking hall was ablaze, the fire spreading to wooden panelling, ceiling tiles, plastic ticket barriers and anything else that wasn't made of either metal or concrete. The fire had become what scientists call a 'flashover'.

The explosive nature and intense heat of a flashover means that few people who witness this phenomenon live to tell the tale. Philip Jones is an exception. He and a friend entered King's Cross Underground from street level a couple of minutes before the flashover occurred. As he reached the booking hall area he could see smoke in the air and realised that something was wrong.

'The smoke was not very dense,' said Jones, 'it was bluey white and smelled of a very mild camp fire. It was then that the temperature started to rise and two or three seconds later it was markedly up. The visibility improved. At just about this time the flow of hot air increased further and the temperature increased steadily, the white smoke was blown away and a brown oily smoke came from the direction of the Piccadilly and Northern Line escalators.'

Alarmed, Jones and his friend began to walk back towards the exit but before he did so, he glimpsed a lone firefighter standing in the booking hall: it was Colin Townsley. As they started along the tunnel they were suddenly engulfed in thick black smoke and the temperature began to rise even more alarmingly. With visibility reduced to zero, Jones and his friend were forced to find their way along the passageway using instinct. Eventually they reached the steps leading into St Pancras Station. 'I wondered whether fresh air would ever come,' recalls Jones, 'as the smoke was beginning to affect me quite badly. I would estimate that I was among the last half dozen up the steps. Most of the people on the concourse were in a confused state, breathing hard.'[7]

Seconds after the flashover occurred the air temperature leapt by several hundred degrees, turning the entire area into a burning cauldron of flame.

John Kelly, an insurance writer from north London, was just entering the booking hall via the Victoria Line escalators when the flashover erupted. He had a very lucky escape. 'As I reached the top of the escalator, at the point where it flattens out, I saw the flames shoot across the ceiling from my right to left. The flames were initially quite small and yellow in colour and I ran to where I thought an exit might be. I recall running ten feet before hitting an obstruction and it appeared to me that I had run into a corner as I seemed to have wall on either side of me. By this time I was overtaken by the flames which by this time were like a fireball, having grown to that point in what seemed to be fractions of a second. There was intense heat and thick smoke. It was difficult to breathe.' Holding his suitcase in front of his face to shield him from the heat, Kelly was somehow able to find his way back to the escalator and escaped down to the lower concourse area, but in the process received serious burns to his hands and face.

Those caught in the path of the fireball stood no chance whatsoever, but some people further away were able to escape from the booking hall and into the exit tunnels. They included Colin Townsley, who might have made it to safety had he not attempted to rescue another passenger: he was eventually overcome by the smoke and collapsed just a few metres away from an exit.

Constable Stephen Hanson was at the far end of the booking hall when the flashover occurred. 'A fireball hit me in the face and knocked me off my feet,' he told reporters from his hospital bed. 'My hands caught fire. They were just melting. The skin came off and was hanging down in shreds.' Despite his injuries Hanson somehow managed to crawl away from the fire and along the super-hot, smoke-filled passageway. 'I had to get out as quickly as possible. I just kept thinking of my family; I just couldn't leave them.'

Hanson crawled up the steps and onto Euston Road where he collapsed. A colleague rushed to his aid and put through an emergency call for an ambulance. 'There has been a major incident here,' he said. The time was 7.45 p.m. and 58 seconds. Despite attempts by firefighters and passers-by, Hanson was one of the last people to emerge from any of the street-level exits. Thick black smoke poured onto Euston Road and into the mainline station at King's Cross. There was nothing anyone could do but wait until the fire brigade could gain control of the situation.

CHAPTER TWO

Rescue and Recovery

At 7.45 p.m. Anthony Palmer, a 36-year-old company director from Sheffield, left St Pancras railway station, which is immediately to the west of the King's Cross terminus. As he crossed the street outside, Palmer noticed smoke pouring from the Underground entrance located on Pancras Road. As he watched, the smoke became darker and more dense; seconds afterwards several people stumbled blindly up the steps and, on reaching street level, collapsed to the ground coughing and spluttering. Palmer rushed to their aid and as he did so a loud roaring sound came from the Underground, followed seconds later by a fierce blast of heat and an outpouring of thick black smoke. Other bystanders arrived and began to drag the coughing escapees away from the danger. Although clear of the scene, Palmer thought that he could see another man trying to make his way up the Underground steps, fighting his way through the choking smoke and heat.

'He still had some forward momentum and was making headway to get out,' said Palmer. 'I went forward to the entrance as he held out his hands. I got hold of his right hand with my right hand but as our hands touched I could feel his was red hot and some of the skin came off in my hand. Assisting him by his right arm, I started to lead him out of the smoke away from the top of the steps.'

The man fell to the ground but Palmer and another man were able to drag him to safety; as they did so a woman could be seen trying to crawl out of the same entrance. Her injuries looked severe but Palmer somehow braved the fierce heat and, on reaching her, was able to pull her clear. Convinced that he could hear voices coming from the tunnel, Palmer returned again to the entrance. He couldn't see anyone through the smoke and so he ran to a fire tender that was parked nearby. The firefighters were busy putting on their safety and breathing equipment but gave Palmer permission to borrow a rope. With one end held by a bystander, Palmer grabbed the other and edged his way to the underground entrance.

'I considered whether to tie the rope around myself and try to enter the stairwell to see if I could find anyone at the bottom,' recounts Palmer, 'but I realised the heat, speed and ferocity had substantially increased and I also realised that if I had entered I would not have come out. So I tied a loop on the end of the rope and leaned as far in as I dared; I proceeded to throw the rope in and shouted as loud as I could for anyone there to grab hold of it. I did this several times but to no avail.'

Eventually the heat and fumes began to take their toll and even Anthony Palmer was forced to retreat to safety. He returned to his briefcase and for several minutes sat coughing and retching until a police officer guided him to an ambulance which took him to St Bartholomew's Hospital. Fortunately his bravery had not overly effected his health, and although he was suffering from smoke inhalation and shock he was only detained overnight. [1]

Anthony Palmer's quick thinking and heroic behaviour was responsible for the rescue of the last two people to emerge alive from the street-level exits of the King's Cross Underground system. To those on the surface the smoke and heat being produced by the fire gave them little hope for anyone left below ground. In fact, there were still people alive in the lower levels of the station, trapped on the concourses and platforms below the booking hall. They were spared the worst effects of the fire which was being drawn away from the platform areas and into the aerated passageways that led up to street level.

Many of those trapped below had experienced a lucky escape. At the moment of flashover the Victoria Line escalator had been packed full of people being evacuated into the booking hall from the deep-level platforms. Those who were near the top of the escalator when the flashover occurred were caught by the initial blast, but those further down had time to run back down the stairs to safety.

'I was about halfway up the escalator,' said Andrew Lee, 'when a sheet of flame shot across the top and soon the ceiling was on fire and debris started falling down. The people at the top seemed to be very badly burned.' Londoner John Lincoln was further up the escalator than Andrew. Immediately after the flashover he was greeted by the sight of two people rushing down the stairs. 'One's hair was smouldering, the second had his back on fire. Suddenly the flames leapt from his back to his head and his hair started to blaze. I rushed to him and beat out the flames with my hands.'

With the booking hall turned into an inferno, the remaining passengers moved back down towards the Victoria Line platforms. London Underground staff on the Piccadilly and Northern Line platforms also started evacuating people towards the Victoria Line in an effort to move them as far from the scene of the fire as possible. Within minutes there were over two hundred people, several with bad burns, gathered on the Victoria Line platforms. However, the first few trains to enter the station ignored frantic gestures for them to stop. The train drivers had received an instruction not to disembark anyone at King's Cross and they were following it, even if it meant leaving stranded passengers on a platform that was rapidly filling with black smoke.

One passenger on board a train that didn't stop described the harrowing scene that greeted him. 'We could smell the smoke before the train reached the station and when we arrived at the platform you could see it pouring through the exits. There were about forty or so people on the platform, some were just standing there, others looked terrified, but the train didn't stop, it just kept going. People began hammering on the side but the driver didn't stop. It was a sickening feeling having to leave those people behind, not knowing what was going to happen to them.'[2]

A couple of minutes after this dark smoke began to enter the platform area, increasing the sense of urgency. Among the trapped were several police officers whose frantic gesturing at last managed to persuade some trains to stop and open their doors. Typically, as the fire survivors scrambled on board some of the Tube passengers tried to alight from the train despite being told not to do so.

'I'm going to get my train from King's Cross,' said one man angrily to a British Transport Police constable as he attempted to push past those being evacuated. 'You are getting back on that train now,' shouted the policeman, 'don't be so bloody stupid!'

With some trains now stopping, all those trapped below the fire were swiftly evacuated although several police and fire service personnel chose to remain in the tunnels below the platform to check for casualties and to monitor the situation. As the police radios did not work underground and it took time for them to find a telephone link to the outside world, for a while their colleagues on the surface thought that they might have perished in the flames.[3]

On the streets above the scene was equally chaotic. Two firefighters wearing full breathing apparatus entered the smoke-filled station and managed to pull a burned and blackened young man up to the surface. With no ambulances on the scene the firefighters left him in the hands of a young woman, a solicitor who herself had only just managed to escape the fire. Although conscious, the man couldn't breathe properly and he began to bleed from his mouth. The solicitor attempted to give him mouth-to-mouth resuscitation but no air would go into his lungs; as she watched the man crumpled and slid slowly through her arms to the floor. It was, in her words, a hopeless situation.[4]

Other walking wounded were wandering about in a dazed state. Some were taken to the nearby Northumberland Hotel and offered tea and basic first aid. Others were left to their own devices. One survivor, Frank Reardon, suffered only mild burns and on reaching safety did not know what to do with himself. He walked around for several minutes before entering a police station and, with his hair still smouldering, asked to borrow their telephone.[5]

The volume of smoke was so intense that it could be smelled several streets away. It was this that alerted two off-duty doctors to the unfolding emergency. They had been watching television in their flat on nearby Caledonian Road when the acrid stink of smoke and the sound of sirens drew their attention. Within ten minutes both of them were on the station concourse area where they were joined by two other off-duty doctors.[6] The four medics, all of whom were there by chance, set about treating the injured. As they did so additional police, fire tenders and ambulances began to arrive, turning the scene into a mass of flashing lights, fire hoses, first-aid equipment and stretchers. The emergency services quickly threw a cordon around the whole King's Cross area, removing unwanted bystanders and preparing themselves for the arrival of press reporters, photographers and television crews.

As ambulances arrived, so the process of removing casualties to hospital began. It was evident that the medical services were dealing with a serious situation and so, at 8.16 p.m., King's Cross was declared by the ambulance service to be a 'major incident'. A rehearsed emergency plan went into action with three London hospitals being told to prepare themselves for the arrival of a substantial number of casualties suffering from burns and smoke inhalation. They were also asked to estimate the number of dead bodies that they could hold.[7]

At the scene the first fatality was confirmed: it was Colin Townsley. His colleagues knew he had been caught by the fire and risked their own lives entering the Underground in search of him. Their worst fears were quickly confirmed when Townsley's body was discovered in a tunnel, only yards from one of the street-level exits. He had no severe burn injuries, suggesting that he had succumbed to the effects of smoke. Two doctors spent several minutes trying to revive him but it was a hopeless task. The firefighter's body was placed on a stretcher and was in the process of being taken to an ambulance when a press reporter jumped forward and attempted to photograph it. He was roughly pushed aside by one of the doctors and then pulled away from the scene by the police. With the media alerted to the disaster, much of the police's time would now be consumed in keeping order at the scene, preventing the public and press from obstructing the work of the emergency services.

Less than forty minutes after the flashover had swept through the upper levels of the underground station, all the surviving casualties had been evacuated to University College, St Batholomew's and St Mary's Whittington Hospitals. Here specialist medical teams were prepped and ready to receive the incoming injured, having already cleared their accident and emergency departments of all non-emergency patients. Following a well-rehearsed major incident procedure, the arriving victims were graded by the severity of their injuries and dealt with accordingly. Those with burns and severe breathing difficulties were taken straight to resuscitation rooms, where, after medical stabilisation, they were transferred to intensive care units. Here specialist surgeons made assessments of the damage to their skin, hair and lungs. People with minor burns or suffering from mild smoke inhalation were treated in the main casualty department and were later admitted to the wards for observation.

Most patients were not badly injured and needed only a precautionary overnight stay, but a minority were in a more serious condition. One of these was Police Constable Stephen Hanson who had been caught by the flashover while evacuating people from the booking hall area. Blinded by the smoke and heat, Hanson would probably have died had not one of his colleagues returned into the Underground system and, on finding him wandering in a tunnel, hauled him to safety. Even so, Hanson suffered third-degree burns to his face and hands that would require months of reconstructive surgery. Photographs of him lying in hospital with his scorched face and arms swathed in bandages were widely circulated in the newspapers, ensuring that Hanson became one of the few named heroes of the fire. In total, twenty injured people were admitted to hospital. It is testament to the skill of the doctors and other staff that despite some horrific injuries only one person died after reaching medical care. [8]

At King's Cross the emergency services were beginning to gain a measure of control. The police cordon was in place and holding fast; all living casualties had been evacuated and the fire brigade had started tackling the smoke and flames. To do this they rigged up dozens of fire hoses and worked in teams, taking turns to enter the smoke-filled tunnels, playing jets of water against the burning walls and ceiling.

'It was a very, very severe fire,' said one fire officer. 'The roof was alight, the kiosks were well alight and the walls were well alight. Tiles were exploding off the walls where the concrete was expanding. Roof tiles were falling on top of us. The only way to fight the fire was to get as low as possible. We were lying in the water.' [9]

The combined danger of heat and fumes impeded the firefighters' progress: their position wasn't helped by trains continuing to pass through the tunnels deep below. As each train moved forwards, it pushed fresh air ahead of it which would then enter into the lower reaches of King's Cross Underground and from there be forced upwards into the burning booking hall. Each burst of fresh air fanned the fire, sending waves of intense heat up towards the firefighters. Miraculously, no further serious injuries were sustained and by 9.00 p.m. the fire was out, although damping down had to continue for several hours.

The earlier declaration of King's Cross as a major incident meant that in addition to the usual emergency services, several other more specialist teams and individuals had also been alerted. One of these was the British Association for Immediate Care (or BASICS), a voluntary organisation that had been formed a decade earlier specifically to provide experienced medical staff for disaster scenes. In 1987 there were eight doctors within the London region registered with BASICS but only three were available to attend the King's Cross fire; these were Robin Winch, Peter Ernst and Paul Davis. All three arrived within minutes of each other at around 9.00 p.m. and immediately began to help with the few remaining survivors who had yet to be taken to hospital. With the living all taken care of, there came the matter of finding and removing the bodies of those who had not been lucky enough to make it out of the station.

A little before 9.45 p.m. the fire brigade declared that, with the flames extinguished, they were preparing to enter the network of tunnels in order to search for further casualties. At the Pancras Road Underground entrance (the one where Anthony Palmer had effected his rescues) several fully attired firefighters assembled and, one by one, descended the steps into the smoke-blackened tunnel beneath. With no electric lighting to help them, the men had to use their torch beams to pick their way through the maze of tunnels and help them in the unpleasant task of finding the remains of those not fortunate enough to escape. To most of us the idea of searching for dead bodies in a confined space with just a torch would be a truly terrifying experience, but the firefighters do not seem to have been fazed by the task. In later interviews, they depicted the action of searching the gutted underground in very matter-of-fact terms with none of the sense of shock and fear that is apparent in descriptions provided by other people, including members of the medical and police teams. [10]

Within minutes of entering the tunnel the body of a young man was discovered lying face down on some steps about thirty metres from the exit. He had been within a short distance of safety but had perhaps tripped and, overcome with fumes, had been unable to get up again. The firefighters placed the dead man on a tarpaulin sheet and carried him the short distance to the surface. Peter Ernst, one of the BASICS doctors, pronounced him dead at 9.50 p.m. It was not long before other victims were being found. Several bodies were discovered in the semi-circular passageway that ran around the outside of the main booking hall. These were people who had managed to get away from the original explosion of flame but who had become disorientated and then overcome by the heat and fumes. The position of each body was noted before being wrapped in a tarpaulin sheet and taken to the surface where one of the doctors could certify the death. [11]

The fire crews were not expecting to find any survivors, but among the carnage there was a success story. At around 10.00 p.m. a firefighter heard a thumping noise coming from deep within the station. In the pitch darkness (and without a map) they tracked it down to a narrow side passage and from there to a soot-blackened, but otherwise intact, door. Cowering in the room behind were a man and woman, both London Under-ground employees, who had been taking an irregular break in a mess room when the flashover occurred. Unsure what to do, they barricaded themselves inside the room and sat in total darkness drinking wine and vodka while the inferno raged outside. They remained there for over two hours, drinking, until the noise of the firefighters caught their attention. The relieved but shaken duo were brought to the surface and treated for minor smoke inhalation. Outside the blackened mess-room door lay the body of a man who had not been so lucky, something that served to highlight the fortuitousness of their survival. [12]

There was a further moment of hope when a firefighter entered the public toilets at the base of the Pancras Road exit. Here he discovered two bodies and, on examining them, thought he could detect a heartbeat. He shouted up the stairs, 'I've found one alive!' and began mouth-to-mouth. A few seconds later Dr Winch rushed down and helped to move the body to the surface. Resuscitation was attempted for several minutes but the man was declared dead and, according to Winch, had probably been so for some time. This victim, and the other man found with him, had managed to get away from the fire but, blinded by smoke, blundered into the public toilets and had suffocated there. Had they carried on for another few feet they could have reached safety. The body count was steadily rising. [13]

The first bodies recovered had been taken by ambulance to University College Hospital but the two body holding rooms there quickly became full. This meant that back at the station a backlog of bodies was building up. On the concourse area the remains of ten other victims, all inside body bags, were lined up and waiting to be moved. Conscious of the presence of press and television crews, all of whom were anxious for pictures, the decision was taken to erect a temporary body holding area away from the disaster scene. The site chosen was a Methodist church located in Birkenhead Street, almost directly opposite King's Cross Station. The Methodist minister gave his approval and two soldiers, who had been passing the scene when they stopped to volunteer the use of their truck, were asked to take the bodies there. Even as the army truck was being loaded, the firefighters were bringing more dead people to the surface. Each was certified deceased by a doctor, placed in a body bag (complete with a sticker reading 'DEAD') and then put in the truck. Eventually a total of thirteen bodies were taken to the body holding area. [14]

By this time it was approaching three hours since the fire's ignition and, with the flames extinguished and the majority of human remains recovered, some of the firefighters were told to stand down and return to their headquarters. From that moment onwards the emphasis switched from firefighting to getting King's Cross Underground prepared for the various accident investigators, engineers and forensic staff who would need to work out how, when and why the blaze had started.

The first priority was to get emergency electrical lighting into the tunnels and booking hall area. Without it the search for evidence would have to be conducted by torchlight, which would inevitably lead to missed clues. The task of rigging the lights went to a team of eight London Underground duty electricians who had been called in from other jobs. None of these men had ever experienced a disaster on this scale and there was much unease when, shortly after 11.00 p.m., they were ordered into the tunnels to erect the lighting rigs. Their unease increased when, after being underground for barely ten minutes, everybody was ordered back to the surface. The firefighters believed that they had detected asbestos in the air and wanted to make further tests. It was after midnight by the time the all clear was given and the electricians, police, doctors and investigators could return into the scene. What they saw shocked them.[15]

'My first impression of the scene was of darkness,' explained Dr Ernst later. 'There was a lot of water and a terrible smell with debris everywhere.' The whole Underground was a mess but the worst scene of all was to be found in the booking hall area where the heat and smoke had been at their most intense. As the lighting rigs went up, so the full horror of the scene came into full view for the first time.[16]

A little later on a newspaper reporter was to describe the devastation in graphic detail. 'I stood at the stairway to hell and saw the blackest nightmare imaginable. Nothing but a burnt-out shell remained of the escalator where the blaze began. And not a single scrap of metal, wood or tiling in the booking hall escaped the ravages of the smoke and flames. Charred and twisted debris lay strewn across the floor of London's busiest Underground station. A tangle of melted wires and light fittings hung from the ceiling. But the most sickening reminder of the disaster's grim toll was the stench of burned flesh that infested every corner.'[17]

With adequate lighting available, the various investigators and doctors set about examining the scene. An obvious area of interest were the three Piccadilly Line escalators where the fire had started; the police and a specialist engineer immediately set about examining these. In the meantime the three doctors from BASICS started to make a systematic search of the booking hall area, looking for any further human remains or discarded personal items. This search upset at least one of the electricians who later said that he 'found the experience very disturbing. In fact, I did not sleep for two days afterwards'.

Further bodies were discovered; they had been so badly burned that they had not been spotted by the firefighters during their earlier search. 'I saw a group of firemen looking at an object on the ground,' said one of the duty electricians. 'It was about three foot in length, black and grey and a funny shape. One of the firemen noticed me watching this object and looked at me. He told me it was the remains of a body. I was shocked to think that this was a person once and made my way out for a bit of fresh air. Once I found out that there were bodies still on the station I tried to stay up the top.'[18]

Nearby was a 'mass of charred remains' that was, if anything, in an even worse state. This turned out to be two bodies belonging to a young boy and his mother, and was one of the most distressing discoveries of the evening. The remains of all three people were removed and sent to St Bartholomew's Hospital.[19]

The various crews and investigators continued to work into the early hours of Thursday morning, taking pictures, making notes, recording video footage and doing other tasks. At around 3.30 a.m. Dr Peter Ernst was about to leave the booking hall in order to go home when he spotted a firefighter trip over something on the ground. 'I shone my torch in the area he stumbled,' said Dr Ernst. 'I saw on the ground what I believed to be human remains of the chest. There were no arms or legs and no head.' He called his colleagues over, all of whom agreed that these were parts of a body. A bag was brought over and the remains placed into it. A second pile of debris was spotted nearby which contained some ladies' shoes, some white training shoes and possibly some further human remains. These too were bagged and taken away.[20]

Exhaustion was evident on the faces of all those present and so, at 4.30 a.m., the station was evacuated and the scene closed down for the night. Only the police remained on duty, guarding against the attentions of curious bystanders and the media.

Shortly before the closing of the disaster scene, the acting Chief Inspector for the British Transport Police made an assessment of the fire's casualties. He spoke to staff at the three main hospitals and to those who had staffed the temporary body holding area at the Methodist church. After collating the figures he had been given, he radioed his superiors at the police's Incident Control centre. There were, he said, twenty injured people in hospital and a total of thirty dead. With no further casualties on the scene, the need to give each victim a name took priority.[21]

CHAPTER THREE

Identifying Characteristics

In 1987 King's Cross was Britain's busiest station. The Underground served two large mainline stations (King's Cross and St Pancras) and received trains along five different Tube lines. On an average weekday around 250,000 passengers would pass through the booking hall area. Given the importance of King's Cross and the scale of the fire, it was inevitable that there would be a major investigation into the events of the evening of 18 November. [1]

Most major incidents in London are investigated by the Metropolitan Police (often referred to as Scotland Yard after the address of their old headquarters) who hold sway over the majority of the capital's streets. However, King's Cross Underground is a train station and as such does not fall under the remit of the Metropolitan Police. Instead, all of London's train and Tube stations are the provenance of the British Transport Police, a separate division whose origins date back to the early nineteenth century. Thus the majority of officers involved on the night of the fire were from the British Transport Police (although the scale of the incident and its knock-on effects in the surrounding streets meant that many Metropolitan Police officers were also involved) and it was they who would be tasked with co-ordinating the investigation into the fire. This meant gathering evidence relating to both the cause and spread of the fire and to the actions of those people caught up in it. It was also the British Transport Police's job to handle the investigation into the fire's fatalities, and this included finding a name for each of the victims so that their next of kin could be contacted.

Those who had survived the fire were, in most cases, able to give the police or hospital staff their names and also the contact details of their next of kin. Unfortunately the same was not true for any of the fatalities, all of whom arrived at their respective body holding facilities without a name. Even those who had been brought to the surface alive but had died shortly afterwards had been unable to divulge any personal details. Given that members of the public were already ringing up to report missing friends and relations, the police had to attach a name to each of the thirty bodies and they had to do so quickly.

The process of identification began almost as soon as the first bodies had been recovered. An attempt had been made to identify some of them while they were stretched out on the station concourse but with the fire still raging and the large number of casualties, the police only got as far as noting the sex and ethnicity of four or five of the victims. It was decided that the bodies had to be moved to calmer, more formal surroundings where the task of identification could take place in controlled conditions.[2]

After being certified dead, the first fatalities were ferried by ambulance to University College Hospital where some of the burns victims were already being treated. Two officers from the British Transport Police were at the hospital when the first bodies arrived. They were in the process of setting up a permanent 'casualty bureau' in the reception area which would provide a central point through which information relating to the victims of the fire (such as their names, details of their next of kin and condition) could be gathered and managed. Once the casualty bureau was up and running, the two police officers were taken to a temporary body holding area which had been hastily erected in a small basement storeroom. This was where the bodies were to be taken in order to be 'processed' by the police.

After being shown in, the officers discovered that the cramped room already held one unidentified body, that of a young woman. One of the officers recognised her; he recalled having seen her at King's Cross stumbling out of the Underground with her clothes and hair smouldering, screaming loudly. He had tried calming her before the medics arrived and took her to an ambulance, but evidently the extent and severity of her burns had placed her beyond the realm of help. As they stood there, the two officers were joined by a policeman and a woman from the Metropolitan Police; together they set about searching the dead woman's body for any clues that could reveal her identity.

When confronted with an unidentified body, especially one that is in some way injured or disfigured, it is vital that those examining it note any potential clue to its identity. Typically an examination will begin by noting the person's sex, ethnicity (as judged by skin colour), height, build and approximate age. As we shall see, even basic details such as these can be invaluable when trying to match a body to a known person. Next a note will be made of the hair and eye colour, the type and make of clothing, shoes, jewellery or other accessories. Then a detailed search is made of the clothing for any personal possessions such as name tags, credit cards, chequebooks, monogrammed pens or other objects that could be used to track down further information on their owner. Finally, any immediately obvious distinguishing features such as tattoos, scars or missing teeth will be noted, although physical features such as these are often left to the pathologist to describe in detail.

The four officers in University College Hospital noted the dead woman's physical features and then set about searching her clothes for anything that might give them a name. With most victims of accidental death (such as those involved in traffic incidents) this would produce objects like a work ID card, wallet or driving licence with a name on it, but the dead woman's clothes had been made of nylon, a flammable synthetic material which had mostly melted in the heat. However, to one side of the body an officer made a grisly discovery: partially fused to her skin were the remains of her handbag, the contents of which had survived the fire. Among some cosmetic items, there was a small piece of paper that gave the dead woman's name and address. This, together with her jewellery and the presence of a scar from appendix surgery, would be enough to allow the police to secure a positive identification from her next of kin.

As the dead woman was being processed, further bodies were being brought into the room, forcing the small police team to quicken their pace. Soon so many casualties were coming in that there was a danger of the bodies, and the notes made about them, becoming confused. To avoid this each new arrival was given a number which was written on two tags: one attached to the toe, the other to the wrist. This number would also allow the hospital and, later on, the pathologists to keep track of where each body had been found, which body holding location it had come from and who had examined it en route. It also meant that any loose possessions could be labelled with the same number as the body they came from, a vital factor in the prevention of mistakes.

Each body was processed in turn but after the initial success of identifying the badly burnt woman, the police experienced mixed results. Like the first body, some of the victims could be identified straight away from name tags, identification cards or personal papers, but others proved to be more problematic. The third body to arrive was, according to the policeman that handled it, so badly burnt 'that it was impossible to identify it other than the fact it was a male about 5'9" tall.' No possible means of identification could be found on it and so for the time being it could only be referred to by its mortuary number. The same was also true for most of the severely burnt victims.

The processing and attempted identification procedure continued for hours and, after the body holding room in the basement became full, it had to be completed in the hospital's chapel. University College Hospital had received the first fatality at 8.30 p.m. and thereafter took another thirteen bodies, but by

10.20 p.m. all available space was taken. The hospital authorities radioed through to the incident unit at King's Cross to tell them that there was no more room in their body holding facilities. [3]

This was not welcome news as the firefighters were still bringing dead people up to the surface. A backlog soon developed, leading to full body bags being lined up in a row on the station concourse. This was when the decision was taken to open the body holding area in the nearby Methodist church on Birkenhead Street. In total thirteen bodies were taken from King's Cross to this church where the business of processing them could take place in secure and private surroundings.

In comparison to the hospital, where the bodies had been placed in two confined rooms, the expanse of the church's interior made the police's job much easier. The bodies were laid out on the floor with each being given a number from one to thirteen. They were then taken, one at a time, to a central table where a team of doctors and police systematically removed and labelled all the clothing, which was searched for identifying items before being bagged. While the clothing was being dealt with, doctors examined the bodies, making notes about physique, injuries and other characteristics. After processing, each body was placed back inside its body bag, labelled and lined up along the floor. Many of the fatalities in the church had come from the area inside or adjacent to the booking hall, where the fire had been at its most intense. The severity of the burns inflicted on the majority of the bodies was horrific; in most cases the fire had removed all traces of clothing, hair and other identifying features.

Despite intensive examination, names could only be found for four of the thirteen bodies at the Methodist church. The whole process took over two hours with the bodies finally being removed by undertakers at 1.30 a.m. The church was cleaned and decommissioned as a body holding facility, allowing it to be returned to its usual function as a place of worship. [4]

Meanwhile, back inside King's Cross Underground Station, an intensive search by doctors and firefighters had revealed a further three bodies. All were discovered in the booking hall area and all were very badly burned indeed. With University College Hospital's body holding areas full and those at the Methodist church closed, the newly recovered remains were taken to St Bartholomew's Hospital. Here police and doctors examined and logged them, but the extent of their injuries meant that all three bodies could not be identified.

That night a total of thirty bodies had been recovered from King's Cross Underground Station and processed by the police. By dawn on 19 November all thirty had been taken from their body holding areas to the public mortuary attached to St Pancras Coroner's Court, Camley Street, where they would undergo a post-mortem examination.

CHAPTER FOUR

Dr West's Examinations

In the aftermath of a major disaster, such as the one at King's Cross, the responsibility for any subsequent investigation is divided between various official organisations. The onus of exploring the circumstances surrounding the cause and effects of the fire falls to accident investigators and the police, but the investigation into when and how its victims died is the responsibility of the coroner. Following a disaster the coroner will take charge of any bodies and then co-ordinate the necessary investigations and examinations; part of this process includes establishing an identity for each victim. Given that there were thirty fatalities from the fire, the coroner's office had a major task to perform in the succeeding days and weeks.

The position of coroner in English law dates to medieval times and although it has undergone much refinement, its role in establishing cause of death can be traced back over several centuries. In modern times a coroner must be informed of any deaths that have come about by suspicious, unusual or accidental means. (A suspicious death does not only include obvious actions such as murder, but also fatalities caused by suicide, drug overdose, industrial accident, neglect or while under anaesthetic as well as those that occur in prisons, care homes, etc.) The process of alerting the coroner of a suspicious death usually begins with the medical doctor who has been called in to certify the death of an individual. If the doctor believes there are suspicious or unusual circumstances associated with the death then the Registrar of Births, Marriages and Deaths must be informed – it is the Registrar's job to issue death certificates – but in most cases the doctor will also inform the coroner at this stage. Once alerted to a possible suspicious or unusual death, the Registrar cannot issue a death certificate without the cause of death having been investigated by a coroner. To initiate such an investigation the Registrar will ask the coroner to open an inquest into the death. It is the function of a coroner's inquest to gather evidence relating to a suspicious or unusual death and then offer a verdict as to how it was caused (for example, 'death by misadventure' or 'unlawful killing'). As part of this process the coroner must also establish that the identity of the victim has been proved beyond all reasonable doubt. This had a serious bearing on the police investigation into the fire.[1]

The victims at King's Cross had died in a location that comes under the jurisdiction of the Inner North London Coroner's Office. This meant that the inquest into their deaths would take place at St Pancras Coroner's Court, located in nearby Camden Town. In November 1987 the Inner North London Coroner was Dr Douglas Chambers who has been described as a 'small, business-like figure'. The unnatural means by which all the King's Cross victims had met their death meant that a coroner's inquest was an inevitability. Shortly after the first fatality had been confirmed, Dr Chambers was telephoned and made aware of the situation. From that moment onwards he was duty bound to oversee the treatment of the bodies and to open an inquest into the cause of death of each of the victims.

The involvement of the Inner North London Coroner meant that once all the victims' bodies had been processed by the police, they had to be removed from their temporary holding areas and taken to the public mortuary attached to St Pancras Coroner's Court. The need to identify a specific cause of death for each person necessitated that each body undergo a post-mortem examination, a process that is also known as an autopsy. In historical times the coroner (who was not necessarily medically trained) would have inspected a corpse in person, looking for obvious wounds and other injuries. By the late twentieth century the post-mortem examination was the job of the pathologist, a medical doctor who is trained to gather medical and scientific evidence from a corpse. As well as gathering evidence relating to the cause of death, the pathologist will also obtain information that can be used by the police and others to help find a name for an anonymous body. As soon as Dr Chambers became aware that there were fatalities at King's Cross, he telephoned the most experienced pathologist he could think of to ask if he was available to perform the post-mortem examinations.[2]

In 1987 Dr Iain West was arguably the foremost forensic pathologist in Great Britain. Born in Glasgow, Scotland, Dr West received his basic medical training at Edinburgh University. Afterwards West moved to southern England where he worked in hospital accident and emergency departments; here his interest in pathology was stimulated after working with haemophiliacs and rhesus babies. He then went to work with Professor Austen Gresham at Cambridge University, a world-regarded pathologist who once referred to West as the best trainee in forensic pathology he had ever taught. From there came a move to St Thomas's Hospital, London, where he took up a post in forensic medicine and where, a few years later, he took up a senior consultancy post at nearby Guy's Hospital.[3]

By 1980 Dr West already had a reputation for brilliance within the field of forensic pathology and he began to get called in to some major incidents. The first of these was the 1980 Iranian Embassy siege in central London which was ended in spectacular fashion, and in front of the television cameras, by the British SAS. Five terrorists and one hostage died, and in the weeks afterwards Iain West's ballistic work on this case received much praise. He became involved in further headline-grabbing cases including that of PC Yvonne Fletcher, shot dead outside the Libyan Embassy in London, and several IRA terrorist bombings, including the 1984 Brighton bomb by which the IRA attempted to assassinate senior members of the British government. His fame frequently led to him working abroad, especially in the Middle East, and he was involved in the investigations surrounding murders, massacres and killings in several countries.

Dr West attributed his popularity with the authorities to the fact that he had been formally trained as a pathologist (apparently not all forensic pathologists are) and to his meticulous note-taking, a habit he learned from Keith Simpson, one of his mentors. Consequently, by the late 1980s Dr West's name was top of the Home Office's list of trusted pathologists and in the event of a serious incident he could expect to be called upon. This was certainly the case with King's Cross.[4]

At around midnight on the night of the fire, Dr West was at home when he received a telephone call from Dr Chambers asking if he was prepared to carry out the post-mortem examinations on the victims of the unfolding King's Cross disaster. Dr West agreed but chose not to visit the scene of the fire itself. It is a decision he has since regretted.

'Everyone learned from mistakes at King's Cross,' said Dr West several years later, 'and one mistake I learned from it was not going there on the night. But, by the time I heard about it, it was quite late in the evening and I didn't think I could con-tribute much by going there. In retrospect, that was probably a mistake.'[5]

In the early hours of Thursday, 19 November Dr West arrived at St Pancras mortuary, a place that has been described as cramped, badly lit and outdated. Undertaking thirty post-mortems in a single sitting is quite a task but fortunately the examination process is relatively straightforward, its chief aim being to provide a cause of death for the coroner's inquest.

The police had asked that some of the bodies be prioritised for post-mortem examination. They had particular concerns about the body of a young woman who had lost part of one lower leg. Her foot appeared to have been blown clean off, an injury that is commonly associated with bomb blasts; this caused the police to wonder whether she had been the victim of terrorism. If so, then this would have a serious bearing on the investigation into the cause of the fire.

Dr West examined the woman's body and was quickly able to reassure the police that she had been hit by falling debris within the station and could not have been the victim of a bomb blast. Immediately afterwards he was asked to examine the body of Station Officer Colin Townsley, which he did with a degree of sadness. West judged that the firefighter's soot-filled airways and lack of burns meant that he might have spent a few minutes wandering the Underground tunnels trying to find an escape route before finally succumbing to the fumes. After this West was free to examine the bodies in any order that he chose.[6]

The identification numbers that had been attached to each body had been assigned earlier in the evening in one of the body holding areas. Because they had come from separate localities, some of the bodies being examined by Dr West had identical numbers. To avoid confusion, a decision was taken to label the fourteen bodies from University College Hospital with numbers 1 to 14, while the remaining sixteen were labelled with numbers 101 to 116. Each would receive a basic pathological examination.

Dr West would typically have begun a post-mortem with an external visual description of the body including a measurement of its height. Any injuries, old and recent, would have been noted as would the person's approximate age, sex, race and eye colour. At this stage photographs and X-rays would be taken and a time of death estimated although, in this case, this last formality was not really necessary as the exact time of the flashover was already known: all the victims would have been dead within a few seconds or, at most, minutes of this.

The next part of the post-mortem process would have been more time-consuming and problematic: this was the internal examination which, in blunt terms, means dissecting the body to study its major organs. The dissection would have begun with the pathologist making two cuts at each shoulder and then drawing them down to a meeting point around the lower part of the breastbone. A third cut would then be made from this point down the middle of the body to the lower abdomen. When viewed from above this incision is Y-shaped and, once the ribs have been cut, permits access to all the body's major organs.

The heart and lungs would have been the first organs to be removed, usually as a single unit. They can then be examined for any signs of disease or abnormality as can many of the other major organs in the abdomen, some of which would have been weighed although this did not seem to occur with the King's Cross victims. The stomach contents would be looked at and, if necessary, sampled as would any liquid inside the bladder. Finally, the head and brain would be assessed, a rather grisly process that requires removing much of the forehead of the skull so that the delicate cerebral organ can be taken out and examined. As a final act, Dr West took blood samples from each body which were sent away for laboratory analysis.

Dr West had to perform this procedure thirty times and on each occasion a series of detailed notes was taken. There was much variation between the condition of each body; some were almost untouched by the fire while others were so badly incinerated that their human characteristics were barely recognisable. One of the most badly damaged of all was a body that came from St. Bartholomew's hospital; it had lost almost all its skin and had deep charring to most of its muscles. The heat had been so intense that it had fractured some of the bones and dehydrated the body's muscles causing them to contract, pulling the arms and legs in towards the torso. Pathologists call this the 'pugilistic position' because the fists end up tucked beneath the chin, making the body look like a boxer. The internal examination revealed that the high temperature had even managed to cook some of the internal organs. It was startling proof of the fire's ferocity.[7]

It was late in the day when Dr West finished the last post-mortem examination. The notes that he had made about each fatality were revised and summarised into a standard post-mortem report which finished by stating the cause of death. The reports were then submitted to the coroner so that they could be used as part of his inquest. Copies of the reports were also passed on to the British Transport Police so that they could use the information gathered during the examinations to help in their quest to identity the victims.

CHAPTER FIVE

The Search for Names

On Thursday 19 November a priority for the British Transport Police was to find a name for each of the fire's victims so that their relations and next of kin could be made aware of the situation and, even more unpleasantly, be able to confirm the identity of the deceased.

The preliminary searches made by the police, doctors and others on the night of the fire had found a probable identity for twelve of the thirty bodies.[1] For each of these probable names, police officers tried to trace where the person had lived or worked and, once this had been established, to locate the whereabouts of their next of kin. It was police policy to break the bad news to the victims' relatives as quickly as possible, preferably by a personal visit, but in some cases a telephone call was necessary. In all instances, a victim's relations, friends or work colleagues would be asked to come to London to identify their personal belongings. If there were no personal items to identify then the police would seek out the victim's medical records and try to match them with the forensic information given in Dr West's post-mortem report. Only in the most extreme cases is a relation ever asked to go into a mortuary to visually identify a dead body and, as far as I can gather, this did not occur with any of the King's Cross victims.[2]

The remaining eighteen unidentified bodies had either carried no means of identification on them or, if they had, it had been burnt beyond all recognition. The situation was made more complex by the large number of bags, briefcases, shoes and other personal items that had been recovered from the Underground station. Some of these could have belonged to the fire's victims, but they might equally well have been dropped in panic by those who fled for the exits and managed to get out alive. Sifting through these belongings yielded few useful clues and did not offer up any new names. There was little the British Transport Police could do other than to wait for the names of potential victims to be suggested to them. 'In many cases it will be a matter of people ringing to say their relative has not come home and us trying to identify them that way,' said Police Inspector Geoffrey Thornes. 'It could take some time, but it will be done slowly and surely.'[3]

On the night of the fire the police established a national telephone number for those who were worried about a loved one who might have had cause to be in King's Cross Underground that evening. Such telephone helplines are a regular feature in the aftermath of a disaster as they are the quickest and most convenient means of gathering potential names for victims, but they can be both a blessing and a curse. It is usual for helplines to be jammed solid with incoming calls for hours, with many of those people phoning simply being over-anxious because a friend or relation is home a little later than usual or because they haven't heard from them for a while. This was true of the King's Cross telephone helpline which was oversubscribed with callers until the early hours of the morning, and which received a surprising number of calls from people enquiring about friends or relations who were not even known to be in London at the time. By the morning after the fire the police had already been given the names of several hundred people, each of whom would have to be investigated. Among these were almost certainly the names and details of the majority of the fire's unidentified victims but separating those who were genuinely missing from those who were simply late home or were not even in London would take time.

Teams of police officers worked their way through the list of names, getting back in contact with those who had rung the helpline either to eliminate the name from the enquiry or, if they were still missing, to elucidate more details. In the majority of cases the missing people had found their way home again after having had their journey back delayed by the knock-on effects of the fire, or because they had decided to go for an after-work drink without telling their wife, husband, parents or flatmates. Of those that still remained unaccounted for, priority was given to those missing persons who had a record of being punctual and reliable but who, for some reason, had not returned home the previous evening.

In some cases the physical description given by the relations was sufficiently close to the attributes of one of the unidentified victims for the police to ask the next of kin to travel to London. This was certainly true in the case of one woman whose husband unexpectedly did not return home on the Wednesday night. She describes the tortuous but necessary process that she had to undergo before her worst fears were confirmed: 'I expected my husband home by about 9.00 p.m.,' she told the police. 'He had not arrived by 10.00 p.m.; I was beginning to get a bit anxious but not too worried. While listening to the ten o'clock news I heard about the fire at King's Cross Tube Station and I thought that perhaps he had to go via another route. About 10.45 p.m. I got more worried and decided to ring a friend for help. My friend, his wife and I tried telephoning the emergency number and finally got through about 2.15 the next morning. [My husband] would never go anywhere without letting me know first. He is not a drinking man and I know he would not have been to the pub or to visit any other person without letting me know.

'At 9.00 a.m. on Thursday we telephoned his office and spoke to his supervisor. He told me that [my husband] had left the office at 7.24 p.m. on Wednesday. We also contacted the Thames Valley Police; they told me that the car was still parked at Slough railway station. Throughout Thursday we telephoned all the people he could have gone to. We also telephoned hospitals in that area of London.

'About 4.30 p.m. the police contacted me and asked me to go to London [where] I was shown a silver-coloured watch with a blue face. I was not able to say whether this watch belonged to my husband. On my return from London I looked through some recent family photographs which I can say show a watch similar to the one I had been shown by the police. I was now sure that my husband had died in the fire at King's Cross.'[4]

This poor woman's husband turned out to be one of those who had been caught in the booking hall area by the initial blast of the flashover. He had died instantly but the searing heat had removed all trace of his clothing and other belongings which, according to his wife, would have included his driving licence, train season ticket and work identification card. The man wore no jewellery and only his steel digital watch managed to survive the fire. This, plus the wife's description of his perfect teeth (so perfect, in fact, that he had never visited a dentist so no dental records were available), confirmed the identification.

The same sad process was happening to other concerned families who had also rung the helpline and who were being asked to provide physical descriptions of their missing relations and details of what they might have been wearing the night before. The police were remarkably efficient at matching these often scant details to the even scantier information gleaned from a victim's body. By the Thursday evening they had positively identified twenty-four of the thirty people, a remarkable feat considering the disaster had only occurred a day previously and that the cosmopolitan nature of London meant that the victims could literally have come from anywhere in the country – or even anywhere in the world.[5]

With their print deadlines approaching, newspaper editors were anxious to be able to name some of the victims for their high-circulation weekend editions. In fact, journalists had already discovered some of the victims' names either through tip-offs or through unofficial releases from people working in the emergency services and connected government bodies. Biographies had been prepared for a few people, which included photographs provided by their families, but the newspaper editors still wanted to be given the official go-ahead by the police to release the names. Permission came late on the Thursday evening when Scotland Yard police confirmed the name, age and general address of eighteen victims. Another six names were withheld until relatives could be brought to London to confirm their identity.

The next morning the newspapers carried stories about the deceased. Some of the stories were utterly tragic, such as the death of a boy of seven who, together with his uncle and his mother, was travelling to Great Ormond Street Hospital to see his ten-year-old brother when they became trapped in the booking hall area. The mother and child were killed in the flashover but the uncle almost managed to make it to one of the exit tunnels before succumbing to the smoke.[6]

There were also tales of heroism. Lawrence Newcombe, a nurse from London, had just left the station when the flashover occurred. Without hesitation he plunged back into the station to see if he could help others and somehow managed to fight his way to the booking hall before he was overcome by the heat and fumes. His mother was not surprised to hear of her son's selflessness. 'He wouldn't have given a second thought for his own safety,' she said. 'As a nurse he knew it was his duty to help others and save lives. We are very proud of him.' Many of the papers splashed the story of Lawrence Newcombe the hero, but their coverage became tainted when it was later revealed that he was HIV positive which, in 1987, was still regarded by some people as being in much the same light as having bubonic plague. Despite the extremely low risk of transmission, all 250 people involved in the disaster were told to get medical check-ups, just to be on the safe side.[7]

As the British Transport Police continued to release the names of victims, so the newspapers continued to relay details about their lives but despite all the publicity the identifications had yet to be confirmed by the coroner's inquest. That was going to be the next major hurdle for the British Transport Police.

CHAPTER SIX

Inquest

The unnatural and premature death caused by the fire meant that all thirty victims had to be subject to a coroner's inquest before their bodies could be released from the mortuary for burial or cremation. Within two days of the King's Cross fire, Dr Douglas Chambers, the Inner North London Coroner, announced that the inquest into those who had died would open on Tuesday 24 November. This was less than a week after the disaster and put serious pressure on those who had been charged with identifying the dead as the Coroner would expect the majority of victims to have been given a name by this time. The short time span forced the police to work round the clock, sifting through the hundreds of names they had been given in search of those few that matched. Remarkably, by dawn on Tuesday morning they had found names for all but two of the victims.

St Pancras Coroner's Court is housed in Camden Town, north London, in a converted chapel on Camley Street close to Camden's famous clothes market. Ordinarily it is a perfectly adequate building, but on 24 November the small courtroom was by no means large enough to accommodate the crush of journalists, police and relatives that had turned up. People struggled to gain entry into the courtroom, forcing those inside to squeeze themselves into every available space and corner. It was an uncomfortable squash, especially in the public areas. Faced with this over-crowding, Dr Chambers chose to begin the inquest earlier than scheduled in the hope of relieving some of the pressure.

The inquest was set to hear the cases of twenty-eight of the thirty deaths caused by the King's Cross fire. The aim of that day's

45

proceeding was solely to establish an identity for each victim so that the bodies could be released to their families. The more complex task of establishing a cause of death would have to wait until after the fire investigators had done their work. However, establishing a person's identity to the satisfaction of the coroner is not a simple task; it requires that evidence be produced in court which shows that a body can be matched to a person once alive beyond all reasonable doubt. Only after satisfying this criterion would Dr Chambers be in a position to release a body to any next of kin.[1]

Dr Chambers endeavoured to make the process as quick and as anguish-free as possible. 'This is the most sorrowful occasion I can remember in this court,' he said before formally opening the inquest.

Once the Court was in session, each victim was dealt with individually. The Court required that for each victim there was a person at the inquest who was familiar with them in life, such a relation, close friend or work colleague. They had to testify that, based on the evidence offered to them by the police, they were certain that the body could be identified as the person named. It was a harrowing occasion which required parents to testify to the identity of their dead children, children to identify their dead parents and employees to identify dead workmates.

The inquest began with Station Officer Colin Townsley, the heroic firefighter whose image had occupied many newspaper pages during the previous few days. His divisional officer came forward and was sworn in to the court. Before asking any questions, Dr Chambers tried to reassure him as to the inquest's function. 'In the circumstances of this tragedy,' he said, 'I have got to make inquiries to establish the identity of everybody. I shall sign a form for burial and then adjourn the matter for further enquiries to be made.' He was to say these same words to every person sworn in that day.

Given the high stakes, the formality of establishing a victim's identification was actually quite quick. Once the nature of the relationship between the witness and the victim had been established, it was just a matter of their confirming that they had seen enough evidence to establish the dead person's identity beyond all reasonable doubt. This evidence took many forms: most witnesses were able to confirm identifications based on visually identifying clothing or possessions that had been found on the body but in more extreme cases forensic evidence, such as dental records and fingerprints, was needed to confirm a match.

Naturally, many people found the process extremely traumatic. One woman, who had lost three members of her family, took the oath, confirmed that the police had correctly identified the bodies and then collapsed into the arms of a friend. Another distraught witness had to be physically helped into and out of the witness box. Sometimes entire families came to testify, at other times it was just a lone employee.

Particularly poignant was the case of Ralph Humberstone, whose identity had been established by documents found on his body that night. The police had been able to trace him to the *Blind Beggar* public house in east London, where he had been a cleaner, but then the trail went cold. Try as they might, the police could not track down any of Mr Humberstone's living relations. In the absence of any close family, Mr Humberstone's publican employer came to the inquest and testified to his identity. Following this, a plea was issued by the Court to the press, asking them to publicise the case in the hope of alerting Mr Humberstone's living relatives as to his fate. A public appeal did follow but no relatives ever came forward, something that would have a bearing on events later on in this story.

Dr Chambers remained true to his word and ensured that the inquest proceedings were handled speedily and efficiently. A little over an hour after starting, the last case was heard and the inquest was adjourned while evidence was gathered concerning the cause of death. A spokesman for London Transport expressed 'profound sympathy for all those who have suffered bereavement' while Dr Chambers expressed his belief that the families would be grateful that the funerals could commence. 'It is not going to bring the dead back,' he said pragmatically, 'but it means the families can get the necessary things done.'[2]

Twenty-eight of the thirty King's Cross victims had been given names and within a day the first of the funerals had taken place, with the rest coming over the following week. It was generally agreed that taking only five days to identify most of the victims had been a stunning achievement for the police, but the task was not yet complete: they were still left with two unidentified male bodies.

It was decided that more detailed medical information was needed about these two men and so the day after the inquest Dr Iain West, the Home Office pathologist who had carried out original thirty post-mortem examinations, was recalled to St Pancras Coroner's Court. Dr Chambers asked him to perform a second, more detailed post-mortem examination, the objective being to scour each body for any evidence whatsoever that might offer clues as to their identity, no matter how small or insignificant.

The two unidentified bodies had been given the mortuary numbers 103 and 115. Both were found lying in the booking hall area where they had experienced the full intensity of the fire. Body 103 had been recovered close to the top of the Victoria Line escalators while Body 115 had been found beyond the ticket barriers next to the steps that lead up to a tunnel known as the 'Khyber Pass'. All that was known about them was that both bodies were male, that 103 was a black youth and that 115 was middle-aged and white.

The initial post-mortem examination had been a standard one that focused on the cause of death with close attention being paid to the internal organs and the fire-related injuries. The second examination would permit Dr West to make a more thorough assessment of each body and, as a consequence, to collect detailed forensic evidence.

In the case of Body 103 little new information could be obtained although Dr West was able to get some fingerprints. The process of obtaining fingerprints from a fire victim is difficult as the hands are often clenched shut. This reflex is caused by heat shortening the tendons and turning the hand into a fist, an action which protects the skin on the fingers (and thus the prints) from heat damage but which makes it difficult to open the hand. It is frequently necessary to remove the entire hand at the wrist and even cut off individual fingers before a print can be made. This is a specialist job and, on this occasion, Dr West was helped by a fingerprint expert from Scotland Yard. These fingerprints, together with a single metal bracelet recovered from the body on the night of the fire, were the only further clues to Body 103's identify.[3]

Dr West had more luck with Body 115. The older man was notably short (only 5'2" by Dr West's measurements) and had managed to accumulate some interesting forensic pathology during his life. The most obvious of these was a large circular scar on the right-hand side of his forehead, the result of a serious brain operation that must have taken place some years previously. Dr West had noted this operation scar during Body 115's first post-mortem examination but had not had cause to explore it further; this time he paid closer attention. The brain operation had been very invasive, requiring the removal of a large, roughly circular piece of bone from the skull, directly above the right eye. The degree of healing suggested that it had been some years since the operation had taken place but even so the wound still retained several small gaps between the edge of the circular bone flap and the skull.

An X-ray of Body 115's head revealed that at the site of the operation, and embedded in the brain, was a small piece of metal. Dr West investigated this further and found a small surgical clip which, when cleaned, proved to be made of wire, a centimetre or so in length and shaped a little like a thin clothes-peg. Dr West recognised it as an aneurysm clip, a surgical device used for repairing damaged arteries. This indicated that the brain operation had almost certainly been carried out in response to a sudden medical emergency such as a stroke. Dr West noted that some of the arteries in Body 115's brain showed signs of furring, a condition known as cerebral atheroma. This confirmed that in life the gentleman would have been prone to strokes or seizures. Having been removed from its location, the metal clip was placed to one side; it was perhaps something that could be looked at in more detail later on.

A second useful discovery occurred in Body 115's mouth, a place which pathologists would routinely examine in order to obtain a dead person's dental pattern. After prising the jaws apart (a process that is often necessary to break the rigor mortis) Dr West found that the man's teeth had long since gone and in their place was a full set of dentures. All dental evidence can be used as an aid to identification and so, like the aneurysm clip, the dentures were removed from the body and set aside for further examination.

Finally, Body 115 was examined for fingerprints by the Scotland Yard expert. The fire had caused extensive charring and the skin had been removed from both hands. Nonetheless, on the tip of the middle finger on the right hand was a small patch of reasonably intact skin from which a partial print was obtained. Given the importance of fingerprints in identifying people, this was considered to be a major find. If nothing else, it could be used to exclude some people from the list of possible names being investigated by the police. With the second post-mortem examination complete, Dr West returned the bodies to the mortuary where they would remain in storage until somebody was in a position to claim and bury them.[4]

As it turned out, it was not the second post-mortem examination that was to resolve the identity of Body 103. Instead it was diligent police work which, thanks to the man's age and ethnicity, narrowed down the list of possible names to only a handful from the more than 10,000 that had been suggested to the police since the night of the fire. On Friday 4 December the father of a man who had vanished on the night of the blaze was brought to central London and asked to view the metal bracelet that had been recovered with Body 103. He recognised it as having belonged to his 23-year-old son. The Coroner was informed and a few days later, following another inquest, Body 103 was released from the mortuary for burial. [5]

The identification of Body 103 meant that there was only one unnamed victim from the King's Cross fire: Body 115. Based on past experience, there was a general belief that the mystery of this man's identity would be quickly solved. Nothing could have been further from the truth.

CHAPTER SEVEN

The Unidentified Body

On 1 December 1987 the St Pancras Coroner's Court opened an inquest into the King's Cross fire's thirty-first victim. He had been a stockbroker who managed to escape from the booking hall to the surface but, sadly, his burns were so severe that he died in hospital several days later. The man's death caused some newspapers to print a revised list of all the fire's fatalities ending with the nameless victim. Officially, the unnamed victim was being referred to as the 'unknown' or 'unidentified' man but behind the scenes those involved in the King's Cross fire investigation were referring to him as Body 115 (pronounced as 'one one five').

This 'moniker', which sounds quite clinical on first hearing, came into use purely as a practical means by which the police could refer to this unidentified victim. For a short while the body had received the nickname 'Michael', after it was suspected that he might be a missing Irishman of that name. However, the post-mortem results excluded the missing Michael and so the police started to refer to the unnamed man by the number that had been given to him by the St Pancras mortuary staff. When dealing with an unidentified corpse 'Body 115' is as good a title as any and so it stuck.[1]

Given the problems associated with giving unidentified bodies a nickname, there have been moves in Britain to adopt the system used in the United States where unidentified bodies of men are routinely called 'John Doe' and those of women 'Jane Doe'. This standard practice takes away the danger of someone giving a nameless body a nickname that later turns out to be disrespectful. Thus an equivalent situation in the United States would have seen Body 115 automatically being called John Doe, an action that would have afforded it a name and yet, perversely, also a degree of anonymity.[2]

In the weeks following the fire both the Metropolitan and British Transport Police had made concerted efforts at finding a name for Body 115 but by mid-December 1987 the investigation had encountered its first major setback. In the days following the fire the police had been given the names of 10,500 people who, according to the friends and family that phoned them in, might have had cause to be in King's Cross on the night of the fire. It was from this pool of names that most of the victims had been identified but, despite early optimism, it was evident that Body 115 was not a good match for any of them.

The known physical characteristics of Body 115 automatically ruled out most of the names given to the police. The dead person's short stature, sex, Caucasian ethnicity and age automatically excluded those who were female, tall, young or non-white, while his dentures excluded those with their own teeth. With no matches on this list, it became evident that whoever Body 115 had been, his friends and family (assuming that he had any) had not missed him enough to associate his disappearance with the King's Cross fire. This suggested to police that he might have been a loner, or someone who through work or estrangement was separated from his next of kin. He may even have been someone whose presence wouldn't necessarily be missed in this country, such as a tourist, or perhaps someone who had cause to keep his identity a secret, such as an illegal immigrant or fugitive. With the list of names provided by the public exhausted, the police returned to the pathological evidence in the hope that this might tell them something about Body 115's lifestyle. It was an option that appeared to hold much promise.

When referring to Dr West's second post-mortem examination Superintendent Ian Blair of the Metropolitan Police said: 'I would have thought that 115 had more clues about it than most of the rest of the bodies. I had no impression that this was going to be a difficult case.'[3] The police did indeed have a number of excellent clues that Dr West had managed to elucidate during the two post-mortem examinations, clues that offered a good impression of the sort of man that Body 115 might have been.

The basic physical characteristics told the investigating police that they were dealing with a white man who would have been noticeably short in stature, perhaps standing between 5'0" and 5'4" tall. (Although the body's measured height was 5'2", allowances were made for age and error.) This was between eight and four inches smaller than the average male height in Great Britain at this time.[4] It was estimated that the man could have been as young as 40 but was more likely to have been in his fifties with an upper age limit of 60. He was well-nourished but not overweight.

Some of the pathology associated with the body gave clues to his probable lifestyle, habits and state of health. The man's dentures were thought to be old, as judged by their general state and the amount of tartar that had built up on them, but they were well made and had probably not come from an NHS dentist. Both dentures showed evidence of severe tobacco staining, suggesting that Body 115 had been a heavy smoker. A toxicology test on the blood reinforced this by revealing a carbon monoxide saturation level of 12 per cent, about what would be expected for a regular smoker. The blood also revealed an alcohol level of between 73 and 94 mg per 100 ml, suggesting that the man had been drinking moderately in the hours before the fire although he was not actually drunk at the time of death and would probably have passed a breathalyser test.

Further hints as to the man's lifestyle came from the state of his internal organs. The lungs showed signs of moderate emphysema and bronchiectasis, both of which would have left him with a constant cough and, at times, very short of breath. The emphysema was yet more evidence that the man had been middle-aged or older and that he had been a heavy smoker, although it could also mean that he had spent much of his life working or living in areas of high air pollution such as inner cities.

Additional evidence of Body 115's general ill health came from his heart which revealed that the coronary artery was partially obstructed, a condition technically known as aortic atheroma. The obstruction had been caused by the build-up of fatty deposits inside the artery which had made it constrict over time, lessening the flow of oxygenated blood to the heart. With Body 115, this furring of the blood vessels had become severe, causing them to narrow to a point where the arteries would not have been able to supply the heart muscle with enough oxygenated blood for its needs. During exercise, when the heart muscle demands more blood and oxygen than is available from the blood supply, this would have produced a stabbing pain in the chest: the classic symptom of angina. The unhealthy state of Body 115's arteries suggested that he could have suffered from regular angina attacks, something that would have affected the degree to which he could move about and/or exert himself. This condition is also commonly connected with heavy smoking but can also be a function of a diet high in saturated fats and a poor general state of fitness. Associated with this was evidence from Body 115's brain and other organs that he had suffered from abnormally high blood pressure, or hypertension, possibly dangerously so.

The final medical clue was the brain operation that, to judge by the scarring, had been performed some years previously. The operation had been in response to a mild stroke generated by a haemorrhage at the site of a small arterial blockage (or cerebral atheroma) in the brain. Again, this is often associated with an unhealthy lifestyle but can also be linked to heavy drinking.[5]

Aside from the pathological evidence relating to Body 115's medical health, there was little other information available that could help with finding a name. All the body's clothing, hair and most of its skin had been destroyed. This meant that not only was any documentation, such as a credit card, missing but basic information such as hair colour and style, eye colour and the presence of any skin blemishes and tattoos was not available. The destruction of the clothes was also a blow as these can normally say something about someone's financial status, age, profession and even their religion or cultural background. The intense heat of the fire had certainly done a remarkable job at creating an anonymous body out of a once living, breathing, human being.

Although there was a general lack of evidence relating to Body 115's specific identity, it was at least possible to suggest something about the man's circumstances. Dr West's pathological evidence painted a picture of Body 115 as someone who had not taken a great deal of care of himself. The diseased parts of the heart, lungs and brain suggested that Body 115 had been a heavy smoker whose diet was poor and who may also have been a regular, if moderate, drinker. This, combined with the stained dentures and a lack of jewellery or even a watch, meant that he was probably not from a privileged background. The fact that no one had reported him missing after the fire hinted that he had no close friends and family or, if he did, that he was estranged from them.

When asked to give his general impression of the man behind Body 115, Dr West confirmed all of this: 'He was quite a short man, was white and, looking at him, he appeared to be between 55 and 65 years of age. He suffered from coronary artery disease and may well have been aware of it, suffering heart pains in the chest. He may even have been treated for it. He would have had a chronic cough bringing up sputum, he may have been wheezy; his chest condition would have been noticeable to those who were well acquainted with him. We looked at his alcohol level; he had been drinking that evening but he had only been drinking a moderate amount and was under the legal limit for driving. The fact that he has had neurosurgery in the past could suggest that he perhaps is an individual who has suffered previous injury to his head or who following neurosurgery has become a bit of a loner.'

The idea that Body 115 might have been a loner was of great interest to the police. They had already raised the possibility he might have been an immigrant to London and/or that he was part of the city's sizeable community of casual workers. 'The search has been narrowed down to a tourist or someone with few friends or relatives,' said a British Transport Police spokesman.

This idea gained credibility because of the circumstances associated with Ralph Humberstone, another of the fire's victims. Mr Humberstone's body had been discovered in a passageway leading away from the booking hall and had been identified on the night of the fire because of documents discovered on his body. The extent of his injuries led Dr West to conclude that he had been caught in the flashover but that he 'had managed to make some escape'. Through his place of work, the police were able to trace Humberstone's residential address in London's Elephant and Castle and, from information provided by other people living at the address, tracked his childhood roots to Lincolnshire. Local and national appeals were made for his friends or relations to come forward but his body remained unclaimed. Humberstone appeared to have led a solitary existence and had it not been for the documents found on his body then he, like Body 115, might have remained unidentified.

Police discovered that Ralph Humberstone had lived a casual lifestyle. His job was a public house 'potman' which meant that he collected glasses, cleaned the toilets and emptied the ashtrays. He was known to have had other work as a temporary kitchen hand in an Italian restaurant near to Waterloo Station. The descriptions given to the police by his employer and housemates gave the impression that Mr Humberstone was a very down-at-heel character whose lifestyle occasionally bordered on vagrancy. This raised an interesting possibility: could Body 115 have lived a similar sort of casual lifestyle? Could Body 115 have even been a vagrant? The ill health, absence of jewellery, possible drinking habit and apparent lack of concerned relations suggested that this might at least be a possibility. In the absence of many other clues, it was a prospect that the police took seriously. [6]

Throughout December and January officers from the Metropolitan and British Transport Police scoured the streets surrounding

King's Cross and Euston Stations, searching out the beggars, tramps, down-and-outs and other people that make up London's transient community. On encountering a vagrant the police would ask whether any of their friends or acquaintances had been missing since the date of the fire. Each time the answer was negative although, given the distrust that vagrants have of the police, exactly how co-operative they were being has been questioned. The search revealed no new potential names for Body 115 and there were no reports of any of the King's Cross 'regulars' having vanished. With the vagrancy theory having come to nothing and the number of new names being suggested down to just a trickle, the search for Body 115's identity was in trouble.

CHAPTER EIGHT

Sugita No. 5

The investigation into Body 115 had taken place in parallel with the other police investigations into various aspects of the King's Cross fire. Predictably, the scale of the disaster and its location in central London had led to an instant media outcry. This placed enormous pressure on the managers of London Underground, London Regional Transport and the Westminster government, all of whom wanted to be seen to be taking action in the aftermath of the fire but, at the same time, did not want to accept any liability for it. Conversely, the media were actively searching for people to blame. They did not need to look far.

On the morning after the fire the national newspapers carried basic descriptions of the flashover and its casualties but they had little other information to go on. By lunchtime radio and television news programmes were reporting that the fire had begun on one of the escalators and that there had been 'chaotic scenes' following its discovery. As more information became available and as eyewitnesses came forward to be interviewed, it became apparent that the scale of the disaster may well have been exasperated by failings associated with the management of the entire London Underground network.

An editorial in the *Daily Mirror* summed up the situation: 'Nobody knew what to do. In spite of official inquiries, reports and recommendations, nobody had taken any notice. There were NO smoke outlets or sensors, NO loudspeaker alert to broadcast instructions in the warren of tunnels, NO emergency lighting of emergency exit signs.'[1]

In the following days, further unsavoury facts about safety management on the Tube emerged. A smoking ban had been widely flouted, both by staff and passengers, while the general age and poor condition of station equipment had led to a general build-up of newspapers, plastic bags, grease and other flammable litter. Perhaps most shocking of all was the revelation that each year the Underground experienced hundreds of fires. Indeed, fires were such a frequent occurrence that London Underground staff were instructed to play down the issue by referring to them as 'smoulderings'.[2] Most of these were small affairs involving litter on the track that had caught fire as a result of sparks from passing trains, but a few were more serious. It was revealed that in 1980, the last year for which statistics were collated, there had been 1246 fires reported on the Tube, sixty of which had been on escalators.[3] Furthermore, in the three years before the King's Cross fire there had been six 'serious fires', five of which occurred on the aging wooden escalators. It was, however, an incident at Oxford Circus that should have alerted people to the potential danger of fires in the Underground.

Oxford Circus Tube Station is the gateway to Oxford Street, one of the biggest and busiest shopping areas in the world, and as a consequence receives some of the highest passenger numbers on the entire network (although not as many as King's Cross). On 23 November 1984, at around 10.00 p.m., a fire broke out in a contractor's storage area on one of the deep platforms. Staff attempts at fighting the fire by hand quickly failed and the station's tunnels began to fill with dense smoke. Thirty fire engines arrived and a complete station evacuation was ordered but the instructions came too late; below the blaze a number of Underground staff and firefighters had become trapped. Ordinarily they would have been taken to safety by passing trains but, to compound the problem, an electrical failure had brought all lines leading into the station to a standstill. As the tunnels filled with smoke, 700 passengers had to walk down the tracks to the next station. It was considered to be a miracle that nobody had been killed and there was wide agreement that had the fire occurred at rush hour, there would have been fatalities.

The cause of the fire was thought to be a discarded match that had fallen among rubbish which had in turn ignited some flammable material in the contractor's store. The disquiet caused by this incident ultimately led to the creation of a Fire Safety Task Force which helped to implement some of the recommendations that resulted from an investigation of the fire. In February 1985 smoking was banned on most of the Tube network and a closer collaboration began between London Underground and the Fire Brigade. The official investigation into the fire concluded that: 'Only luck is preventing further fire tragedies on the Tube and luck has a habit of running out.'[4]

The media used the Oxford Circus fire and several other incidents as proof that responsibility for the King's Cross fire could be laid on London Underground's management team. They also blamed a lack of modernisation on the Tube which they said was the result of decades of national underfunding. The government was quick to react to the public's disquiet; the day after the fire Margaret Thatcher, the Prime Minister, was taken around the booking hall which was still detectably hot. 'I am horrified,' she said as a firefighter shone his torch about the blackened scene, 'It is one of the worst disasters we have had for some time.'[5]

Later the Transport Secretary, Paul Channon, made a statement to the House of Commons about the fire. In it he announced that there would be a public enquiry. 'I have decided that a formal investigation should be held into the disaster,' he announced to a very sombre Parliament. 'The evidence will be heard in public [and] the report will be published.'[6]

The announcement of an investigation into the King's Cross fire was welcomed by everyone and the fact it was to be held in public and its findings published reflected the seriousness of the disaster. Britain's authorities have a reputation for secrecy with even the most mundane of official papers often being subject to disclosure restrictions. When it came to politically sensitive issues, governments had been known to conduct any investigations behind closed doors with the findings remaining unpublished, something that inevitably leads to accusations of a cover-up. The scale and horrific nature of King's Cross made this option politically impossible but, given the potential criticism that could result, the government did not want to make life too difficult for itself. Thus, on 23 November, it was announced that the investigation into the King's Cross Underground fire would be headed by Desmond Fennell.

The appointment made some in the media feel uneasy. It was not Mr Fennell's qualification for the role that was in doubt – he was an experienced and well-regarded lawyer and a member of the Queen's Council – it was his connection with the ruling Conservative Party. Mr Fennell, who was aged 54, was not only a Conservative Party activist, but also the president of his Conservative Association in Buckinghamshire. Some commentators implied that the Conservative Party had installed a chairman who might prefer to see things from the government's point of view, possibly lessening the final report's impact on Parliament. Mr Fennell tried to calm his critics by announcing that his investigation would be exhaustive and that his recommendations would be made 'independent of cost'.[7]

From the start Desmond Fennell decided that he should look not just at the physical cause of the fire but also into the actions of those staff and passengers involved on the night of the disaster. He also wanted to examine the issue of safety across the whole London Underground network. The wide scope of this investigation immediately placed a large burden of work onto the British Transport and Metropolitan Police, both of whom were in charge of gathering witness statements and other evidence associated with the fire. That process had begun on the day after the fire and continued for weeks afterwards, taking up hundreds of working hours.

By the time of the inquiry's official opening on 2 December, over three hundred witness statements had been gathered and transcribed but there were dozens more still to collect. Added to these were documents being submitted by all the emergency services involved, by London Underground investigators and by various specialists who had been brought in to examine or advise on certain matters associated with the fire. The public-hearing phase of the inquiry, during which witnesses would be cross-examined under oath in court, was set for February 1988. By this time the British Transport Police had to have gathered all their evidence, catalogued and sorted it and acted on any new leads that were uncovered. They also had to act on any outstanding issues from the night of the fire that remained unresolved. One of these was Body 115.

It was in January 1988 that officers in British Transport Police became aware that all attempts hitherto made at finding a name for Body 115 had failed. A senior officer said: 'We found one of the casualties that night had no name and we were struggling as a Service to actually find a next of kin due to the difficulties in identification.' Another person associated with the case said that the presence of Body 115 was 'an embarrassment' to the police and that in light of all the other problems associated with the fire, it was also 'the final straw'.[8]

Rather than allow the Body 115 case to progress as part of the background inquiries into the fire, a decision was taken to make it the subject of a separate investigation by a dedicated team of British Transport Officers. That team was to be headed by Chief Inspector John Hennigan who already had considerable experience with the King's Cross investigation. Hennigan had attended the scene of the fire and afterwards managed the police incident room, co-ordinating the inquiries into the cause of the fire as well as preparing and collating material for the coroner's inquest and for Desmond Fennell's public inquiry. He was thus intimately acquainted with all aspects of the King's Cross disaster and had even seen Body 115. 'I wouldn't want anybody to come across that sight,' he said. 'How can you describe a really badly burnt body? Someone said that it looked like a tailor's dummy that got caught in a fire.'

Below Chief Inspector Hennigan was Detective Sergeant Ray Turner who was in charge of co-ordinating the day-to-day investigation. Several other officers were also assigned to the case on a full- or part-time basis; they were in charge of gathering evidence and chasing up leads.

A review of progress to date revealed that the standard method of matching names submitted to the police against the characteristics of Body 115 had failed to find a match. To progress the investigation, Hennigan and his team needed to be able to use evidence associated with the body that would eventually lead them to its identity. This meant that they were going to be reliant on the forensic evidence recovered during the post-mortem examinations.

The forensic information from Body 115 had already been used to gain a general understanding of the man's lifestyle and habits but the body also possessed several unique pieces of evidence, such as his fingerprint and dentures, which might help in the search for his identity. A review was undertaken with the aim of identifying which items of evidence were most likely to produce a result in the shortest possible time. Fingerprints, as we shall see, are a reliable form of identification but finding a match in the various national fingerprint databases is a costly and time consuming process; the same was true for other items of evidence, such as the dentures. On balance the most promising was a piece of evidence related to the brain surgery performed on Body 115 several years before.

Finding evidence of medical treatment on a body can be an immensely useful means of narrowing the search for its identity. This is because if a person needs to visit a GP or hospital to have a wound, disease or biological abnormality attended to, then details of their condition, and its treatment, will be recorded on their NHS medical record. Thus injuries found on a body, such as cuts that require stitches, broken bones, surgery on the internal organs and the implantation of artificial objects such as false hips or heart valves, can be matched to procedures in an individual's medical record. If the police have a probable name for an unidentified body then the nature and location of any old wounds or surgical scars can be compared with those noted on the person's medical history; if the two match, identification can then be confirmed.

The evidence of brain surgery in Body 115 had in fact already been used to eliminate a number of potential candidates whose medical records had shown no trace of them having undergone this procedure. However, as well as confirming or denying potential matches, in some circumstances medical evidence can also be used to find a name for a person. This is especially true in cases where artificial objects (such as false kneecaps) have been implanted into the body as some of these have serial numbers on them that have allowed the police to trace the hospital where the surgery took place and, from there, obtain the deceased's name and medical records.

Body 115 was missing most of its skin which meant that any evidence of scarring had also been destroyed; there was also no sign of any old traumas such as broken bones, heart surgery or an appendectomy. The body held evidence of only one major surgical procedure: the brain operation. On its own the surgery offered few clues to the man's identity; it is a standard procedure, routinely carried out on hundreds of people each year in the United Kingdom. It was also difficult to say precisely when the surgery had been carried out. Dr Iain West told the police that, in his opinion, the surgery 'was done at least nine months or a year ago but it could have been done several years ago and probably was.'[9]

The procedure itself may not have been very diagnostic but what caught the investigation team's attention was the presence of the small but distinctive aneurysm clip that had been inserted into the skull by the surgeon. According to Dr West this had been done 'in order to control some bleeding on the right side of the brain.' The need for aneurysm clips during brain surgery is explained by pathologist Professor Christopher Milroy who worked on the latter stages of the Body 115 investigation: 'If there is a little blister, or balloon on a blood vessel, and the blood vessel bursts then the surgeon therefore needs to clip that artery. To do that he has to get in at the artery which is at the base of the brain, which is of course encased in the skull. Therefore, he has to cut around the side of the skull, produce a flap that he can then open to look in ... Then there is surgery to the skull which is laid apart, the clip is then placed on the artery and then everything is closed back up. That leaves a defect in the skull which never heals completely, so one can always tell when someone has had neurosurgery.'[10]

The aneurysm clip recovered from Body 115 by Dr West was of a type that he could not readily identify, which suggested that it was rarely used by brain surgeons. The investigation team hoped that the clip's rarity would allow them to trace where and when the brain surgery had occurred. If so, then it ought to be possible to find Body 115's medical records and hence also his name.

In late December 1987 the investigation into the aneurysm clip was placed in the hands of Detective Constable Robin Smith of the British Transport Police. His enquiries quickly took him to a neurosurgery expert based in Northern Ireland who was able to identify the aneurysm clip's exact make and model: it was known by surgeons as a 'Sugita No. 5'. This proved to be a significant discovery and led the police into the unusual and specialised world of aneurysm clips.

Aneurysm clips have been used in brain surgery since the 1930s, but advances in microsurgery during the 1960s led to the development of smaller and stronger clips that were angled to give the surgeon a clearer view of the aneurysm. As techniques progressed, surgeons were able to operate effectively on aneurysms that were located deep inside the brain but the commercially available clips were proving inadequate for the job. By the late 1970s some neurosurgeons were frustrated with a lack of commercially available clips and began to make their own modifications. At this time the Japanese neurosurgeon Kenichiro Sugita happened to be visiting London when he heard his colleagues' frustrations and, fascinated by their complaints, made notes on some of the ideas they had to improve the clips. On returning to Japan Sugita began to manufacture his own aneurysm clips which, according to one competitor, 'turned out to be a best-seller'. Sugita clips became commercially available in 1977 and were generally used for large and deeply located brain aneurysms. Several different models were produced including the Sugita No. 5, a so-called 'long clip' (in fact it is only a couple of centimetres from top to tip) with a pronounced bend in it. The No. 5 was a specialised clip and was manufactured in Japan between 1977 and 1982 before being superseded by other designs. Within this narrow time range the No. 5 clip was not widely used outside Japan and especially not in Europe, something that ran in favour of the police investigation into Body 115.[11]

Detective Constable Smith was able to determine from the Sugita manufacturing company in Japan that there had only ever been one importer of No. 5 aneurysm clips into Great Britain, a large medical supply shop called Downs Surgical located on London's New Cavendish Street. The police contacted Downs Surgical and asked for help in tracking down which British hospitals had bought supplies of the Sugita No. 5 clips from the shop. Ray Hedges, who was then Downs Surgical's general manager, agreed to the request. 'We looked at our records and found that between 1978 and 1982 we must have imported something like between 300 and 400 of this type of clip from Japan,' he recalls.[12]

To be precise, Downs Surgical were able to confirm that exactly 120 Sugita No. 5 aneurysm clips had been imported into the country between 1980 and 1982. They suspected that another 140 to 180 had been imported between 1977, when the clip was first manufactured, and the start of 1980 when the shop's records began. This gave a maximum of 300 Sugita No. 5 aneurysm clips that could have been used in brain operations in the United Kingdom between 1977 and 1982. Assumedly the clip that had been implanted into Body 115 came from among this number.

These odds were low enough to warrant further investigation by the British Transport Police team; if the medical records relating to all 300 people who had received Sugita No. 5 clips could be tracked down then, by a process of elimination, it ought to be possible to identify Body 115. Other factors associated with the surgery would help narrow down this pool of people further. Given that Body 115's operation had been performed on the right-hand side of the skull of a male patient, it was calculated that probably only around ninety operations would match these criteria (the rest were either on the left-hand side or on women). Of these ninety or so patients, a good many could be eliminated because their age or height did not match those of Body 115; some would doubtless be found to still be alive or have traceable graves. Others would also be eliminated because of mismatches with Body 115 concerning the dentures or other factors. Suddenly the small and apparently insignificant aneurysm clip had become the best hope of identifying Body 115.[13]

Downs Surgical were asked to provide the police with a list of the people to whom they had supplied the aneurysm clips. 'We would have to have sold them to any one of sixteen, or maybe all, sixteen health authorities and probably to forty or so of the neurosurgical centres in this country,' said Ray Hedges. This number of health authorities and hospitals, while not exactly small, was equally well not prohibitively large either. Checking them all would take time but it was not an insurmountable task, especially if it meant that Body 115 could be given a name and, hopefully, be returned to his next of kin.

The process of contacting all the health authorities and neuro-surgery centres on the Downs Surgical list began in earnest but it was soon apparent that tracing the whereabouts of each individual Sugita No. 5 clip was going to be nigh on impossible. Most of the medical institutions contacted had records which showed that they had bought Sugita No. 5 clips from Down's Surgical but none had kept an inventory of where, when and on which patient each individual clip had been used. Given the often pressured nature of neurosurgery, keeping track of individual clips was simply not possible. When in the operating theatre, a neurosurgeon would select an aneurysm clip by its shape, size and suitability for the brain injury concerned. In most cases the choice of clip was unplanned and instinctive and there was no medical need for anyone to write down the clip's make and model either on the patient's records or in the surgeon's notes. Once inserted into the skull, an aneurysm clip would become anonymous. This news placed the Body 115 investigation team back at square one.

Without a list of names, they had no way of differentiating those patients who had been given Sugita No. 5 clips from the thousands of people who underwent brain operations in Britain during the late 1970s and early 80s. Trying to identify Body 115 from a pool this large would be like looking for the proverbial needle in a haystack. It was frustrating; although Body 115 almost certainly had a medical file stored in the archives of one of the forty hospitals that had used the Sugita No. 5 clips, there was no ready means of finding it.

Chief Inspector Hennigan expressed this frustration: 'We felt quite confident that having gone to the right hospitals we should be able to trace somebody fitting the body who had an operation but there was no record of their usage. A surgeon would require a clip; a clip was handed to him and obviously it was used during the procedures. Therefore unless we could go to the hospitals with a name [for Body 115] and trace it against a particular type of operation we were going to be struggling.'[14]

In late January 1988 the enquiries into the aneurysm clip came to an abrupt halt. Without further information, such as a possible name for Body 115 and an approximate idea of where and when the surgery took place, it was impossible to proceed. The investigation into the aneurysm clip had narrowed down roughly where and when Body 115's brain operation had been performed but it was not going to provide the unknown man's name. With this avenue closed off, the police were forced back to Dr West's pathology report which still contained valuable forensic information. On balance, the next most hopeful piece of evidence was the single partial fingerprint that had been obtained from the middle finger of Body 115's right hand.

CHAPTER NINE

A Lone Fingerprint

For over a century the swirling, hypnotic patterns that make up our fingerprints have been the most widely used means of personal identification, chiefly by the police, but also by other authorities. It is a well known fact that the patterned skin on every one of our fingers is unique to ourselves and is not shared with anyone else. Even the fingerprints of identical twins differ from one another. It is also common knowledge that the police routinely use fingerprint evidence to help locate, identify and, in some circumstances, eliminate suspects in criminal cases. In recent years innovations such as computer-readable biometric passports and national identity cards have led to our finger-prints being used as a means of establishing our identity as part of anti-fraud and anti-terrorism measures. However, what is often overlooked is that fingerprints are also a useful tool in forensic pathology, especially in cases where a body arrives at a mortuary with no ready means of identification associated with it.

This was true in the case of Body 115, even though the horrific circumstances of the fire led to only a single fingerprint being obtained. In the weeks after the fire this lone fingerprint had been used to eliminate a number of potential names from the inves-tigation. A mismatch between the fingerprints of a candidate name (usually obtained from criminal or armed service records) and that of Body 115 would instantly eliminate them from the inquiry. However, the police believed that the fingerprint could be used to do more than just eliminate names: they hoped that it might be able to provide a name for Body 115 by utilising the unique way in which the police have found to exploit the physical properties of human fingerprints.

Fingerprints are made from small raised ridges of skin which run in patterns across not just our fingers, but also our palms, toes and the soles of our feet. These patterns develop while we are in the womb and then stay with us, unaltered, until death (barring any severe skin damage). Experts divide the skin that forms fingerprints into ridges, which are the raised bits, and furrows, which are the valleys between the ridges. The characteristic fingerprint pattern that is produced when we place a dirty hand on a clean surface or push our fingers into soft clay is formed chiefly by the ridges which will make contact with an object while the furrows in-between generally do not. It is this system of ridges and furrows that allows us to pick up a relatively smooth object, such as a glass, by creating a rough surface against which the glass can be gripped; it has also been suggested that fingerprints may originally have evolved to help our forebears climb in trees. [1]

The fingerprint has long been recognised as a means of personal identification. Pottery from China dating to around 2000 years ago seems to show that even then individual potters were using their fingerprints as a form of personal signature. It would, however, be a good many centuries before the fingerprint received any form of serious scrutiny and even longer before their potential value to science and criminology would be recognised. The first person to describe a fingerprint pattern was the British physician Nehemiah Grew who, in 1684, provided the world with the following observation:

'For if anyone will but take the pains, with an indifferent glass to survey the palm of his hand, he may perceive innumerable little ridges, of equal bigness and distance, and everywhere running parallel one with another. And especially, upon the hands and first joints of the fingers and thumb. They are very regularly disposed into spherical triangles and elliptics.' [2]

Nehemiah Grew accompanied this most basic of descriptions with two illustrations, one of which showed the patterns on the fingers and palm of a hand and the other an extreme close up of the ridges and furrows that comprise a fingerprint, complete with uniform rows of sweat pores. Two years after this the Italian anatomist Marcello Malpighi made a similar observation, describing the intricate pattern of loops, ridges and spirals that make up our prints. However, neither Grew nor Malpighi made any mention of the uniqueness of a person's fingerprints and therefore did not see their potential for use as a means of personal identification. [3]

For more than a century little further progress was made. This, in the opinion of one modern doctor, was probably because, in comparison to other parts of the body, patients do not complain of fingerprint-related ailments. As a result biologists and anatomists rarely had cause to notice them. This was not true of the Czechoslovakian physiologist Jan Purkinje who in the 1820s studied a great many of his patients' fingerprints and was the first to recognise that their patterns had a certain geometry to them. In 1823 he published the first known scheme for classifying finger-prints which recognised nine 'varieties of pattern' including ellipses, loops, curves, stripes and three types of whorl. Purkinje's work was admirable but because he failed to notice the individuality of fingerprints, his peers could see no practicable application for it. At the time of his death, in 1869, fingerprints were still regarded as a curiosity with their patterns having no more relevance to science or society than sand ripples on a beach. [4]

The scientific community continued to be ignorant of the hidden potential of fingerprints until as late as 1880. In that year everything was to change, but it was not as a result of a sudden major discovery or scientific revolution. The break-through came as the result of a short letter written to the British science journal *Nature* by an unassuming doctor named Henry Faulds.

In 1872 the recently graduated Faulds had accepted a missionary post in a Tokyo hospital. In 1878 he was handed some antique Japanese pottery and noticed that some of the shards held faint impressions of the potters' fingerprints. Faulds was living in a post-Darwinian age where talk of evolutionary relationships dominated scientific thinking. Given the row over man's alleged descent from apes, Faulds thought it would be interesting to see if there were any discernable differences between the fingerprints of humans and those of monkeys and chimpanzees. He quickly developed a system of obtaining physical prints using printers' ink and white paper and, after gaining access to some barbary apes, was able to declare that there were similarities between their fingerprint patterns and those of humans. Only when faced with a lack of further ape specimens did Faulds begin to take prints from humans, with the aim of gathering specimens from as many different nationalities as possible. In doing so Faulds hoped that each nationality might hold certain characteristics in their fingerprints and that these could be used to 'aid students of ethnology in classification'.

It was largely on the strength of his 'ethnology' work that Faulds eventually wrote to *Nature*. He explained his methodology and his belief that there were characteristics in the patterns of Japanese fingerprints that could be used to differentiate them from European ones and that, more bizarrely, there were similarities between the patterns on the fingers of barbary apes and Europeans. However, it was the final, almost incidental, paragraph that was to be the real eye opener. In this Faulds briefly describes his involvement in a criminal case that occurred in the summer of 1879 where a thief had made good his escape by scrambling over a recently painted garden wall, leaving behind a dirty handprint. This, naturally, drew Faulds's attention and led him to take the fingerprints of a man whom the police had arrested as a suspect. The prints did not match, leading Faulds to declare the suspected man innocent – much to the hilarity of the police, all of whom thought him to be quite mad. However, a few days later another man confessed to being the thief. His prints matched those on the garden wall, validating Faulds's theory and silencing the sceptical Tokyo police.

In another separate case, Faulds was able to identify a person who had been sneakily drinking spirits by the fingerprints left on the bottle. These two cases, which were summarised in only a few sentences, led Faulds to declare that 'when bloody finger-marks or impressions of clay, glass, etc., exist, they may lead to the scientific identification of criminals'. He also noted: 'Other cases might occur in medico-legal investigations, as when the hands only of some mutilated victim were found. If previously known [their fingerprints] would be much more precise in value than the standard mole of penny novelists.'[5]

Although not stated in so many words, Faulds was the first person to declare the possibility that a person's fingerprints are unique to themselves and that, consequently, they could be used as a means of personal identification at crime scenes or with unidentified bodies.

Faulds's remarks were insightful and caught the attention of one William Herschel, a middle-aged civil servant who had spent many years working in British-administered India. Herschel came from a family with much scientific kudos; his grandfather was a highly regarded astronomer and the discoverer of the planet Uranus while his father had invented the means of fixing photographic plates. Although not himself a scientist, William was inadvertently to continue the family tradition. In 1853 he became a government administrator in India but was immediately confronted with a system that was open to fraud and mismanagement on a grand scale. A large part of the problem came from not being able to identify the people who, on payday, would come to claim their wages. As a result money was being paid out to the wrong people or, in some cases, to people who, it turned out, had died some years previously. After a time Herschel noticed that many illiterate natives would use their thumbprint in place of a written signature and that, on looking back through the files, no two prints were the same. He designed an experiment whereby each claimant had their thumbprint taken and placed on file so that, come payday, a fresh print could be taken and a comparison made. It was an instant success, reducing instances of fraud to almost zero. Herschel widened the experiment:

'When I found all room for suspicion effectually removed, I tried it on a larger scale in the several registration offices under me, and here I had the satisfaction of seeing every official and legal agent connected with these offices confess that the use of these signatures lifted off the ugly cloud of suspiciousness which always hangs over offices in India. It put a summary and absolute stop to the very idea of either personation or repudiation from the moment half a dozen men had made their marks and compared them together. I next introduced them into the jail, where they were not un-needed. On commitment to jail each prisoner had to sign with his finger. Any official visitor to the jail after that could instantly satisfy himself of the identity of the man whom the jailor produced by requiring him to make a signature on the spot and comparing it with that which the books showed.'[6]

During his Indian posting Herschel collected thousands of such prints and saw his system adopted by various parts of civil service. In 1879 he retired back to England and was in the process of thinking about how best his thumbprint system could be used in Britain when he read Faulds's letter to *Nature*. Although slightly crushed that someone else had beaten him into print, Herschel wrote an immediate reply to Faulds's letter that was published by *Nature* a few weeks later. In it he outlined the uses of the thumbprint as a means of guaranteeing an individual's identity but, because he had over twenty years' experience with finger-printing, he was also able to state with certainty two facts: that no two thumbprints for different individuals are the same and that the thumbprint does not change with time but remains constant throughout life.[7]

In less than a month Faulds and Herschel had given all the information needed for people to begin using fingerprints as a means of personal identification. Faulds had provided evidence of their potential use for identifying unknown persons in instances where their fingerprint could be obtained; Herschel provided proof that the fingerprint was a highly reliable means of personal identification. However, the world chose to ignore their findings and it seems that few of their peers could be convinced of the potential of the fingerprint. In the coming years Faulds offered to quit Japan and return to London in order to set up (free of charge) a fingerprinting unit at Scotland Yard. The police declined his offer; they could not be convinced that fingerprints had an application to criminology.[8]

At around the time he had written to *Nature*, Henry Faulds also penned a letter to the naturalist Charles Darwin, asking him whether he could help him obtain fingerprints from lemur monkeys. Darwin regretted that he could not but commented that he had forwarded Faulds's letter to his cousin Francis Galton, who took more of an interest in genetics than he.[9] Galton did not reply to the letter and so Faulds assumed that he had taken no interest in its contents. It was therefore of some surprise when, several years later, Galton gave a talk on fingerprints to members of the Royal Society where, as well as advocating their use as a means of personal identification, he also suggested that there was the need for a scientific and universal means of classifying fingerprints.

Without acknowledging Faulds's work, Galton set about devising a means of describing fingerprints that made extensive use of Herschel's knowledge and data. To do so he built upon Purkinje's 1823 classification system but also made use of work of the Parisian police chief Alphonse Bertillon, who had developed a means of using various body measurements to identify an individual. Bertillon's science of 'anthropometry' had already been used to create 'Bertillon cards' which were slips of paper containing the vital statistics of thousands of known criminals. These were routinely used by police forces around the world to give names to hardened criminals who would use disguises and pseudonyms to hide their identity.

The result was Galton's comprehensive 1892 book, entitled *Finger Prints*, in which he outlined his new classification scheme and used statistics to reinforce the uniqueness of each person's fingerprints. The odds of two individuals sharing an identical fingerprint were, wrote Galton, 1 in 64 billion. The likelihood of two individuals sharing identical prints on all ten fingers were 'far beyond the capability of human imagination'. Galton was soon to be proved correct, but not in his own country.

In the year that *Finger Prints* was published a brutal murder took place in Necochea, a coastal village close to Buenos Aires, Argentina. The victims were two children, aged four and six, who had been beaten to death at their ramshackle home. Their mother, Francesca Rojas, was also slightly injured but she accused her boyfriend, named Valasquez, of the crime. With no independent eyewitnesses, the only clue was a bloody fingerprint left on the door frame. The investigation stalled until the detective in charge, Eduardo Alvarez, declared that he could match the prints with those of Francesca Rojas. Faced with this, she broke down and confessed to the crime. Alvarez had taken his lead from the work of his police superior Juan Vucetich, an immigrant from Croatia, who had followed the growing debate over fingerprints and had developed his own basic classification system.

With the potential use of fingerprint evidence so obvious, the British Home Office agreed to use Galton's classification scheme to add details of criminals' fingerprints to their Bertillon cards but there was a problem. Galton's system would permit only 20,000 different prints to be held on file, a number he believed sufficient to cover the whole of England's criminal population. However, as Faulds and Herschel had long suspected, the use of fingerprints proved so useful to the police that the 20,000 permissible references was predicted to be sufficient for only a few years.

In 1901 Scotland Yard took a bold decision and founded a dedicated Fingerprint Bureau which saw the abandonment of most of Bertillon's 'anthropometry' body measurements in favour of fingerprinting. Galton's classification method was also abandoned in favour of a new streamlined system developed by policeman Edward Henry. The Henry system, as it is still known, takes key features, such as whorl patterns, from a full set of ten fingerprints and assigns them numerical scores depending on where these features occur. Simple mathematics then gives each set of prints an overall numerical value which would be used to allocate a person's fingerprint pattern into one of 1024 groups. Thus if the police can calculate the overall numerical value of a suspect's fingerprints, it will tell them which grouping of fingerprint pattern to look in. Thus the Henry system greatly narrows down the number of prints that the police need to search in order to identify specific ones, although the final identification must still be made by visual comparison.

The Henry system made searching so much easier that in the first year of its operation 1722 positive identifications were made compared to only 400 in the previous decade. However, the Henry system can only be used when a set of all ten fingerprints has been obtained which means that it is less useful for crime scenes, most of which provide only one or two individual prints. To find a match for an individual fingerprint means manually searching the file cards, a task that could be prohibitively time-consuming (unless a list of suspects is known to the police).

The first conviction based on fingerprint evidence came in London in September 1902 after a left thumbprint was recovered from a newly painted windowsill at the scene of a break-in. The three detectives assigned to the Fingerprint Bureau spent hours going through their file cards until a match was obtained with the card of one Harry Jackson, a 41-year-old labourer and known burglar. The court accepted the fingerprint as evidence of Jackson's presence at the crime scene, leading to a sentence of seven years in custody. Similar convictions followed including, in 1905, the first one for a murder; a year later Edward Henry received a knighthood for his services to police work. [10]

Police forces around the world started to adopt the Henry system and, like Scotland Yard, immediately saw its benefits. The invention of the telegraph allowed a suspect's fingerprint details to be transmitted across the world but before long many police force fingerprint databases became victims of their own success.

By 1946 the FBI, on its own, held over 100 million fingerprint cards in manually maintained files; by 1971 it was double this number.[11]

Although not on the same scale, the British police were suffering from a similar problem so that by the early 1960s there were several million cards in the National Fingerprint Collection. In 1966 preparations were made for a computerised fingerprint retrieval system, following in the footsteps of several similar systems then being constructed in the United States. The system, known as Videofile, was based around digitally scanning in the fingerprints then held on file cards so that trained officers could retrieve them from the computer's database and view them on screen. This was a vast improvement on the old method of manually searching index cards and when Videofile eventually went live in 1978 it held images of over 2.5 million fingerprints. Although Videofile allowed trained officers to retrieve individual fingerprint files in an instant, its role in finding matches for individual prints was limited. The computer was not sophisticated enough to be able to take a fingerprint from a crime scene and then search its own database for a match. Instead it relied on a trained officer sitting in front of a computer monitor making visual comparisons which was certainly a vast improvement over the card files. However, it still meant that searching for individual prints was a time-consuming process.

In 1980 the police Fingerprint Bureau was subdivided into the National Fingerprint Office, which was in charge of comparing sets of prints and making identifications based on criminal records alone, and the Scenes of Crime Branch, which was tasked with making comparisons and identifications based on prints taken at crime scenes. In the year of the King's Cross fire over 40,000 fingerprint identifications were made by the police force although this represented only 2 per cent of criminal cases. 'The proportion of crimes where identification might be made using fingerprints is certainly greater than this,' concluded a Parliamentary Audit Commission in 1988. Even so, at the time of the King's Cross fire fingerprints were the most widely used means of establishing an unknown individual's identity, a fact that was very relevant to the Body 115 investigation. [12]

The single fingerprint taken from Body 115 came from the tip of the middle finger on the right hand but it was far from perfect. The central part of the print shows a classic 'single loop' pattern which points to the left but beyond this the rest is obliterated by the cracked pattern of the body's charred skin. In technical terms, the print is generally described as having a 'group 1 radial loop', which is not that uncommon, but its finer features, such as the points where the ridges join or divide, made it more distinctive. The Scotland Yard specialist who first examined it was able to say that Body 115's fingerprint was 'unusual' and that, although imperfect, there was enough information to allow a comparison to be made with the millions of other prints on record.

In 1987 there were approximately 5.5 million fingerprints held in the police's national collection. The majority of these had been taken from people who had been arrested and then subject to criminal proceedings within the British justice system. If Body 115 had ever been apprehended or had spent time in jail then his fingerprints ought to be on file, permitting a match to be made with the print taken at the post-mortem examination. It was agreed that the entire police collection should be searched in the hope of finding a match with Body 115.

Such a search of the whole national fingerprint collection is a vast undertaking in terms of staffing and the costs associated with this. The millions of comparisons can only be carried out by trained specialists at the police's dedicated Fingerprint Office. Had Body 115 produced a complete set of fingerprints then the task would have been easier; they could have been classified under the Henry system which would have allowed staff at the Fingerprint Office to narrow their search down to only a few thousand people. Unfortunately, having just one print made the task exponentially more difficult. To find a match, Body 115's lone fingerprint would have to be compared with every other middle finger, right hand print in the system. Even with the computerised Videofile system, it was a labour-intensive job that had to be fitted around more immediate tasks such as identifying fingerprints left at crime scenes.

It was estimated that a complete search would take several months or more to complete and there was, of course, every possibility that Body 115 would have no criminal record and that a match would not be made. Rather than waiting in hope that the fingerprint would drag a name out of the criminal record system, the Body 115 investigation team continued to pursue other leads. They were prepared to try anything that might give them a name, and thus a decision was taken to employ a high-risk strategy. The investigation team would attempt to give Body 115 a recognisable face. [13]

CHAPTER TEN

Do You Know This Man?

The era of forensic facial reconstruction in Britain began in 1983 when a young woman's skeleton was uncovered in some Oxfordshire woods. Evidence associated with the scene led police to suspect that she had been murdered. However, there was no clue to the woman's identity and so, after weeks of fruitless appeals, the police contacted Richard Neave, a forensic artist based at Manchester University who had developed a technique for reconstructing facial likenesses from the skulls of Egyptian mummies, prehistoric humans and other archaeological exhibits. It was the police's hope that Neave would be able to produce a reasonable reconstruction of the murdered woman's face using only information available from her skull. Richard Neave agreed to give it a try.

A few weeks later saw Neave unveil a sculpture that depicted the face of a European-looking woman with narrow lips and high cheekbones. Police were able to take Neave's sculpture and match it to some photographs of a girl that had been found in a rucksack over two miles away from the body. The rucksack contained other papers that allowed detectives to trace the dead woman's origins to Finland where her dental records were used to confirm her identity. [1]

At this time the use of forensic artistry in criminal cases was unknown but with the police having been alerted to its potential usefulness, Neave's services were called on regularly. In almost all instances Neave would be asked to construct a facial likeness for a murder victim whose identity could not be established using conventional means. Then, in early January 1988, he received a more unusual request from the British Transport Police in London who had a nameless male body that had defied all attempts at identification. However, this man had not been the victim of a violent crime; he had been killed in the King's Cross fire.

Richard Neave is a medical artist who developed his facial reconstruction technique using archaeological specimens, and he acknowledges that working with the police on criminal or missing persons cases is a much tougher proposition. 'As a general rule,' he says, 'what seems to happen is that one creates a face which is very similar to the kind of face which the individual had when alive. There are too many variables for a reconstruction based only on a skull to be completely accurate and it can never be regarded as a portrait.' Despite these caveats, Neave's success rate is good, something that he puts down to a rigorous step-by-step technique that he has developed over time and which, as we shall see, incorporates within it some aspects of other older, more established methodologies.

Having agreed to become involved in the Body 115 investigation, Neave's first task was to see what clues about the unknown man could be gleaned from the post-mortem findings. The pathology report was able to give him Body 115's height, poor state of health and, most importantly, an age of between 40 and 60 years. It also alerted him to the brain operation on the right-hand side of the skull which was relevant because it would have left a highly visible scar on the forehead. These features were crucial to the reconstruction process as they told him about things such as the degree of aging and texture to give the skin, the general size and shape of the ears and the position of the surgical scar.

Neave was able to find other clues from the body that the pathologist had not picked up on. Even though severely burned, Neave was still able to get an idea as to the original shape of Body

83

115's nose and lips plus some other more minor details from the face. More problematic was the absence of any information about Body 115's hair and eye colour, the destruction of which meant that the finished sculpture could not have a wig, eyebrows or any facial hair added to it.

With this basic information at his fingertips, Neave could begin to make the facial reconstruction but he first needed a clean cast of Body 115's skull. To do this required 'de-fleshing', a standard technique that is usually accomplished in the pathology laboratory by 'cooking' the remains until the soft tissues and grease come away from the bones. Once de-fleshed, a mould was made of Body 115's skull from which a cast was prepared and sent to Neave's laboratory at Manchester University. Here he put into effect a technique that had taken him nearly fifteen years to perfect but which was based on a tradition dating back nearly a century.

The event that would lead to the first forensic facial reconstruction occurred on 28 July 1750, with the death of the famous German composer Johann Sebastian Bach. Three days later Bach was laid to rest in the Johanniskirche graveyard in Leipzig but no headstone was erected and in time the grave's exact location was forgotten, much to the annoyance of his many admirers. In October 1894 a planned enlargement of the Johanniskirche graveyard meant sinking foundations in the area where Bach's grave was traditionally thought to lie. It was decided that this would be an ideal opportunity to try and locate the great musician's final resting place.

Although the exact burial spot was not known, there were some clues. It was recorded that the grave was located six steps from the church's south door and that Bach's body had been encased in a fine oak coffin. Of the 1400 people buried in 1750, only twelve had gone to their graves in wooden coffins. With this knowledge the diggers went to work and, after three days, had recovered not one but three wooden coffins, one of which contained the skeleton of 'an elderly male, well proportioned, not large of stature, with massive skull, receding forehead, shallow eye-sockets and heavy jaws.'[2]

A comparison of the skull with portraits of the musician suggested that the skeleton was that of Bach, but rather than make a mistake it was decided to get the opinion of Dr Wilhelm His, Germany's foremost anatomist. Dr His had a reputation for innovation but even so the approach he took to identifying Bach's remains was remarkable. He decided that the best solution would be to use the shape of the skull to recreate a three-dimensional clay likeness of the deceased person's face and then compare this with Bach's portraits.

Although there had been some previous attempts at making facial reconstructions from skulls, these had been accomplished without any formal scientific methodology and the results had been somewhat mixed. His turned his mind to the problem and decided that if he could find out the depth of skin tissue at certain specific points on the human skull then this information could be used on other skulls to create lifelike reconstructions of their faces. With the help of over two dozen cadavers His used a needle to measure the depth of skin at twenty-one standard points across the face and forehead. Returning to Bach's supposed skull, His took the tissue-thickness measurements and modelled clay across the skull to the same depth, smoothed it out and then added details such as eyebrows and wrinkles so as to form a recognisable face. The bust was finished in 1895 and compared to contemporary paintings of Bach; the similarity was unmistakable, permitting His to declare that Bach's skeleton had been recovered. Dr His's work was later used by the sculptor Carl Seffner to create a monument to Bach that was placed on public display in Leipzig. [3]

Wilhelm His provided the world with a scientifically controlled technique for reconstructing the faces of people who had been dead for many years. In the coming years Dr His's work was taken up by others and expanded to include more tissue-depth data on a greater number of reference points on the skull. However, rather than using this new-found technique on the unidentified victims of murder or accidents, almost all facial reconstructions were performed on archaeological specimens dating back thousands or even tens of thousands of years. There was particular interest in reconstructing faces from the skulls of Neolithic and Neanderthal humans but it was noticed that different scientists were producing markedly different results, even when working on the same skull. Mutterings about the unreliability of facial reconstruction led, in 1913, to anatomist H. von Eggeling devising an experiment which involved asking two different sculptors to make facial reconstructions from a skull that he had measured and de-fleshed. The result was a disaster: the two facial sculptures not only looked entirely different from each other but also bore no resemblance to the original face. Eggeling concluded that there were fundamental flaws in the whole facial reconstruction procedure. He was not alone, and the technique quickly fell out of favour with the scientific community. [4]

At around the time of Eggeling's experiment, a young Russian boy named Mikhail Gerasimov was developing a fascination with the many mammoth bones and other Ice Age fossils that were being unearthed close to his family home in Siberia. By his teenage years his interest had spread to include skeletons of all kinds. He was locally famous for mixing and matching bones creating Frankenstein-like creatures: the cat's skull that he mounted on the body of a duck caused some disquiet in his village.

Eventually Gerasimov studied archaeology and went on to specialise in Russia's prehistory, ending up in Leningrad in 1932. Like other archaeologists before him, Gerasimov gazed at the skulls of long-dead Neolithic men and women and wondered what they looked like. To the displeasure and scepticism of his colleagues, Gerasimov began to make facial reconstructions based on skulls at his university. Although initially following the discredited techniques as laid down by His and others, Gerasimov soon began to develop his own style that relied upon his own measurements and which took into consideration elements such as race and facial expression. The results were impressive and on at least one occasion led to Gerasimov correctly reconstructing the racial characteristics on three skulls that had been given to him as a test by his colleagues. Gerasimov did not just use his new-found skills for scientific purposes, he would charm women by complimenting them about their lips. 'He'd actually be looking at their anthropological structure, but the women would be terribly flattered,' said his colleague Andrei Velichko.

It was not just the flattered women who took notice of Gerasimov's endeavours. In 1941 Stalin despatched him to Uzbekistan to exhume and reconstruct the remains of several Mongol leaders, including the famed warrior Tamerlane. After the second world war Gerasimov was given his own 'Laboratory for Plastic Reconstruction' in Moscow where he was permitted to follow his own research.[5] Over several decades Gerasimov created what became known as the 'Russian School' of facial recon-struction which paid particular regard to the musculature of the head and neck. Gerasimov was to teach his method to many others and it would be used to reconstruct the faces of hundreds of archaeological specimens and famous characters such as Ivan the Terrible and the playwright Schiller. Only rarely was Gerasimov asked to put a face to unidentified modern bodies but it was for this forensic work that he was immortalised as the fictional scientist Andreev in Martin Cruz Smith's novel *Gorky Park*.

'Whether beautiful or ugly,' said Gerasimov once, 'the human face is always harmonious.' By the year of his death, in 1970, facial reconstruction was an accepted scientific technique in the Eastern Bloc but was virtually unknown in the West.[6]

It was also in 1970 that Richard Neave was to become drawn into the realm of facial reconstruction. This involvement was to come about as a result of a decision taken by Manchester Museum to undertake a wide-ranging and systematic study of all the ancient Egyptian mummified remains in its possession. From early on it was decided to ask for the help of anatomical and forensic experts from the affiliated Medical School at Manchester University. The resultant mixture of medical practitioners and archaeologists went under the nickname of the Manchester

Mummy Team. By 1973 much of the basic work had been done and thoughts turned to the Museum's Egyptology display and how it could be enhanced. One suggestion was to get a medically trained artist to look at the ancient skulls and to use anatomical knowledge to make drawings of how their faces might have looked in real life. The skulls chosen were those of Khnum-Nakht and Nekht-Ankh, two middle-aged brothers who had died over four thousand years ago and had remained entombed until their discovery in 1907. They were handed to Richard Neave, an artist attached to the Medical School who had already had some involvement with the Mummy Team's work.

In the book *Making Faces*, Neave admits that he had never heard of facial reconstruction techniques but had nonetheless independently suggested the idea of making casts of the Egyptian skulls and then adding clay to them to build up a face. A colleague drew Neave's attention to the pioneering work of people like Wilhelm His and so, armed with their soft-tissue measurements, he set about delicately adding layers of clay to the replica skulls. From the outset Neave recalls being obsessed with sticking to a rigid scientific method. 'Every attempt was made to ensure that these measurements were accurate,' he said. 'Right from the beginning I had endeavoured to ensure that I was not relying merely upon intuition; what was always irritatingly referred to as "artist's licence".'

The result was two sculptures which, even with the blank expressions that Neave had purposefully given them, still looked striking and met with the approval of the Mummy Team – but there was to be a further test of their accuracy. Entombed with the brothers had been two small statuettes that showed the men as they looked in life. Given that Neave had not been shown these, would his reconstructed heads bear any resemblance to them? In fact, the likeness was remarkable, especially in the case of Nekht-Ankh where the similarities between the two faces was deemed to be uncanny. Facial reconstructions may have been out of favour generally in the 1970s, but their potential was certainly recognised by the Manchester Mummy Team.[7]

The initial success with the Egyptian heads led to further facial reconstructions. Richard Neave's fame grew but all the work was related to archaeological specimens such as the skulls of King Philip II of Macedon (father to Alexander the Great) and 'Lindow Man', an Iron Age body discovered in a peat bog. Perhaps inevitably, as news of these successes was covered by the newspapers and television, so Richard Neave was approached with more arcane requests including some that took him away from the world of archaeology and into the realm of police forensics.

During the 1970s, when Neave was developing his technique, there was still much scepticism about the accuracy of facial reconstruction among western scientists and, consequently, also among police forces. Over the years there had been several attempts at re-establishing faith in facial reconstruction but with only limited success. Especially notable is the work by Wilton Marion Krogman who, between 1946 and 1962, published a number of step-by-step guides to facial reconstruction that used precise skin-tissue measurements. This was in contrast to Gerasimov's 'Russian School' use of facial musculature and so Krogman's ideas became known as the 'American School'.[8]

When Neave was asked to complete his first reconstructions he had nobody to teach him the necessary techniques and so he relied on information that was over seventy years old. As more commissions came in, so the technique he used began to draw on more influences, most notably the so-called American and Russian school methods that were developed by Krogman and Gerasimov. Rather than go exclusively one way or the other, as many others had done, Neave took elements from both Krogman and Gerasimov to create a logical and scientific step-by-step approach to making accurate facial reconstructions that couldn't be too biased by the artist's own feelings.

By the time he agreed to undertake a facial reconstruction of Body 115, Richard Neave was Assistant Director of Medical Illustration at Manchester University and head of a team of three people. His laboratory was housed in the Medical School behind the Department of Anatomy's dissection suite and was recognisable because its shelves were lined with rows of skulls. A visitor at this time described it as 'not a place for the squeamish' and had been warned not to open any drawer without checking the label first, just in case the contents turned out to be 'shockingly gruesome'.[9]

With a cast of Body 115's skull and the basic information gathered from the pathology report, the process of reconstructing the face could begin. Neave started by selecting the set of soft tissue depth measurements that best fitted Body 115's biological profile. Thanks to an upsurge of interest in facial reconstruction, accurate measurements were available by 1988 for a wide variety of ethnic groups including Caucasian, Afro-Caribbean and Japanese people. It was known that Body 115 was a white person with European-style features and so he fell into the Caucasian category. Within this broad group there were further sets of figures that took into account the sex of the individual and whether they were thin, normal or obese in shape. Body 115 was known to be male and 'well-nourished' but not overweight; this last point was a great help to Neave who normally found himself confronted with a naked skeleton from which it was virtually impossible to judge a person's weight.

With the most suitable set of measurements selected, Neave went to the cast of Body 115's skull and began to mark the thirty-four anatomical points that are used to indicate the skin's depth. This, it may be remembered, was the approach favoured by Americans like Krogman but experience had allowed Neave to refine the procedure. Rather than relying on approximation to get the right depth, at each of the thirty-four chosen sites on the skull Neave would drill a small hole and insert a small wooden peg that had been cut to exactly the right skin depth at that place. Doing this gave an accurate skin-depth guide for the artists to work to; prior to this innovation, skin depth had to be measured manually, a process that led to occasional errors. At the same time, a series of short wooden pegs would be placed on the nose to indicate its rough shape and width. With the basic guide markers in place, the clay was then applied to the skull. [10]

Although Neave was using Krogman's American skin-depth measurements for consistency, his technique for applying clay to the model was derived from Gerasimov's Russian methodology. Rather than applying the clay in a uniform layer, Neave paid close attention to the marks that the facial muscles leave behind on the skull. Amongst other things, these muscles control our expressions and help to give the face its definition, and so getting an idea of their rough size and strength during life can help make the reconstruction that much more accurate. Consequently, Neave adds his clay in long strips that mimic the size and length of individual facial and neck muscles.

The first muscle to be modelled by Neave is always the temporalis, the large muscle that runs across our temples, followed by the masseter, the powerful muscle that attaches the jaw bone to the cranium. Together these two muscles help us chew our food but their size and strength also gives a face much of its definition. With these in place the smaller muscles are added and smoothed onto the skull, gradually giving the face its basic form. Later on the nose is moulded onto the skull, as are the lips, eye muscles and ears. Naturally, as the skull is symmetrical, this process must be done twice for the muscles on each side of the face. In the case of Body 115, allowance also had to be made for the brain operation which would have left a visible circular scar on the right side of the forehead.

The muscle reconstruction process is slow and deliberate, often taking several days to complete, and leaves the face covered in thin strips of clay that are layered around the mouth and neck but much thinner on the top and sides of the skull. This makes the sculpture look a little like a skinless figure from a horror film; it is the next stage that turns it into a recognisable face.

Neave admits that the final stage in the reconstruction sees 'art and science blend before separating again at the end of the process'. This is because all the musculature detail that has been painstakingly added to the skull gets covered over with a smooth clay layer that gives the face its skin-like texture. The depth of this smooth layer is controlled by the wooden pegs inserted into the skull at the beginning of the process but the artist must also learn to interpret how the muscles beneath would have made subtle, but visible, changes to the outline of the face. It is during this stage that the face comes to life, joining together key features such as the nose, lips, eyes and ears, and hopefully making it recognisable to those who would have known the living person.[11]

In total, Body 115's facial reconstruction took Richard Neave three days to produce but the end product was less complete than he would have liked. A lack of information about the hair, all of which had been burned away by the fire, meant that the sculptured head had to be presented completely bald with no eyebrows, moustache or beard. The absence of such features might lessen the chances of somebody recognising the face but it was judged better to omit them than to guess at what they might have looked like. Nonetheless, Neave was generally happy with the result. 'It's very similar to the kind of face that the man would have had,' he said at the time. 'It's not 100 per cent accurate, you can't make a completely accurate portrait. On a scale of one to ten, perhaps seven.'[12]

The completed facial reconstruction was handed over to the British Transport Police in late January 1988: it revealed the solid but well-proportioned face of the middle-aged man that was derived from Body 115's skull. The prominent bones and sunken cheeks gave the face a gaunt appearance while the addition of sagging skin beneath the eyes contributed towards a slightly haggard expression. Given the ill health, age and rough lifestyle that had been ascribed to Body 115, the result was entirely believable.

The police were pleased with the result and hoped that the likeness was close enough to Body 115's original face to strike a chord of recognition in a member of the public so that the body, at last, could be given a name. To ensure that the sculpture could be seen by as wide an audience as possible, a publicity campaign was organised around Neave's work. The centrepiece of the campaign was to be a large poster containing a single striking image: Neave's sculpture photographed against a black background. The face is turned slightly away from the lens allowing the harsh lighting to emphasise the high cheekbones and sullen features of the face as well as the prominent circular scar produced by the brain operation. Although the image made the face appear somewhat harsh, it was clear enough to allow anybody who knew Body 115 in life to recognise him.

On 27 January, the large white posters containing the reconstructed face were put up around the King's Cross area. The design was simple. Underneath a headline bearing the words 'British Transport Police Appeal for Information' was the photograph of the sculpture, offset to the left hand side. Next to the photograph, written in bold capitals, was a direct question: 'DO YOU KNOW THIS MAN?'. At the bottom of the poster was a phone number and a guarantee of confidentiality.

One theory held by the police was that Body 115 was someone who had frequented the King's Cross area and so, while people might not have spoken to him, he could have been known by sight to commuters or local shopkeepers. It was thought possible that the facial reconstruction might jog someone's memory and cause them to phone in with a detailed physical description of the unknown man, if not his actual name.

On the day that the first posters were put up, the British Transport Police held a press conference to help publicise the issue of Body 115's anonymity. In a large room Richard Neave sat at a table flanked by two British Transport Police officers. After being introduced to the assembled newspaper and television journalists Neave held up the photograph of his sculpture. 'It is a strong face belonging to a slim sort of man,' he said. 'His features may be even thinner than we have recreated. Our hope is that it will jog the memory of someone who will remember him from a pub or paper shop and that that person will contact the police.'[13] The police too were hopeful. They described the man has having had 'a good strong English face' while adding that he may also have suffered from chest pains.

The publicity drive worked and the next few days saw pictures of Body 115's reconstructed face appear in the national press as well as across all the television news programmes. New names were put forward but it did not take long to exclude most of them as potential matches for Body 115. The majority were the wrong height or age while others could be excluded because of their fingerprints or because they weren't denture wearers. However, among the many unsuitable candidates put forward there were two names that members of the Body 115 investigation team earmarked for further investigation.

The first of these was Thomas Barnard, whose last reported sighting had been more than two decades before the King Cross fire since which time his brother had been searching for any trace of his sibling. When he saw Richard Neave's sculpture he believed that, after allowing for twenty years' aging, Body 115's gaunt face looked like his brother Thomas and so phoned the British Transport Police. He was contacted by Detective Sergeant Ray Turner and Constable Helen Spears, both of whom were dealing with the investigation into the new names being suggested to them.

On paper, Thomas Barnard proved to be a good match for Body 115. He was 5′4″ in height and would have been 58 years old at the time of the fire. Barnard's dental records were traced which revealed that all his teeth had been extracted in November 1964. The Barnard case looked promising and concerted efforts were made to trace his medical records. These were found and led the officers to Thomas Barnard's doctor in Clacton, Essex – and it was here that the investigation stopped. 'We managed to trace a doctor who had seen Mr Barnard,' said Detective Sergeant Turner, 'we contacted him and he stated from his files that Mr Barnard was alive and that he was living locally. He was not far from his brother, in fact.' After two decades of estrangement, the British Transport Police were able to reunite the two brothers. It was a personal success for the Barnard family but yet another failure in the search for Body 115's identity. [14]

Another name suggested to the police was Paul Quinton who worked as a pub cleaner in Chingford, east London. At 75 he was older than the estimated age for Body 115 but he was 5'2" tall and had the sort of ill health and transient lifestyle that had been deduced by Dr West. Quinton's name had been suggested to the police by a friend of his who had last seen him drinking in a public house about a week before the King's Cross fire. Again, there were strong physical similarities between Body 115 and Paul Quinton but despite extensive enquiries, Turner and Spears could find no physical or circumstantial evidence to connect the two. 'We did the usual checks but there was no further information to assist us,' explained Turner. Quinton's name joined the list of candidates which, through a lack of evidence one way or the other, could not be fully excluded from the investigation.

As each name was crossed off the list, the initial optimism expressed by some members of the Body 115 team began to fade. It was apparent that although the facial reconstruction had given the issue of Body 115 some much-needed publicity, it could not give them the name they so urgently needed. The decision to commission the facial reconstruction had been a gamble that appeared not to have worked, but its true worth would only be appreciated with time. In the years to come the haunting image of Neave's medical artistry became an iconic one for the Body 115 investigation. It would be shown again and again in newspapers, magazines and on television, giving valuable publicity to the investigation team in their attempt to resolve the identity of Body 115.

Writing several years later, Richard Neave referred to Body 115 as being perhaps the saddest case that he had worked on and he especially lamented the fact that his reconstruction could not have been of more help. Neave acknowledges that this is not necessarily because of faults with the facial reconstruction process, but can be due to events beyond the control of the artist, the police and the media.

'Such reconstructions,' he wrote in *Making Faces*, 'are usually publicised through the news media and through posters, but there still remains the fundamental question of who actually sees the reconstructed head or face. Despite the best efforts this must depend largely on chance: just because a body is found in the south of the country does not necessarily mean that it did not originate in the north and vice versa. It therefore follows that the exercise will not be successful if the reconstructed image is circulated in the south while those more likely to recognise it live in the north. Again, not everybody reads the newspapers, or watches television news programmes. Not infrequently those whose remains are found in circumstances where such investigations become necessary had few friends and may have lived a wandering and irregular lifestyle.'

The failure of the facial reconstruction was disappointing but the British Transport Police officers investigating Body 115 did not have much time to dwell on their lack of success to date. The public hearing into the King's Cross disaster was looming and that was an event which required the full attention of all those associated with investigating the fire and its after-effects.

CHAPTER ELEVEN

The Public Hearing

The opening of the public hearing phase of Desmond Fennell's investigation into the King's Cross fire took place on 1 February 1988. For over two months the British Transport Police and others had been gathering and submitting evidence relating to the fire. At the opening of the hearings Mr Fennell had seen 60,000 pages of submissions, including some 500 witness statements, as well as a wealth of technical and scientific evidence. It is little wonder that when Mr Fennell first addressed the hearing it was with some exasperation at the size of the task he had been afforded.

'When I opened the investigation,' he said, 'I said I wished to proceed with speed but I had no idea, indeed I suspect that no one could have had any idea, of the scale and depth that the inquiries in this investigation would involve.' He then outlined the objective of his investigation which was to be threefold: firstly, to establish how the fire happened; secondly, to find out why the disaster occurred and, finally, to make recommendations that would ensure that 'a disaster of this magnitude never happens again'. With the statement of these aims, the public hearing went into session. It began with an official reading out a list naming all thirty-one of the King's Cross victims which ended, as usual, with the 'unknown man'.[1]

Public hearings are rarely good-humoured affairs but the one into King's Cross fire was to be especially noted for its high tension and occasional episodes of bad temper. At its heart was the need to know what had caused the fire and how it had spread unchecked and with such disastrous consequences. From the outset the evidence gathered by the scene of accident investigators favoured the idea of accidental ignition rather than a blaze started by an arsonist or by terrorists. Their intuition was based on the location of the point of ignition, which being underneath the escalator is a difficult place for a person to reach, and also because the fire's slow start suggested that no form of explosive or accelerant, such as petrol, was present. To test this theory, members of the Health and Safety Executive returned to King's Cross Underground Station, which was still gutted, and performed an experiment on one of the surviving wooden escalators. Video footage from the experiment was one of the first exhibits to be shown during the public hearing.

The film shows the men dropping lit cigarettes down the side of the escalator into the layer of grease and fluff which had gathered underneath the steps: these had no effect whatsoever. Next a lighted match was dropped into the same space. It took only a few seconds for small curls of smoke to start rising from underneath the wooden steps. Within minutes flames were shooting up from the treads, apparently being fanned by the air blowing up the shaft. After just seven minutes the fire had hold of the escalator in such a way that the watchers below began to look concerned. One shouted, 'Are you getting unhappy about this?' His colleagues nodded in agreement, and so firefighters moved in and doused the blaze. It was noted that had any trains being moving through the tunnels below, the increased air flow could have helped the fire to spread more quickly.[2]

After showing this film Roger Henderson, the counsel to the inquiry, made it clear that the most likely explanation for the fire's cause was a discarded match. This conclusion was to spark the first of many disagreements in the trial when representatives for London Regional Transport, who were in charge of running the Tube, insisted that arson could not be ruled out as a cause. Indeed, they used the large number of fires occurring on London Underground to postulate the idea that there may have been a serial fire-starter at large on the Tube network. 'I do not conceal our very serious concern that an arsonist may be at large with a predilection for starting fires in the Underground,' said a London Regional Transport representative.

The Tube's managers had good cause for wanting the inquiry to keep its options open. If the blaze had been started accidentally by a match then awkward questions were going to be asked about the Underground's supposed no-smoking policy, its escalator cleaning and maintenance schedules and its firefighting capabilities (the newspapers had already been highly critical on all these points). If London Underground were able to deflect the blame onto an arsonist then this would remove some of the pressure from the Tube's staff. [3]

In the following days the hearing heard eyewitness testimony from dozens of people who had been present on the night. Most of these were either London Underground staff or members of the police and fire services but some members of the public who had become involved in the fire were also invited to speak. From the outset it became obvious that a series of blunders had helped turn an ordinary fire into a blaze that had killed and injured dozens of people.

Early on, Tube staff testified that there had been a fire hydrant in the passageway at the foot of the burning escalator but that none of the staff knew it was there or recognised it. A leading railman told the hearing that he had forgotten what a fire hydrant looked like while another admitted that there was another fire hydrant and thirty metres of hose that had been hidden behind a hoarding in the main booking hall for five months. A firefighter confirmed that no one could direct him to a hydrant and that this caused him a significant delay: 'I could have put that fire out easily from the bottom [of the escalator],' he said sorrowfully. Even more surprisingly, the firefighter admitted that while the escalator burned, he and a policeman had enjoyed a smoke at its base. 'There was time for the police constable and myself to have a cigarette,' he told his astonished audience. [4]

Other blunders were revealed. The only escape tunnel from the platforms to the surface had been closed off by two sets of locked gates, with two different sets of keys that were not held by staff on duty. Thus, through a lack of any other route, people evacuating the station were forced to travel up the escalators and into the smoke-filled booking hall. It also meant that after the flashover had occurred, the only escape route was via passing trains. A number of surviving passengers described how they were herded towards the inferno by police and Underground staff. It was postulated by Roger Henderson that some of the fatalities had resulted from people being evacuated from the lower platforms, where they were waiting for trains, and up into the booking hall.[5]

After Easter the inquiry moved away from the fire's cause and onto more complex arguments associated with the organisation of the Tube, with its funding and with its safety procedures and equipment. The managers and directors of London Underground were called to give evidence; some admitted that there had been problems, others denied there had been anything wrong. One manager, on hearing details of the fire, even cried in the witness box.

Finally, on 24 June 1988, the public hearing finished. It had taken 91 gruelling days in session and had included the testimony of 150 witnesses and the submission of 100 written reports, 15 videos and a final total of 80,000 pages of technical information.[6] The overrun had placed Fennell's inquiry weeks behind schedule and had created a near-continual stream of controversy for journalists to feed upon. The hearing painted a picture of a Tube system that was almost totally unprepared to deal with a disaster such as the one that had occurred the previous November.

The Underground staff were shown to have had no firefighting training, little or no knowledge of evacuation procedures and some didn't even know where the firefighting equipment was located. The fire burned for fifteen minutes with no sustained attempt at putting it out even though there were fire hydrants above and below the Piccadilly Line escalator. Even worse, the only platform-level escape tunnel was locked, forcing evacuation to take place via the booking hall.

Even after the fire brigade had arrived at the scene there was no one to guide them to the fire and while there were many examples of bravery, it looked very much as though no one had been working to a rehearsed procedure. One senior fire chief suggested that had they had another three minutes ('three unforgiving minutes' as he called them), the flashover could have been prevented. He suggested that the brigade should have been called at 7.30 p.m. by London Underground staff, when the fire was first spotted, rather than several minutes later by the British Transport Police.[7]

One journalist summed up the mood of the hearing and the nature of material it had covered:

'The tragic nature of the investigation has been underlined by the fact that in nearly 200 hours of hearings there has been virtually no humour, an aspect emphasized by the sepulchral tones of some of the lawyers; but the inquiry has been enlivened by the occasional vignette, ranging from the poignant to the incongruous. There were the policeman and the fireman who were feared to be dead but who, having done what they thought they could and being unable to get back to the surface, paused for a cigarette. There were the two London Underground employees taking an unofficially extended meal break, which meant there were only two ticket collectors on duty. They found themselves trapped in a mess room just off the burning ticket hall for two hours, and comforted themselves by drinking vodka and wine. There was the woman who struggled through asphyxiating smoke and collapsed at the foot of some stairs, thinking herself "a goner". She "had a little word with God", saying "I don't really want to die yet". She then struggled up the stairs and to her astonishment found she had escaped.'[8]

However, although the hearing had established (to most people's satisfaction) that the cause of the fire was a dropped match, scientists could not agree amongst themselves about how a medium-sized blaze could suddenly have been transformed into the deadly flashover that engulfed the booking hall. A scientific committee was convened and asked to undertake further research using scale models and more complex technical experiments. While Desmond Fennell and his small team of four people were waiting for these scientific results, they began to sift through the mountain of evidence they had gathered in preparation for writing their report about the fire.

With the public hearing no longer in session, the many British Transport Police officers who had contributed to it were free to return to more normal duties. For some, this meant carrying on the investigation into Body 115.

CHAPTER TWELVE

Vagrancy

The search of the national fingerprint collection that had been initiated just prior to the start of the public hearing was a vast undertaking that took months to complete. By the end of the summer it was apparent that Body 115's single fingerprint did not match any of the over 5 million prints held in the collection. A further search of the fingerprints held at the Scottish Criminal Records Office was ordered but this too drew a blank. The logical conclusion was that Body 115 did not have a criminal record, a situation that rendered obsolete any hope of tracing his name through the police's extensive archives.

Chief Inspector John Hennigan explained the implications of this failure: 'This means that Body 115 did not have a set of fingerprints within the records office which usually indicates that he had not been arrested for an offence for which his fingerprints would have been taken, or his fingerprints had not been taken for any other reason, for elimination purposes, for instance.' He later added, 'If we'd got a match on the fingerprint we'd have had a name and an area, we would have had a lot more of information with which to go to the hospitals and say please check on that person, that name, that address.'[1]

The lack of a fingerprint match was a serious setback because it represented the last independent method of obtaining a name for Body 115 using just forensic evidence. The investigation team had no option but to use the remaining evidence at their disposal to try and identify new areas in which to search for people who might match the physical characteristics of Body 115. Finding new investigative avenues was not an easy task so it was fortunate that one of the first to emerge came as a result of some comments made during the public hearing.

During Desmond Fennell's inquiry the issue of Body 115 was not raised directly (establishing the identity of the King's Cross victims was not within the inquiry's remit) but there was an incident that touched upon the matter. While being examined in the witness box a British Transport Police officer, Patrick Balfe, recounted an incident that had occurred while he was in the booking hall trying to stop people travelling down the burning Piccadilly Line escalator:

'I would like to add that whilst directing members of the public away from the Piccadilly Line escalator, one male person particularly stands out in my memory. This was because I was obliged to turn him away repeatedly (approximately two or three times) as he seemed intent on descending the Piccadilly Line escalator in order to catch his train. He spoke to me with a London accent and said, "I have to get to Highbury and Islington." I said, "The escalator is closed: it's on fire." He said, "Well, how am I going to get to Highbury and Islington?" I said, "I suggest you catch a bus or something." He then turned away, but as I was engaged in directing other people away, he attempted to squeeze past me when my back was turned. I again told him to get away from the escalator and pointed him in the direction of the station exit. He seemed slightly vague in his manner and the way he spoke I would describe him as being in his mid-fifties, approximately 5′6″ tall, scruffy appearance, white, European-type, proportionate to slim build, brown hair which was receding on the forehead. His complexion was pale. I did not notice his eye colour. He was wearing a brown jacket, dark trousers and leather shoes. He walked with a short slightly shuffled gait. Generally I would describe him as being of the vagrant type, though I do not remember smelling any traces of intoxicants. I have seen the artist's impression of the unidentified deceased person in the fire, and have read the accompanying description. I would say that it matches or is similar to the person who I turned back from the escalators on the night of the fire.'[2]

Constable Balfe only remembered this 'vagrant type' at the end of January 1988 after he had been shown a picture of Richard Neave's facial reconstruction of Body 115. Did Balfe's belief that there was a similarity between the two make him the only known person to have seen the man whose remains were later to be labelled Body 115? If so, then his description of the scruffy, shuffling, middle-aged man would be invaluable. This had the potential to lead to further revelations.

The suggestion by Balfe of a possible link between Body 115 and a 'vagrant type' was well timed, for the investigation team had obtained other evidence that was pointing them in the same direction. The first clue had come from Dr Iain West who believed that the general ill health of Body 115, his heavy smoking and possible drinking, all pointed to him being a transient character. Then there was the fact that nobody had missed Body 115 after the fire which suggested that he was estranged from his family and had no close friends. However, the most compelling piece of evidence suggesting Body 115 could have been a vagrant came from a member of the public.

In 1988 Terrance Morgan was a young man living in central London. After work one evening he went for a drink at the Calthorpe Arms public house, just down the road from King's Cross station; while there he had an encounter that was to have great relevance to the Body 115 enquiry. Morgan later recounted his experience to a television reporter: 'I went in the loo and whilst I was in there I noticed a vagrant was in a very distressed state, going about his business with his head on the wall and obviously very upset about something. So I tried to comfort him to find out what the problem was and all he kept saying to me was that his friend Eddie had died in the fire.'[3]

Thanks to the publicity that accompanied Richard Neave's facial reconstruction, Morgan was aware that there was still an unnamed victim from the fire. He contacted the police who were keen to hear his story not least because the name 'Eddie' made sense of the 'E.H.' engraved into Body 115's dentures – perhaps they were the man's initials? Suddenly there was an urgent need for the police to find and talk to the man that Morgan had encountered in the *Calthorpe Arms* toilet.

Morgan was asked to help produce an identikit picture of the vagrant he'd seen. The result revealed an unkempt man with a prominent nose, long scruffy hair and a full beard. He looked like a great many of the other long-term down-and-outs that haunt London's streets; picking him out by sight alone was not going to be easy but a concerted search was made nonetheless.

'Then police asked me if I would be prepared to go with them to the usual haunts of vagrants in and around central London,' explained Morgan, 'This took in the railway stations, soup kitchens, parks – the places that vagrants go – in the hope that we might find him but unfortunately that wasn't the case.'

Despite efforts like this, the London police could find no trace of the man who had been so upset by the loss of his friend Eddie but Mr Morgan's encounter was not a complete waste of time. The incident inspired the two officers running the Body 115 case, Detective Sergeant Turner and Constable Spears, to make a full investigation into the movements of vagrants in and around King's Cross station on the night of the fire. Given the distinctive appearance and behaviour of some vagrants, they wondered if any of the eyewitnesses on the night might have seen 'Eddie'; if so, then they might have inadvertently seen the man who was to become Body 115. With over 800 eyewitness statements to search through and with there having been so much confusion on the night itself, the task was not an easy one. It was made all the more complex by the large numbers of people then living as vagrants in the King's Cross area: London in the late 1980s was at the centre of a homelessness crisis.

During the 1980s London experienced the steepest recorded increase in its numbers of homeless people. By the time of the King's Cross fire there were some 75,000 people registered as homeless with local authorities, plus an estimated 4000 people who were sleeping rough on the streets. According to the charity Centrepoint, people were being attracted to the capital by the thought of jobs or the excitement of city living but most ended up broke and either sleeping in hostels or on the streets. Statistics revealed that the average homeless person was a 16-year-old man who had typically spent most of his childhood in care homes and who had come to London from a small town in the Midlands, usually in search of work.

One 1989 survey of seven people sheltering in a doorway on the Strand revealed the tragedy associated with London's vagrants; all were under 20 and all were huddled together for warmth and their own protection. Most had been ejected by their families or were running from the police. 'The police are after me for aggravated burglary,' said a young girl. 'I was sitting in my boyfriend's car when he robbed this shop. I'm too frightened to go home. My step-dad hits me and my mum's dying.' Others had come in search of employment but were not finding it easy. 'I can't work at the moment,' said a man named Jeff, 'because I'm sick. I had a place in Lancashire, but I got behind with the rent.' One of the girls, aged only 15, had been raped earlier in the week; all were living by begging or stealing.

These cases were by no means unusual and by the late 1980s the numbers of young people 'flocking to London' was proving of such concern that the government began to take draconian measures to put people off coming to the capital, such as stopping local authorities from housing people who came from outside their area. [4]

Amid the masses of young people that make up the majority of London's homeless community, there is a minority of 'old timers'; middle-aged and elderly men and women who have spent years or even decades living as vagrants. Many are alcoholics and, surprisingly, some are on the streets by their own choice, periodically returning to their families when the occasion warrants it.

Large communal areas such as train stations have always acted as magnets for vagrants and this is certainly true of King's Cross. The large volumes of people passing through a station offers a good opportunity for begging or scavenging food and cigarettes while the inside of the terminus offers shelter from the British climate. The Victorian design of most of Britain's railways provides a profusion of archways, bridges, tunnels and other places that can be used as overnight shelters should the need arise. The Underground system, which is particularly warm and dry, offers an excellent refuge from the elements and, given the cold weather on the day of the fire, it is unsurprising that many vagrants found their way down there.

London Underground does not tolerate vagrants on its property and it is the duty of the British Transport Police to find and eject them as quickly as possible. Despite the best efforts of the police, King's Cross Underground is a large area that contains a warren of tunnels making it difficult to patrol. The station almost always contained a few vagrants so the idea that one of them could have been caught up in the fire was a realistic possibility, but amid the chaos of the night did anybody actually see a man fitting Body 115's characteristics?

Mapping the movement of all the vagrants within King's Cross Underground Station on the night of the fire was a daunting task made more difficult by the lack of a closed-circuit television system. In the absence of any video footage from within the station, Detective Sergeant Turner had to check through the 878 eyewitness statements taken after the fire as well as the notebooks of the British Transport and Metropolitan police officers on duty in the area that night. Any mention of a vagrant, tramp or other person who might loosely be termed as such was noted. In total Turner was able to find thirty reports of vagrant types hanging around King's Cross station in the hours before the fire. The location of each sighting was plotted onto a large floor plan of

King's Cross Underground Station and the descriptions of the vagrants' behaviour and appearance were cross-referenced against one another. The process took weeks to complete but eventually a broad picture of the whereabouts and movement of individual vagrants on the night of the fire did emerge. [5]

Some sightings concerned vagrants who had been seen in or around the mainline train station and not in the Underground system itself. This included, for example, one known trouble-maker who was arrested outside the overland station only a short while before the fire started. Incidents like this, which occurred away from the Underground, were ignored; this left around twenty eyewitness reports concerning vagrants seen inside the Tube system itself. Several of these involved individuals who had been seen in the Underground several hours before the fire but not immediately before it, suggesting that they were probably well clear of the area before the flashover occurred. These sightings included a group of two women and one man seen begging at 5.00 p.m. and some scruffy-looking buskers observed around an hour later. With no evidence placing them in the Underground at the time of the fire, these sightings were also discounted. Eventually Turner was left with a hard core of reports concerning just three individuals, all of whom had been seen in the King's Cross Underground network immediately prior to the fire. If the investigation team's hunch was correct, then Body 115 could have been one of these people. [6]

The most numerous sightings concerned two male vagrants who had been seen in and around the booking hall area by thirteen separate eyewitnesses. The earliest sighting was by passenger Roy Holbrook who described seeing 'two drunks' near to the travel enquiry office in the main booking hall area; it was around 6.20 p.m., about an hour before the fire started. Holbrook was in a hurry but observed that 'one was flat out unconscious, clutching a bottle, and the other was getting into the same state. Both were male.' [7] A few minutes later and two more witnesses remembered seeing the vagrants. One described the unconscious tramp as being 'white, aged between 40 to 50 years old. He was wearing either a fawn or brown overcoat, and a scruffy shirt and trousers. He also had a bottle in his hand. I also saw a younger man bending over this tramp.'[8]

Between 6.20 and 7.15 p.m. these two vagrants appear in seven separate eyewitness statements but the descriptions are for the most part vague. They are called variously vagrants, alcoholics, drunks, tramps and scruffy types with occasional references to their approximate age ('middle- to old-aged'), relative height (one tall, the other shorter) and clothing (scruffy dark overcoats). Other than the fact that there were two of them and that one was consistently reported as being unconscious through drink (or possibly asleep), it was difficult to make a match with the known characteristics of Body 115.[9]

Just after 7.15 p.m., these two vagrants stirred from their position on the floor in the booking hall. At this time Christopher Fisher, a passenger exiting from the station, saw the two of them standing up in the passageway leading from the booking hall to the mainline station. Fisher got a good look at both men and was later able to give the police a full description of their appearance and behaviour. 'I would describe them as follows,' says Fisher in his statement. 'The taller one was white in colour, aged 35 yrs to 40 years, height 5' 10", dark black shiny hair, with a black untidy beard, a Scottish accent, slim build, wearing dirty, dark-coloured clothes. I might possibly recognise him again. The second one was white in colour, aged about 50 years, height 5'7", dirty grey unkempt hair, slightly stocky build, wearing dirty clothing. Both were unsteady on their feet, and in my opinion they were drunk.'[10]

Could either of these men have been Body 115? Their approximate ages (one about 40, the other 50) were within its given age range but the heights (5'10" and 5'7") were potentially too tall for the diminutive Body 115 (only 5'2"). However, experience has long established that when it comes to estimating height, weight, age, etc., members of the public are notoriously unreliable, especially when they are describing people who are glimpsed once and only briefly. It was thus possible that Fisher's heights were exaggerated, which could perhaps place the shorter of the two men within the height range of Body 115.[11]

Christopher Fisher was the last known person to see the two vagrants standing together. Shortly after his sighting the British Transport Police became aware of their presence and attempts were made to remove the men from the booking hall area. As he passed by, Fisher heard the taller man say to the shorter one, 'If you stay down here, you get moved on,' while, at around the same time, another witness remembers him saying 'You don't want to go down there mate, they don't want you'.[12] After this the two men parted company. A few minutes later on the platform area below the booking hall a vagrant was seen sleeping in a tunnel between the Northern Line and Piccadilly Line escalators. It would appear that it was this man, evidently the more inebriated of the two vagrants, who was found by two members of the British Transport Police and removed from King's Cross Underground. One of the officers recalls that they 'found a male vagrant asleep on the booking hall floor and ejected him, seeing him clear of the station'. It was immediately after effecting this ejection that the first reports of a fire on the escalator were made on the police radios.[13]

This left one known vagrant in the booking hall area at the time that the fire was beginning. With his incapably drunk friend having been forcibly removed from the station and amid the increasing confusion regarding the burning escalator, the second vagrant was not noticed by many people. In fact, there are only two definite reports of him: one, at around 7.20 p.m., describes the man as walking towards the booking hall area. He is then described as being 'about 60-plus years of age, wearing a heavy dark overcoat and about 5'7" tall, of vagrant appearance'. He is thus probably the shorter of the two vagrants seen earlier and indicates that the taller one was the person thrown out by the police. The next sighting is more intriguing.

In a statement made to the police in the days after the fire, a London Underground booking clerk recalled seeing a vagrant trapped behind the set of gates that block off the tunnel known as the 'Khyber Pass', one of the exit routes from the booking hall area. The clerk recalls that he 'noticed that these gates were closed, and I recall a tramp rattling the gates to get them open. The tramp was calling out, "Which evil bastards has locked these gates?".' In this first statement he recalled that this occurred only a matter of seconds before the flashover happened, at around 7.43 p.m.[14]

On the face of it this was a very important sighting as it placed a vagrant in the booking hall area at the time of the flashover. Furthermore, the vagrant's reported position was only a short distance from the spot where Body 115 was discovered. This sighting suggested that the vagrant may have witnessed the flashover and, being trapped inside the 'Khyber Pass' by the closed gates, tried to retrace his steps back down the tunnel into the booking hall area only to be overwhelmed by heat and smoke. The fact that his taller colleague (the one ejected from the station by the police), broadly fits the description of the weeping man who had been seen by Terrance Morgan in a pub toilet lamenting the death of his friend 'Eddie', was also compelling. Morgan's identikit showed an unkempt man with long untidy hair and a beard; the best description of the taller man gives him 'dark black shiny hair with a black untidy beard'.

Given its relevance to the Body 115 inquiry, much attention was paid to the clerk's description of the 'tramp' but all was not what it at first seemed. The clerk was questioned again about his sighting at which point it became clear that there had been some confusion over the timing. On being asked about the exact timing of his sighting as given in his first statement (i.e. 7.43 p.m.), the clerk replied: 'They have got this the wrong way round. The tramp was rattling the gates when I was on the way down to the Metropolitan section, not on the way back.'

'So this had occurred earlier, had it?', asked an examining lawyer.

'About twenty past seven, roughly that area,' was the clerk's reply.[15]

This moved the sighting of the tramp rattling the gate back from the time of the flashover to about the time when the fire was just beginning. This rescheduling was problematic. The clerk was still the last known person to have seen the vagrant, but there was a gap of approximately twenty minutes between his sighting and the event that killed Body 115. In that time the vagrant might easily have left the station and/or other vagrants may have entered it. Although there were similarities between the description of the short vagrant and some of the known characteristics of Body 115, any link between the two could only be supposition. Again, what had once been a promising lead had transformed into a speculative possibility.

There were, however, two additional sightings of a lone vagrant type who was seen in the period immediately after the escalator fire had been noticed. This was the man who had attempted to push past policeman Patrick Balfe and whom he later identified as looking like Richard Neave's facial reconstruction. Balfe described the man as a 'vagrant type', white-skinned, in his mid-fifties, approximately 5'6" tall, of slim build with brown receding hair and wearing a brown jacket. He placed his sighting at around 7.33 p.m., almost quarter of an hour later than the last sighting of the short vagrant.

Just two minutes later Julie Taylor, a passenger waiting for a train on the Piccadilly Line platform, recalls being approached by a man who asked her for money. Given the brevity of her encounter, she was able to give a remarkably full description of the man. 'I would describe this man as being a white male, aged between 45 and 55 years. About 5'9" to 5'10" tall. He was of slender build. He would have weighed about 10 stone. He had red/brown hair, more of a copper colour, cut above the collar and curling at the ends. The hair was receding and combed forward. He was thin-faced, shaven but he had a weathered facial appearance, he was not dirty, his face narrowed at the chin. He did not wear spectacles and had light-coloured eyes. He wore a dark blue woollen coat, it was grubby but in reasonable condition. He was wearing trousers and a shirt. He was not poorly dressed and seemed as though he looked after himself. He did not smell, nor could I smell, intoxicants on his breath. This man begged me for money; he spoke with a slur as though he had an impediment. I refused to give him money and he walked on. I noticed he held a walking stick which I believe he held in his left hand, he had a definite limp. It was a dark wooden stick. He left me and walked to the far end of the platform begging. He then turned and walked back past me.'[16]

This was probably the man seen earlier by Patrick Balfe at the top of the escalators although there are discrepancies between Balfe and Turner's statements concerning height and clothing. If the sightings did refer to the same man, then he had evidently found his way down to the platform area but, despite having told Balfe that he wanted to travel to Highbury and Islington (a station on the Victoria Line) he had made his way to the Piccadilly Line platform to ask passengers for spare change. It was what Julie Taylor had to say next that proved to be of real significance to the Body 115 investigation.

'I believe,' she recalls, 'that he may have had a head injury which he may have been trying to disguise by combing his hair forward. I gained this belief as he leant over to ask me for money. I recall when he held out his hand he was holding three 2p pieces.'[17]

Here there was an obvious and very real connection to Body 115 whose serious brain operation would, according to Iain West, have left a visible scar on the side of his head. Could the head injury described by Julie Taylor in fact have been the circular operation scar? It seemed to be a possibility. Balfe's belief that the man he had seen was similar to Richard Neave's facial reconstruction added weight to this idea but other elements from the two statements were not so promising. Although the scruffy-looking man was about the right age (mid-fifties) and build (slim/slender build) for Body 115, his height was a problem. According to the two witnesses he was somewhere between 5'6" and 5'10" in height, significantly taller than Body 115, and did not smell of alcohol, whereas Body 115 was known to have been drinking (albeit moderately) prior to his death.

The close proximity in time between Julie Taylor's sighting of this man, at 7.35 p.m., and the flashover, ten minutes later, was hopeful but, as with the short vagrant seen earlier, there was still a sizeable time gap in which anything could have occurred. A real possibility was that the man seen by Taylor may have left the station on a train. With no further sightings and no closed-circuit television footage to help them, it was impossible to say.[18]

At the end of this process the police had two separate reports of vagrant types in the station in the minutes prior to the fire but there was no physical evidence that could link either man to Body 115. Detective Sergeant Ray Turner summed up his findings: 'I was able to pick out the descriptions of all the tramps and vagrants and the movements of the vagrants on King's Cross station that evening. There were a number of police officers at the scene before the fire and they took away or ejected a number of those vagrants from the area but of course we can't be positive that all those vagrants were taken away that particular evening or were ejected from the station.'

Despite a widespread belief that Body 115 was someone who had lived a transient lifestyle, the investigation team could find no hard evidence to back this up, leaving the issue wide open. To some people associated with the inquiry this was no surprise as they had never believed in the theory that the unknown man had been a vagrant. Superintendent Ian Blair of the Metropolitan Police was adamant on the matter. 'I'm reasonably certain that he's not a vagrant,' said Blair, 'because we carried out a lot of enquiries in the initial stages into the vagrant community around King's Cross and Euston [train stations] and they are telling us that none of their regulars were missing. Secondly, the fact that he had not appeared in the national fingerprint collection indicates to me that he's not a vagrant as sooner or later most vagrants commit criminal offences.'[19]

The investigation into Body 115 had absorbed a serious amount of police time and money and yet, despite some hopeful leads, there was a feeling among the officers that they were no nearer to finding out the man's identity than they had been in the days immediately after the fire. With the various public appeals having failed to produce a name, the fingerprint search coming to nothing and the enquiry into the vagrants being at best ambiguous, the options open to the British Transport Police had narrowed to one unexplored piece of evidence: the set of dentures removed from the body.

CHAPTER THIRTEEN

Dentures

The King's Cross fire was typical of a situation where the use of forensic dentistry can be of crucial importance. The searing heat of the fire reduced many of the victims' bodies to a state where they could not be visually identified and where fingerprints could not be taken (assuming, of course, that there were reference prints to compare them with). In such circumstances matches made using dental patterns are a crucial factor in establishing a positive identification.

Although the temperatures inside the booking hall reached more than 900°C, the teeth of most victims remained intact. Prolonged burning will eventually destroy teeth but in King's Cross, where temperatures were intense but only for a brief period of time, they were preserved by being inside the mouth – where the cheeks, lips and tongue offer protection against the heat and the saliva, which turns to steam, prevents the teeth from cracking. The ability of teeth to withstand fire is legendary. In 1944, for example, a crash between a petrol tanker and a train in Norway led to an intense fire that burned for twelve hours and yet the majority of the victims' teeth survived even though other parts of their skeletons were reduced to ashes.[1]

Like the other King's Cross victims, Body 115 was expected to have its dentistry preserved after the fire. However, although the mouth area was intact, there were no teeth inside it, only a set of artificial dentures, both upper and lower. These were examined by Dr West and, as has been mentioned already, were found to have a pair of initials inscribed on them which read either 'E.H.' or 'F.H.'.

The discovery of these initials was greeted with optimism by the British Transport Police. Chief Superintendent John Hennigan thought that they were a major step forward. 'It was almost like a signature on the material,' he explained, but given other failures associated with Body 115, he was also aware of the limitations of this evidence: 'Unfortunately E H or F H could have been anything. They could have been the initials of the owner, the technician who made them, the dentist or even the dentist's department of a hospital.' The dentures were also noted as being old and displaying 'technical idiosyncrasies'.[2]

Although Dr West had made a preliminary examination of the dentures, he was not an expert in this field and could make only basic observations. When the Body 115 investigation team turned their attention to the dentures, Chief Inspector Hennigan approached Dr Bernard Sims, one of Britain's leading forensic dentists. Dr Sims had already been associated with a number of high profile cases including the controversial 'dingo baby' case in Australia where a couple camping in the outback claimed to have had their baby snatched and killed by a wild dog. Hennigan asked Dr Sims if he was willing to examine the dentures with the aim of finding any features whatsoever that could be used to help in the search for Body 115's identity. Dr Sims agreed, and on being given the dentures found them to be highly unusual. He believed that some of the dentures' features were so distinctive that they might just be able to jog the memory of the dentist or dental technician that made them. He also believed that they were distinctive enough to allow a comparison to be made to Body 115's dental records, should they ever be found. This was an important statement given the usefulness of dental records in establishing a person's identity.

There are many reasons why teeth are helpful to forensic pathologists but the most important of these relies upon the premise that inside each person's mouth are certain features that are unique to them alone. Even though most humans will grow up to have the same number and types of teeth, variations in their

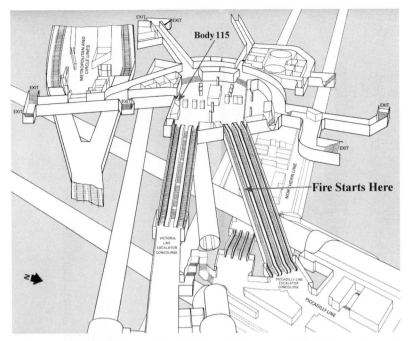

A three-dimensional plan of King's Cross Underground Station as it was in 1987. *Courtesy of the Department of Transport.*

The top of the Piccadilly Line escalator after the fire. *Courtesy of the Department of Transport.*

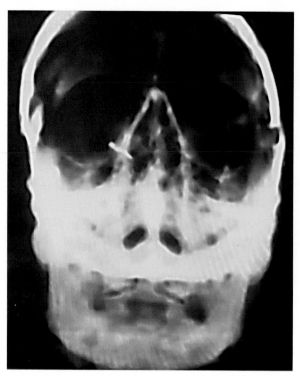

An X-ray image of Body 115's skull showing the position of the surgical clip. *Courtesy of the British Transport Police.*

The Sugita No. 5 surgical clip taken from Body 115. *Courtesy of the British Transport Police.*

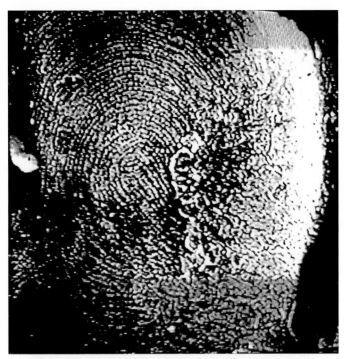

This fingerprint was the only one to be obtained from Body 115. *Courtesy of the British Transport Police.*

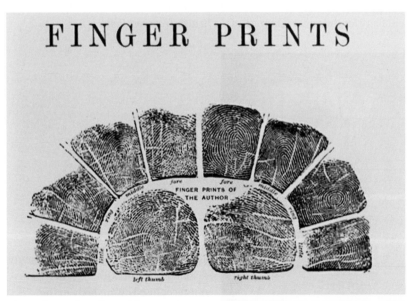

The police only adopted fingerprinting in the late Victorian era. These prints came from Francis Galton, a fingerprint pioneer. *Courtesy of the Author.*

Richard Neave's facial reconstruction of Body 115 generated much-needed publicity for the police. *Courtesy of the British Transport Police.*

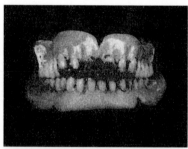

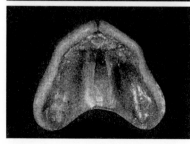

The dentures from Body 115 had many distinctive features and yet they were not recognised by anybody in the British dental industry. *Courtesy of the British Transport Police.*

An artist's impression of a vagrant whose best friend Eddie was allegedly killed in the fire. *Courtesy of the British Transport Police.*

For over a decade the seaman Hubert Rose was considered a prime candidate for Body 115. *Courtesy of the National Archives.*

James Brown shortly before he went missing in 1984. He shared many of Body 115's characteristics. *Courtesy of Kathleen Wilson.*

This photograph shows Alexander Fallon when he was in the army during World War II. *Courtesy of Mary Leishman.*

A picture of Mr Fallon taken shortly before his disappearance in the autumn of 1987. *Courtesy of the British Transport Police.*

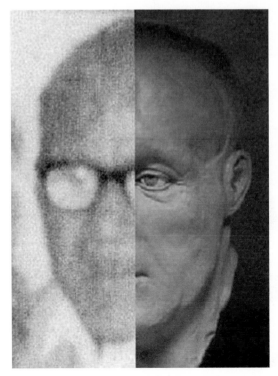

A comparison between a photograph of Mr Fallon and Richard Neave's facial reconstruction of Body 115 revealed a noticeable similarity. *Courtesy of the British Transport Police.*

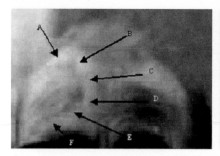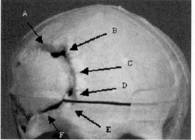

A detailed study was able to match the surgery performed on Body 115's skull to photographs that show the scars on Mr Fallon's head. *Courtesy of the British Transport Police.*

KING'S CROSS DISASTER FUND

IN MEMORY OF THE 31 PEOPLE
WHO DIED
IN THE TERRIBLE FIRE
AT KING'S CROSS
UNDERGROUND STATION
ON THE NIGHT OF
18th NOVEMBER 1987

BETTY AFUA AGYAPONG	MICHAEL HOLDEN
TERRENCE ALONZO BEST	RALPH HUMBERSTONE
MARK DAVID BRYANT	BERNADETT KEARNEY
ANDY BURDETT B.A.(HONS)	M.A.BOBBY KEEGAN
ELIZABETH N.BYERS	MOHAMMED SHOIAB KHAN
TREENA CHAPPELL	MARCO LIBERATI
DEAN T.COTTLE	PHILIP G.MARKS
SUSHEILA N.COTTLE	LAURENCE V.MORAN
FELIX DEARDEN	LAWRENCE S.NEWCOMBE S.R.N.
NEVILLE H.EVE	STEPHEN A.PARSONS
JANE A.FAIREY B.A.(HONS)	CHRISTOPHER WALLACE ROOME
NATALIE A.FALCO	RAI SINGH
JONATHAN R.GEORGE	JOHN F.JOSEPH ST.PRIX
KUTTALAM GOVINDARAJAN	IVAN TARASSENKO
GRAHAM D.HALL	STATION OFFICER
	COLIN J.TOWNSLEY G.M.

AN UNIDENTIFIED MAN
LATER IDENTIFIED AS ALEXANDER WILLIAMSON FALLON

On 25 May 2006 a plaque containing the names of all thirty-one victims of the fire was unveiled in the new booking hall at King's Cross Underground. *Courtesy of the author.*

shape, length and width will make them particular to the individual. Add to this the fact that the exact position of each tooth within the mouth also varies from person to person, and it is little wonder that we all have a dental pattern that is ours and ours alone.

As we progress through life our dental pattern can be altered by accidents, illness and visits to the dentist. Teeth may fall out or be extracted leading to gaps, bridgework or surgery. Damaged teeth may need capping, filling or to have other repairs made. Teeth can also be straightened, reshaped or even have cosmetic enhancements (such as the fad for implanting diamonds) or they may be taken out altogether, leading to the use of dentures. Such adjustments to our teeth only serve to make our dental patterns more distinctive and so can be of further help to the forensic dentist.

The majority of people in the western world will make several visits to the dentist during their lifetime. At each visit the dentist will record salient features of a person's teeth and also make a note of any repair work carried out. Often X-rays will be taken of the mouth or moulds made of all the teeth, thus providing a visual record of a person's dental pattern. The dentist will take this information and hold it on file. It is the ability of forensic dentists to compare features recorded in a person's dental file with features seen on the teeth of a dead body that can lead to a person being positively identified. It is not unknown for identifications to be made from just a single tooth.

Despite their uniqueness, dental patterns are normally only used where other means of identification (such as fingerprint evidence) is lacking. Often this means that those human remains requiring dental identification are in some way incomplete or disfigured; it is under such circumstances that teeth come into their own as a useful forensic technique. [3]

There are many historical examples of teeth being used to give names to bodies, especially those belonging to people who met an untimely end on the battlefield. In 1776, during the American War of Independence, the Boston silversmith Paul Revere (famous for his warning cry of 'the British are coming!') was asked to find and identify the body of General Joseph Warren who had been buried in an unmarked grave at the Battle of Breed's Hill (sometimes called the Battle of Bunker Hill) the year before. Revere found Warren's body and was able to identify it because of the silver and ivory bridgework that he had performed on the man a couple of years previously.[4]

A more formal use of teeth came about in nineteenth-century Britain when anti-child-slavery campaigners became exasperated at the means by which people and employers could circumvent the law against overworking those under the age of thirteen. The law in 1819 stated that anybody taller than $51\frac{1}{2}$ inches tall was over thirteen and could thus work 69 hours a week rather than 48. In 1837 abuses in the system led medic Edwin Saunders to undertake a study of the teeth of English schoolchildren through which he was able to prove that the number of teeth is a better gauge of a child's age than height (especially as the latter can be influenced by environmental factors, such as diet). A few years later dental evidence was used to identify the incinerated remains of Aberdeen doctor George Parkman which led directly to the prosecution and execution of his murderer, J. W. Webster. Thus, dental evidence was being used in court long before many of the more famous forensic techniques, such as fingerprinting.

Dental evidence as a means of identification was used increasingly during the late nineteenth and early twentieth centuries but, even so, it was not until relatively recently that it became formalised into a coherent discipline. Problems identifying dead soldiers on the battlefields of World War II (Hitler's burnt body was, for example, identified by the teeth) and Korea led to 'forensic odontology', as this science is officially known, becoming widely used.[5]

One of the greatest values of teeth to forensic pathologists is their ability to survive great trauma and yet still be useful as a means of identification. Teeth are mostly made from enamel and dentine, largely inorganic substances that can withstand high temperatures, violent impacts and years of burial. The same is true of much of the material used by dentists to repair teeth, like gold fillings. Thus, in situations where the soft tissue on a body, such as skin, fingerprints and facial features, has been removed through decomposition, violence or burning, the teeth may remain perfectly intact.

The resistant nature of teeth has led to forensic dentists being routinely called upon in disaster scenarios, such as plane crashes, earthquakes and explosions, where there may be many disfigured victims. Indeed, one of the first formal uses of dental identification was in the aftermath of a fire at a Vienna opera house in 1849 when evidence from teeth was used to give names to some of the victims. [6]

Before the 1950s the chief use of forensic dentistry was to give a name to unidentified bodies, but nowadays it can be used to determine so much more about the deceased individual. For example, if the victim was a child or teenager then the number of erupted teeth (those that have come through the gums) can be used to give an accurate estimate of age. Teeth can also be used to determine ethnic origin. European teeth, for example, exhibit a narrow arch and crowding, while Chinese teeth have a wide arch and five cusped third molars. If the person came from abroad then the style of dental work and types of material used for fillings, etc., can also be used to determine the country of origin. Finally, there have been occasions when marks on the teeth have given clues as to the person's job – for instance, a carpenter had marks on his front teeth where he had used his mouth to hold nails.

It might be thought that a person wearing dentures would present more of a problem when it comes to using their dental records for identification purposes. In fact, the presence of the dentures is not necessarily a hindrance to identification for although there may be no tooth pattern to match, the dentures themselves can still be compared to dentists' records. In particular, because dentures are made to order by individual dental practices, many dentists are capable of recognising their own handiwork. For example, when, in 1932, detectives in Mount Magnet, Western Australia, found the charred fragments of a body in the outback, they suspected that it might belong to one Louis J. Carron who had earlier been reported missing. With the body almost entirely destroyed, the police were left with a handful of artificial teeth and two gold dental clasps. The dental work on these was recognised by Carron's former dentist and compared to the dead man's dental record. A match was made and, later on, a man named Snowy Rowles was convicted of his murder.[7]

So, far from being a problem, dentures can be every bit as useful as normal dental patterns, and identifications based on them are accepted by coroners and the courts. In fact, dentures can have a potential added advantage over natural teeth in that, because they are man-made, they can be marked or stamped with the person's name or the name of the dentist that made them, although this is not a standard practice.[8]

Although a person's teeth or dentures can be used to establish identity, unlike fingerprints there is no central database containing people's dental patterns. Therefore, if the police do not have a list of names to check then finding the dental records to match an unidentified person is virtually an impossibility. The officers investigating Body 115 did not have a list of names to help them but Dr Sims had identified some interesting features on the dentures which might help in the search for the person that made them.[9]

When interviewed about the dentures, Dr Sims summarised his findings. 'The shape of the extension into the mouth, for suction and retention purposes, was a little bit more unusual than the normal sort of dentures that a person makes for a patient; there was a dagger-like chamber, a relief chamber in the upper denture which can be significant in some circumstances and on the heel of the lower denture inside was the obliterated mark or a technician's mark.'

The dentures' most interesting feature was the technician's mark which took the form of two indistinct initials, 'E.H.' or 'F.H.'. It was speculated that this might represent the initials of Body 115's name or perhaps be the mark of the person who manufactured them or the place where they were produced. But with nearly half the population being denture wearers and there being no standardised means of marking false teeth, the initials could have been made anywhere and by anyone. It was not thought prudent to spend time trying to track down individual dentists or their patients based solely on just two indistinct letters that had been engraved into the dentures. Instead the investigation team chose a more general approach that utilised all the dentures' distinctive features; they decided to make an appeal to Britain's entire dental community in the hope that someone would remember having manufactured or handled the dentures. Given that the dentures had a number of unique features and that they were preserved in their entirety, the chances of someone recognising them was thought to be good. If the team could find out who had made the dentures then tracking down the dental records that went with them ought to be a relatively straightforward task.

In March and April 1988 a one-page feature was run in several specialist periodicals including the *British Dental Journal*, *Dental Practice* and *Dental Technician*. The *British Dental Journal* item began with a bold and succinct headline:

Unidentified King's Cross Fire Victim Appeal for Help

Beneath this were three pictures of the dentures, one taken from the front, another of the top of the upper denture and the last one of the initials on the lower denture. A lengthy appeal was then made, outlining the known physical characteristics of Body 115 (height, ill health, etc.) and then giving a highly detailed description of the dentures, much of which could only be understood by dentists and their technicians. One paragraph, for example, described the upper front teeth as being 'approximate to Cosmopolitan Mould T14, and the shade approximates to Shade P on the Cosmopolitan Shade Guide. There appears to be no equivalent on the TNR Shade Guide, but there is similarity with G8 on the Dentacryl Shade Guide ... ' The article ended with an appeal for information although callers were asked to 'note the definite facts' before putting forward any names. [10]

The journals had been chosen because of their wide coverage which would have led to around 25,000 dentists and dental technicians seeing the appeal. Included in this number were a greater majority of working dental surgeries in the British Isles plus a good many in Ireland, America and even further abroad. The dentures had been described with painstaking detail and had accompanying photographs. Even allowing for their age, estimated at around twenty years old, it was thought that the appeal would produce some new leads, if not an actual name for Body 115, but no useful information was forthcoming.

Although there were some suggestions made, no one knew where, when or by whom the dentures were made. The appeal did not move the investigation forward at all which, to the investigating officers, suggested that Body 115's dentist must have long since retired, died or gone out of business. It was also speculated that the dentures could have been manufactured abroad.

Whatever the reason, the negative outcome of the appeal was an acknowledged setback. The dentures had been the last major piece of forensic evidence and, coming on the back of a string of similar failures, there was a risk of despondency developing among those investigating Body 115.

When asked what he felt about a possible future direction for the Body 115 investigation Chief Inspector Hennigan replied: 'Where do we go tomorrow? Where do we start again? Do we start again? Which line do we need to carry on with? Is there one worth carrying on with?' [11]

The exasperation in Hennigan's comment reveals the frustration that was being experienced by him and his colleagues. The most obvious avenues had all been explored and yet by the early autumn of 1988 the body lying in St Pancras mortuary still did not have a name. To make matters worse, the coroner's inquest into the deaths of the King's Cross fire victims was about to resume and the publication of Desmond Fennell's report into the fire was also imminent. One year on from his death, Body 115 was still going to have to be referred to by the Coroner as the unknown man.

CHAPTER FOURTEEN

Accusations and Recriminations

On 4 October 1988 Dr Douglas Chambers, the Inner North London Coroner, resumed his inquest into the deaths of the thirty-one people killed by the King's Cross fire. The original inquest had established the identity of the dead (Body 115 excepting) but proceedings had been adjourned to allow time for further evidence to be gathered. Now, ten months later, the St Pancras Coroner's Court was in session again, its aim being to establish and register a cause of death for each victim. [1]

The inquest opened with the jury members collectively reading out loud the names of all thirty known victims; after a short pause they ended with 'and an unknown male'. The inquest was not permitted to delve deeply into the cause of the fire or the actions of London Underground staff and the emergency services (that was the remit of the investigation undertaken by Desmond Fennell). Rather than dwelling on the events that had led up to the moment of flashover at 7.45 p.m., the inquest focused more on what happened in the minutes afterwards, when the deaths had occurred. To this end testimonies from those present on the night were either made in person or read out to the Court, and these included statements from many firefighters who had attended the blaze.

The inquest process was straightforward and uncomplicated and there were few interruptions or delays, allowing the Court to move through the evidence at a far faster pace than anybody had anticipated. Prior to its resumption, it had been speculated that the inquest would last for about a month: in the end it took just six days.

On 11 October the jury retired to consider their verdict but, in a move that was seen by some as controversial, Dr Chambers limited their options by instructing them not to return an outcome of 'unlawful killing'. This enraged the victims' families, many of whom had been openly campaigning for just such a verdict. They found the decision all the more perplexing given that a year earlier the inquest into the Herald of Free Enterprise ferry disaster, which caused 193 deaths, had found that the victims had been unlawfully killed.

The barrister for the King's Cross relatives argued against the Coroner: 'If the members of the jury in any way suspect gross negligence by more than one person or by corporations it should be open to them to return a verdict of unlawful killing. There is some evidence, albeit imperfect and incomplete, that there has been gross negligence. I refer in particular to the failure to apply a drop of water to the fire in the first fifteen minutes. I refer to the previous eighteen fires on that escalator. The jury have not heard the full story.'

Dr Chambers would not be swayed. 'The Lord Chief Justice has advised me to do this,' he replied before reiterating that the jury should only consider accidental death or an open verdict.

Just over an hour later the jury returned a verdict of 'accidental death' for all thirty-one victims; in each case the cause of death was deemed to be 'asphyxia due to smoke fumes' except for the thirty-first victim who died later in hospital of complications. Dr Chambers ended the inquest by announcing that he would be writing to London Underground to ask that they take action to ensure that a similar catastrophe could not happen again. The Coroner's involvement with the deaths of the thirty-one King's Cross fire victims was complete but with no blame having been apportioned, the reaction of the victims' families was predictably angry.

'The inquest dodged the real issues,' fumed one relative. 'What we want to know is what happened in the fifteen minutes before the flashover. Why, for example, were our relatives directed up to the booking hall at all? Most were simply changing trains below ground. Who directed them? On what basis? These questions were never answered.'[2]

In fact, statements like this were based on a misunderstanding. The role of a coroner's inquest is not to apportion blame, either to individual people or to organisations, but to establish the circumstances relating to the cause of death. To take their action further, the victims' families would have to take out a private prosecution against London Regional Transport, a prohibitively expensive process.

Following the closure of the inquest, those associated with the King's Cross fire began to prepare themselves for the publication of Desmond Fennell's report which was still a month away. However, within only days a most extraordinary allegation emerged that would see the coroner's inquest briefly reopened. The allegation centred around the claim that the fire had taken the life of a thirty-second victim whose body had since disappeared.

At 3.30 a.m. on the night of the King's Cross disaster members of London's fire brigade were inside the burnt-out booking hall area making sure it was safe before the police, forensic investigators and others entered it. On the surface above were, amongst others, Robin Winch, Peter Ernst and Paul Davis, the three duty doctors who had been called in to help recover bodies and certify them as dead. They had been told that all the fire's casualties had been accounted for and were on standby, awaiting further instructions. While the doctors rested, a senior firefighter asked if they wanted to go into the underground station to see the extent of the damage for themselves; all three accepted the offer.[3]

Led by a firefighter, the doctors were taken on a tour of the disaster scene. They were shown where the fire had started, on the Piccadilly Line escalator, and were taken around the booking hall and into the surrounding corridors, shops and offices as well to the platform levels below. [4]

With their tour over, the party was led upstairs and back into the fire-gutted booking hall where the lead firefighter guided them towards one of the exits. The party had begun to climb a small set of steps leading out of the hall when one of the firefighters tripped over something on the floor. The object was initially assumed to be a piece of debris but in the half-light one of the doctors, Peter Ernst, spotted something unusual about it. He called for a torch to be brought over and asked that his colleagues join him. Paul Davis recounts what happened next: 'A call caused torches to be shone on this item and I returned to look at it. This was quite clearly, in my opinion, a part of a human torso, with the inside of the sternum and ribs clearly visible. Additional lighting was called for and a further search was made, initially of the immediate area. Two further items were found, the first being what was thought to be part of a human skull, and the second, a human foot still encased in the remains of some footwear. This last item had been fused to some form of molten plastic at the base of one of the pillars or ticket booths and had to be hacked free from its anchorage. These three items were bagged separately and put into a body bag.' [5]

This discovery prompted a search of the surrounding booking hall area, just in case further remains had been missed, but nothing more was found. The doctors returned to the surface at around 4.30 a.m. and were stood down.

Finding what were apparently disarticulated human remains did not seem very significant. They were, after all, at the scene of a major fire and everybody present was familiar with the chaotic scenes and carnage that these can produce. It was assumed by all that the recovered body parts would be placed with those of the other victims and dealt with accordingly. Over the coming few months the doctors had little cause to reflect on the matter and in their statements to the British Transport Police, the discovery is treated in a matter-of-fact manner. 'We found the remains of a human torso, piece of skull and the remains of a foot,' wrote one of the doctors in his statement of 15 January 1988.[6]

With their part in the King's Cross fire complete, all three doctors had no cause to involve themselves in the investigation that followed. They made themselves available to Desmond Fennell's investigation but were not called as witnesses although a statement by Dr Ernst was read out to the jury.[7] There was little need for the doctors' evidence as the focus of the inquiry was on the cause of the fire and its implications for the Tube network, not on the recovery and identification of individual bodies. However, given the central role they played in certifying the bodies on the night of the fire, the three doctors had expected to be called as part of the coroner's inquest. They told the Coroner that they were available and willing to appear as witnesses at the inquest, scheduled to resume on 4 October 1988, but as this date approached it became clear that their services were not going to be required.[8]

This baffled the three doctors but their perplexity deepened when they realised that at no point had the investigation into the fire taken into account the discovery of the alleged body parts in the booking hall. To them this meant that there could have been additional victims of the fire whose presence had thus far gone unacknowledged. Shortly before the inquest was reopened the doctors' concerns came to the attention of Ian King, the solicitor to London Regional Transport. King obtained copies of the doctors' official statements and, on reading the description of the discovery and bagging of the apparent body parts, became concerned that there was additional vital evidence which had been overlooked by the general investigation into the fire.

On 3 October 1988 King wrote to Detective Superintendent Anthony Clift, the British Transport Police officer in charge of the investigation into the fire. King drew Clift's attention to the doctors' statements, saying that 'this evidence would tend to suggest that another person and possibly another two persons may have died in the fire.'[9]

Clift consulted Dr Iain West, the pathologist who had examined the bodies taken from the scene of the fire, but did not reply to

King until 12 October, the day after the Coroner's inquest had closed. He said: 'It would appear that the parts of bodies referred to by Dr Ernst and his colleagues at the scene, were in fact parts of bodies previously removed to the mortuary and such had been disturbed during the firefighting operation by the fire service.' He added that Dr West was happy that 'all those that perished are accounted for.'[10]

This did not convince the doctors, at least one of whom had a set of the post-mortem examination notes made by Dr West. A check of these revealed that only one body, that of a woman, was recorded as having a missing body part, her foot, but this could be accounted for. It had become separated from her body after its recovery and later discovered by a woman police sergeant in a gutter on the concourse area of King's Cross station.[11] If the remains found by the doctors had been of human origin, then they could not be affiliated with any of the thirty bodies recovered from the station that night. Despite these protestations, it was decided that the issue of potential additional bodies required no further action, much to the doctors' frustration.

The matter remained unresolved until early November when Chester Stern, a journalist working for the *Mail on Sunday*, was tipped off about the situation. For some time this newspaper had been looking into reports of a possible arsonist (a man in blue overalls) seen behaving suspiciously prior to the fire.[12] With the first anniversary of the fire approaching, Stern sensed that the mystery of the missing body parts could make for a potentially revealing story.[13]

Stern was able to obtain the doctors' witness statements and some of the relevant correspondence between London Regional Transport and the British Transport Police. Most importantly, Stern also managed to track down a colour photograph of the alleged human torso, taken as it lay on the floor in the burnt-out booking hall. The photograph showed a large, charred object with what look to be a series of ribs projecting from it, giving it the appearance of a seriously overcooked Sunday joint. As the *Mail on Sunday*'s crime correspondent, Stern already had a good working

131

relationship with Dr Iain West and so he approached the forensic pathologist over the matter.

Dr West was surprised at Stern's news and allegedly told him that he had not seen the controversial remains himself, even though they had been taken to St Pancras Mortuary in a body bag. At Stern's insistence, Dr West agreed to look at the photograph of the alleged remains. Stern remembers that West spent an hour studying the picture and even took some measurements from it. 'It could be human,' he eventually concluded, 'but I can't be certain.' Armed with this somewhat hedged opinion, Stern then approached the Inner North London Coroner, Dr Douglas Chambers, for a comment on the situation. However, Dr Chambers was just as surprised as West had been; he had not been made aware of the building controversy and knew nothing at all about it.[14]

On 11 November, and with the basic facts in hand, Stern approached Doctors Ernst, Davis and Winch for their take on the matter, telephoning each of them in turn. At first all three men were pleased that their concern about a possible missing body was being taken seriously by the media. Stern was able to gather some quotes for a possible article and each of the doctors agreed to be photographed. The journalist remembers that all three were vehement and united in their belief that what they had seen were human remains, and that they were angry and concerned that their testimony was being ignored. Robin Winch, who had worked as an accident investigator for over two decades, said at the time, 'All of us were quite certain that it was a human torso. We could clearly recognise the ribs and the vertebrae and the gelatinised lungs. The base of the skull could also clearly be identified. There was no doubt at all about what he had found.' Ernst concurred. 'I have no doubt at all that what I saw was a human torso,' he said. 'There is absolutely no doubt about it,' added Davis.[15]

A few days after speaking to Stern and being photographed, the three men arranged to meet and speak about the implications of their actions and, more importantly, whether by speaking to the media they might have overstepped the mark. It was at this point that the Coroner decided to open a further inquest into the fire to investigate the doctors' claims. This decision was based on Douglas Chambers having read the statements the doctors had given to the British Transport Police. As the enormity of the situation dawned on them, the doctors contacted a legal representative who advised them to regard the matter as being *sub-judice* and not to say anything further to the media.

By this point Stern had already written his article and the following weekend the *Mail on Sunday*'s front page carried the headline 'MYSTERY OF THE MISSING BODY'. The newspaper had photographs of the doctors with the quotes they had given and an outline of their concerns but although Stern suggested that there may have been another body associated with the fire, he reached no definite conclusion. 'It was a classic whistleblower story,' remembers Stern, 'but without physical proof it was the doctors' word against the authorities.'

The problem of a lack of proof resurfaced at the inquest opened by Dr Chambers into the missing body. At Dr Chambers' request all three doctors made additional statements to the police about their position with regard to the alleged human remains. All three were in agreement about the issue and expressed their feelings using the same words: 'I remain convinced in my belief that what I saw were human remains. I have today been told by Detective Superintendent Clift that what I saw and described as part of a human torso was in fact synthetic material. I find it impossible to accept this.'[16]

Dr Iain West was also requested to provide a statement outlining his view on the matter but what he had to say to the Coroner differed from what he had allegedly told Stern. West had initially denied having seen the problematic remains at all but, in his statement to the Coroner, claimed that he had been shown some bags containing 'no recognisable human remains either on a visual inspection or on inspection of the interior of the alleged remains. They were a mixture of inanimate debris from the scene. The main specimen that I was asked to examine resembled a roughly triangular-shaped piece of debris that I have subsequently recognised in a photograph of the booking hall.'

West continued, dismissing the idea yet further. 'I am satisfied from my examination of the bodies of the thirty-one victims of the fire that none of the victims could have been destroyed to this degree. The duration and intensity of the fire was insufficient to cause total thermal destruction of the limbs and head ... I have considerable experience of the destructive effects of both high explosive and fire, including the cremation of human bodies, and based on this experience can absolutely discount the concept of the disintegration of a body as alleged by Doctors Davis, Ernst and Winch. The alleged torso described by Dr Winch which showed "gelatinised lungs" cannot be correct. The lungs do not gelatinise but progressively decrease in size and solidify when exposed to prolonged heat until ultimately they are either burnt away or start to fragment. No human remains of any substance could have been destroyed by the effects of a high-pressure hose.'[17]

In contrast to Detective Superintendent Clift's earlier belief that the objects seen by the doctors were 'parts of bodies previously removed to the mortuary and such had been disturbed during the firefighting operation by the fire service', West claimed that they were inorganic and that in any case the flashover and firefighting techniques could not have produced such fragmented and charred remains. Dr Chambers accepted these arguments and decided that whatever the objects were that the doctors had stumbled across that night, they were not human in origin. With no physical evidence to the contrary, the inquest was closed and the official body count remained static at thirty-one, although the doctors continued to maintain that what they had found was human and not just debris.[18]

Following the closure of the coroner's inquest there were still two unclaimed bodies from the fire lying in St Pancras Mortuary. One of these was Body 115; the other belonged to Ralph Humberstone, the pub cleaner from east London, none of whose relations could be traced. As part of their investigation into

Body 115, the British Transport Police had traced Humberstone's origins to the town of Horncastle located in Lincolnshire fens. Investigations there revealed that he had been born in 1932 and afterwards lived in Gas Street, Horncastle, with his mother Ada. Despite rumours of family that still lived in the region and much local publicity, no one had come forward to claim Mr Humberstone and so, like Body 115, he had lain in storage for nearly a year.[19] At the end of the inquest the Coroner was satisfied that next of kin could not be traced for either man and so, on 11 October 1988, he handed the care of the remains of both men over to Camden Social Services, in whose borough King's Cross is located.

With the post-mortem examinations completed, the cause of death established and death certificates filed with the Registrar, Camden Social Services saw no need for the bodies to remain in storage and began to make plans their burial. With no next of kin, both Body 115 and Ralph Humberstone were to be given a pauper's burial which, as the name suggests, is a burial reserved for those who do not have any other means of funding a funeral.

Sensitive to the forthcoming first anniversary of the fire, Camden Council elected to bury both men on 11 November 1998. The choice of Armistice Day was deliberate: given their violent deaths, the men were to be laid to rest on a date that is synonymous with peace. Thus, on a cold, damp Friday morning, an entourage made their way to Finchley Cemetery in north London to say farewell to the last two victims of the fire. Attending the service were, amongst others, the Mayor and Deputy Mayor of Camden, members of the British Transport Police and several relations of other people who had died in the fire. It was a quiet, sombre occasion that saw both coffins lowered into the same grave: Ralph Humberstone's went in first followed by that of Body 115. The order of the coffins was purposeful: should Body 115 need to be exhumed, it could be accomplished without disturbing Mr Humberstone's remains. The King's Cross Disaster Fund paid for a simple but handsome headstone to be

135

erected. It read:

RALPH HUMBERSTONE
AND
AN UNKNOWN MAN
WHO PERISHED IN THE TERRIBLE FIRE AT KING'S CROSS
UNDERGROUND STATION ON THE NIGHT OF 18 [TH]
NOVEMBER 1987

The burial of the last two victims of the fire was ignored by the media and with good reason: twenty-four hours beforehand Desmond Fennell had published his findings into the King's Cross fire. There had been speculation that the Fennell Report would be a whitewash, exonerating London Regional Transport, the government and others involved in the organisation of the Tube network of any blame. This turned out to be far from the truth.

The Fennell investigation received its final submissions on 31 August 1988 after which came the gruelling job of writing the report that would summarise the investigation and publish its recommendations. Despite the size of this task, Fennell and his small team managed to do it in under two months, an achievement that is still remarked upon to this day. The finished report was submitted to the Transport Secretary at the end of October 1988 but the media had to wait until 10 November before copies were released to both them and the general public.

It turned out that Desmond Fennell, the man who had been portrayed by some in the media as a government stooge, had in fact presided over a thorough investigation and delivered a report that pulled no punches. Aside from its minute-by-minute analysis of the fire's development and the actions of people on the night, the report made 157 recommendations concerning safety on the Underground. Ninety of these were rated as either 'most important' or 'important'. London Underground chiefs bore the brunt of the report's criticism and were accused of suffering from 'blinkered and dangerous self-sufficiency'. [20] This led to the immediate resignations of Keith Bright, the chairman of London Regional Transport, and Tony Ridley, the chief of London Underground. There were calls for the resignation of the Secretary of State for Transport, Paul Channon, but he managed to ride the public outcry although he did leave his post the next year. Fennell himself summed up his findings in one memorable paragraph:

> For over a century London Underground has run an exceedingly safe railway system. It has a very good record and travel by the Underground remains considerably safer than by almost every other form of transport. But London Underground, and its holding company London Regional Transport, had a blind spot – a belief that fires were inevitable, coupled with a belief that a fire on a wooden escalator, and there had been many, would never develop in a way which would endanger passengers. In my view that approach was seriously flawed for it failed to recognise the unpredictability of fire, that most unpredictable of all hazards. Moreover it ignored the danger from smoke, which is almost certainly more deadly than fire. [21]

The report also put an end to the speculation about an arsonist being responsible for the blaze. Some in London Underground were still talking about a suspicious man in blue overalls being seen near the escalator before the fire but the scientific report was adamant. Experiments showed that an arsonist simply was not needed to explain the fire: 8 per cent of matches dropped randomly on an escalator fell through the gap at the side and of those one in four would land in the accumulated grease and fluff and cause a fire. When dismantled, one of the King's Cross escalators was discovered to have many discarded matches embedded in the grease plus eight separate patches of burning beneath the treads where other fires had started but failed to take hold. [22]

Why the fire should have smouldered for some minutes before suddenly exploding into a flashover situation was initially difficult for investigators to fathom. Throughout 1988 scientists and technicians performed tests using scale models of the escalator and booking hall areas to see if they could produce an effect similar to that reported by eyewitnesses at King's Cross. From this it became clear that the flames seen on the escalator were only a small portion of the actual fire, much of which was lying next to the wooden steps being carried upwards in a fast-moving layer of air (scientists refer to this as the Coandă effect). It was a general lack of visible flames that led some people to believe that the fire was not that serious. As the fire progressed, it heated up the wooden steps and other combustible materials to such a high temperature that clouds of flammable gas were released into the escalator tunnel and the booking hall area above. The temperature in the escalator tunnel continued to rise until it reached around 500°C at which point the flammable gases in the air spontaneously ignited, creating the flashover. Within seconds an explosion of flame engulfed the top part of the escalator and spread into the booking hall area raising the air temperature to around 900°C. The fire continued to burn intensely, reducing anything flammable to a charred mass. It was estimated that almost four tonnes of material was destroyed by the fire, much of which came from the wooden components on the escalator.

The unexpected and explosive way in which the fire developed was such that it later became known as the 'trench effect' after the manner in which the trench-like design of the escalator had allowed the fire to develop into a flashover via the Coandă effect. The scientific report into the fire recommended that the wooden escalators be removed from the Tube system as it was material from these that had fed the fire, allowing it to burn out of control for an extended period of time. The removal of the wooden escalators was deemed to be very important by Desmond Fennell, who set a deadline of July 1989 for their replacement by metal alternatives. Another seven recommendations requested the replacement of other flammable materials, the regular servicing and cleaning of the escalators and stopping the practice of treating the escalators using oil and spirits. [23]

The publication of Desmond Fennell's report and its 157 recommendations was welcomed by the families of those who had died in the fire, some of whom were still considering bringing a private prosecution against London Underground. It was not, however, quite so welcomed by the government who had been financially neglecting the Tube network for some considerable time. Implementing Fennell's recommendations and bringing the Tube up to reasonable safety standards would cost tens of millions of pounds, money that the government did not want to spend. Even so, the public nature of the disaster left them little choice and by the time of the report's publication some improvements were already being made.

First to go across the Underground network were the old wooden escalators and outdated rubberised electrical cabling which were to be replaced with new equipment. Modern smoke-detection and firefighting machinery was also to be installed in all stations. Most importantly, the escalators were to be cleaned regularly and the no-smoking rule on the Underground was to be better policed. At King's Cross itself new monitoring equipment was installed and a passenger alarm button was placed by the gates to the emergency exit that was locked on the night of the fire. A root and branch review of Underground management was also implemented.[24]

As far as the media (and therefore also most of the public) were concerned the Fennell Report drew a line underneath the King's Cross Underground fire. The number and scope of Fennell's recommendations, plus his reprimands, were seen as suitably severe in the light of so many deaths and injuries.

A few days after the Fennell Report's publication a service of remembrance was held at Blessed Sacrament Roman Catholic Church, located close to King's Cross. It was attended by relatives of the deceased, members of the emergency services and many others associated with the terrible events of a year earlier. Thanks to the actions of the church's priest, Father Jim Kennedy, the service of remembrance was to become an annual event. Those involved in the fire would never forget all they had experienced, but the public's attention span is somewhat shorter and as time passed memories of the fire faded slowly from most people's minds.

The closure of the coroner's inquest, the publication of the Fennell Report and the re-opening of the refurbished King's Cross Underground station all occurred around the time of the first anniversary of the fire. During this time the newspapers and television news were full of stories concerning the political fallout of the fire and the feelings and opinions of those who were involved in it or who had lost friends and relations. Body 115 was mentioned only occasionally and, after the passing of the anniversary date, the media attention died down again; from then onwards the King's Cross fire would receive only occasional attention. As far as the public and the media were concerned, the exciting part had finished. The papers had told their lurid stories and had seen the resignation of several transport executives (although the perceived big prize, the Transport Secretary, remained unmoved). It was time to move on and, on 12 December 1988, a train crash close to Clapham Junction gave people a new transport-related disaster to focus on. With thirty-five dead, dozens of serious injuries and arguments over the role of the railway's signalling system, the scale of the tragedy was at least as bad, if not worse than, the King's Cross fire.

When the refurbished King's Cross Underground Station opened its doors to the public, all traces of the disaster had been obliterated. The only reminder that there had once been a terrible loss of life at the station was in the tunnel leading from the booking hall to the south side of Euston Road. Here a stone memorial plaque was erected containing the names of the fire's thirty known victims plus an inscription for the 'unknown man' whose identity had yet to be established. [25]

CHAPTER FIFTEEN

Missing Persons

Diminishing public interest in the King's Cross fire was of little matter to Chief Inspector John Hennigan and his small team of British Transport Police Officers. Their main concern was to find a name for Body 115. In the year following the fire their investigation had continued regardless of Fennell's inquiry, the coroner's inquests and the maelstrom of media headlines. However, by Christmas 1988 it had reached a virtual standstill with all obvious lines of inquiry exhausted. The aneurysm clip, fingerprint, dentures, vagrancy enquiries and various public appeals had failed to produce any concrete leads that might be able to take them to Body 115's identity.

The team were reliant on two possibilities. Firstly, that someone would ring up the police suggesting a name for Body 115 or, secondly, that someone had already reported Body 115 to the police as a missing person. Searching for missing persons is a time-consuming and frustrating business but with no new names being put forward by the public, it was a realistic option for securing Body 115's identity.

At the time of the King's Cross fire the scale of Britain's missing persons problem was mind-boggling. Around 160,000 people each year were being reported to the police as having gone missing from home or work (these statistics include people who were on the run from prison, those who had deserted from the army or left care homes). 'There is nothing easier than going missing if you want to,' said a Salvation Army spokesman, 'although we prefer to call it getting out of touch.'[1]

Each missing persons case is unique but general causes behind such desertions include mental health problems (especially depression), debt and relationship troubles. The sudden disappearance of a loved one is a traumatic experience but the majority of people who are reported missing do return home within a few days. However, each year there are around a thousand people who do not. The idea that Body 115 might have been a member of Britain's large community of missing persons was a realistic possibility but it also presented the British Transport Police with a logistical problem.

When someone goes missing within the United Kingdom, their relations or next of kin can only initiate an official investigation by filing a report with their local police station. The police will record essential details such as the person's physical description, last known address and likely destination, and from these compile a missing persons report. However, further action is rarely taken unless it is felt that the person is vulnerable (for example, a juvenile) or a danger to themselves or others (perhaps mentally ill). 'Police become involved when there is a reason to worry about the individual's safety. Cases of suspected crime, of missing children, the mentally ill and those over 65 fall into that category,' said Roger Tiedeman of Scotland Yard, speaking at the time of the Body 115 investigation. Thus, in most cases it is left to individuals to make their own enquiries into the possible whereabouts of their absent relations: the police simply do not have the time and resources to follow up each case.[2]

In 1987 another problem facing the Body 115 investigation team was the lack of a centralised national database of missing persons. There were fifty-two separate police forces in mainland Britain, each of which would have had dozens, often hundreds, of unresolved missing persons cases on their books but it was rare for this information to be shared between forces. Despite the scale of the missing persons problem, the only dedicated unit was the Missing Persons Bureau, a small section of the Metropolitan Police based at London's New Scotland Yard.

The Missing Persons Bureau was set up in the 1960s to help co-ordinate the increasing number of missing persons reports being made at local police stations across the London area. If a missing persons report remained unresolved after two days then the police station had to pass the file on to the Missing Persons Bureau. In 1986 around 25,000 official missing persons reports were made in London alone but the majority were quickly resolved, with only a few hundred being passed on to the Missing Persons Bureau. To keep track of these reports, the Missing Persons Bureau developed a computerised database into which the details of each missing person would be entered so that should a body be recovered or a person voluntarily hand themselves in, their details could be matched swiftly. This computer database was particularly concerned with storing information on the physical characteristics and appearance of each missing person. It had, for example, 167 different categories under which a person's height, weight, hair colour, complexion, etc., could be entered. In time this computer database gained the rather irreverent nickname of 'Lucan', after Richard Bingham, the 7th Earl of Lucan who was suspected of battering his nanny to death before fleeing Britain.[3]

By the mid-1980s 'Lucan' contained the details of between 2000 and 3000 missing persons, the vast majority of whom had been absent for between one and five years, although some cases dated back a decade or more. However, although the Missing Persons Bureau had been a local success for the Metropolitan Police, the project had not been expanded nationwide to include other forces; this meant that 'Lucan' generally only held information on those reported missing in London and some of its neighbouring counties. In 1990, for example, the Metropolitan Police processed 28,117 missing persons cases from London reports but only received an additional 4898 reports from the whole of the rest of the country. Part of the problem was resources; the Metropolitan Police did not have the time or money to request and process the claims from every other force in the country. As early as 1988 requests had been made by the

Metropolitan Police for extra government funding to allow the Missing Persons Bureau to gain national coverage but it was not forthcoming. Despite the drawbacks, whenever an unidentified body came to light, the Missing Persons Bureau and its computer database were the best place to begin searching for a match. [4]

In early 1988 the British Transport Police approached the Missing Persons Bureau with the known physical characteristics of Body 115. Considered particularly important were his short height, his use of dentures and the fact that he was a middle-aged male. Commander David Stockley of Scotland Yard explained what happened next. 'In the first instance my staff within the Missing Persons Bureau checked the brief details that we received from the enquiry team against the computer database of some 3000 records of missing persons. They came up with 325 possible matches. These were collated and forwarded to the inquiry team for further investigation.' [5]

From a position of having had very few possible names for Body 115, the British Transport Police suddenly had over 300 new candidates. Investigating all these people, some of whom had been missing for years, was a major task; in most cases the police were being asked to succeed where concerted search attempts made by family and friends had failed. Regardless of this, each of the 325 new names would have to be investigated and either eliminated from the Body 115 enquiry or highlighted for further investigation. On paper many of the men put forward by the Missing Persons Bureau seemed to be a good physical match for Body 115, including the case of James Brown who at the time of the fire had been absent from his family for several years.

On a Tuesday evening in 1984 Kathleen Wilson arrived at the *Steam* public house in Brighton where she had arranged to meet her father, James Brown. The meetings were a regular weekly event and so Kathleen was concerned when he failed to show up. She went to the local YMCA, where he had been staying, and asked if anyone knew of his whereabouts. One resident told her, 'Kathy, he's gone to London.' He added that he thought James

Brown had been heading for the Blackfriars area, near to St Paul's Cathedral.

Although alarmed at this, Kathleen was not surprised; her father had unexpectedly moved away from his family before and had taken several months to get back in touch. 'He had a tradition of moving around,' she says, 'you may not see him for a year, but he'd call eventually.' This time, however, there was more cause for concern than usual as her dad was recovering from a minor stroke that had afflicted him earlier in the year. A week later Kathleen had still not heard from him and so reported him missing to the Brighton police.

James Brown was born in 1928 in Glasgow and from the outset his life was unusually harsh. When he was only a child his father died; a short time afterwards his mother remarried and soon fell pregnant. James became jealous and started to act up. 'In those days,' says Kathleen, 'if you didn't tow the line then you were out.' Aged seven, James Brown's behaviour landed him in the local care home and he remained there until his teenage years.

Brown's ambition had always been to join the army and even in his adult years he would sometimes dress in uniform and march about the house. Aged 19, he signed up with the Royal Ulster Rifles but the discipline of army life was harder than expected and so after only a short time he deserted, returning to his native Glasgow. There he met and married Dorothy and sired a family of seven children. He may have spent time in the merchant navy before moving to Aberdeen in the early 60s where he worked as a trawlerman and ship's cook. Dorothy and the children moved from Glasgow to join him but the nature of the job meant that he would be away from home for days or even weeks at a time. A few years after this he and the family moved to Grimsby where he again worked on the fishing boats. Despite the long absences and hard nature of her father's work, Kathleen remembers family life as being happy. 'Dad tried so hard to make mum proud of him,' she recalls, 'he was a comical rogue.'

One by one Dorothy and James Brown's children left home, moving away from Grimsby to various parts of the country.

Eventually Kathleen's brother Jim settled in Edinburgh while Kathleen and her sister Susan elected to live in Brighton, the large resort town located on the south coast of England. Then, in 1982, tragedy struck; their mother Dorothy was taken ill with cancer and, after a short while, succumbed to the disease. This event was to be a turning point for James Brown.

'Dad dealt with it very badly,' says his son Jim. 'Up to then, there was always a home to go to, a place to be. But now she was gone and his kids were grown up, a bit of him died the day she died.' Without Dorothy by his side, James Brown's life began to fall apart.

In 1983 Brown quit Grimsby and went to Aberdeen where he confessed to the police that he had left the army without following the proper procedures. The army interviewed Brown but quickly released him, giving him a travel pass to anywhere in the country. He used it to travel south to Brighton where his daughters Kathleen and Susan were living. They welcomed his arrival and he stayed with them for a while before moving to the local YMCA. Although he had always been a moderate drinker, something that the family say came with working on the boats, Brown's habit appeared to worsen while in Brighton.

'I knew the local community well and once got a message about my father,' explains Kathleen, 'I found him lying on a bench, drunk, in Pavilion Gardens.' She also remembers him sneaking whisky from a bottle in her house, topping it up with tea so that nobody would notice. The increased drinking may have been a contributory factor to the mild stroke that saw Brown hospitalised in late 1984. It may also have led him to make the break with his family and move from Brighton to London, a city where anonymity is easy to obtain. Whatever the cause of his sudden disappearance, by early 1985 James Brown was registered with the Brighton police as a missing person.

In the absence of any news from the police, Kathleen Wilson and her brother Jim began to search for their father. Initially this involved one or both of them making visits to London, searching the streets and hostels for any sign of James Brown.

They particularly focused on the Blackfriars area, his supposed destination in London, but no trace of him could be found. As time moved on and there was still no word, the search widened to include other known haunts in Aberdeen, Grimsby and elsewhere, all without success.

In 1986 Kathleen moved from Brighton to Cornwall, and from there continued the search by phoning hostels and hotels and making enquiries with coroners, mortuaries, care homes, nursing homes, friends, relatives and the Salvation Army. Nobody had heard of her father but it was still Kathleen's hope that he was alive and that he would eventually find a means of contacting his family to let them know he was well. He never did.

While Kathleen continued her search, her father's missing persons report had been passed on from Brighton to the Missing Persons Bureau in London where his details were put on the computer database. He was not considered to be at risk and so no further action was taken until 1988 when his short height caused his file to be highlighted as a potential match for Body 115. His details were passed across to the British Transport Police whose first action was to contact Kathleen, the person who had filed the original missing person report.

In the autumn of 1988, Kathleen was still living in Cornwall when she received a visit from two local policeman, anxious to speak to her about the missing persons report she had filed over three years earlier. 'They said there had been a large fire in London in November 1987,' said Kathleen, 'They wanted to know my Dad's height. I put my hand against my head to indicate his height and when the police officer estimated 5 foot 4 inches, I agreed. They said they had an unidentified body. They asked if Dad had any tattoos, which he didn't. They wanted to know if he'd had any operations and I told them not that I knew of.'

The visit was a short one and, after thanking Kathleen for her time, the two policemen went again. They left Kathleen with plenty to think about, 'Before their visit it hadn't crossed my mind that my father had been involved in the fire.'[6]

Kathleen Wilson was just one of many householders across Britain who had received visits from police officers wanting to know about missing friends and relations. The visits were an important part of the Body 115 investigation because the information given by relations would often eliminate a missing person from the list of possible names, generally because their whereabouts had already been resolved or because they did not match one or more of Body 115's known physical characteristics.

This was not the case with James Brown, whose short height, age, transient lifestyle and probable location in London were all positive matches. Kathleen was able to provide further information about her father, including references to his brief army career and to a couple of brushes he had with the law. Information like this was invaluable as it allowed police to track down officially generated reports concerning individual people, some of which might contain evidence that could be matched to that from Body 115.

Thanks to their visit to Kathleen, the police were able to trace a criminal record relating to James Brown and, from this, get hold of a set of his fingerprints. Experts at Scotland Yard checked Brown's prints against the one from Body 115: they were a clear mismatch which, in the eyes of the British Transport Police, eliminated him as a candidate for Body 115. Brown's name was crossed off the list and the officers moved onto the case of another of the 324 other possible missing persons. Kathleen Wilson accepted this decision but in years to come doubts began to creep in: this was not to be the last time that the police would encounter the case of James Brown.[7]

The police officers in charge of investigating Body 115 were able to eliminate the vast majority of names on the missing persons list using fingerprint evidence alone. For those missing persons whose fingerprints could not be traced, there were other options such as checking their social security and tax records to see if they had claimed benefits or paid tax in the months after the fire. In a number of cases it was found that the missing person was alive and well which sometimes led to estranged family members being reunited. Through the police's actions the list of candidate missing persons dwindled from the original 325 to just a handful; as each name was crossed off the list so the hopes of finding a match for Body 115 faded that little bit more.

Within months the majority of missing men had been excluded or the investigation into their whereabouts had reached an impasse. Even among the list of names of those that could not be completely discounted (usually through lack of further information), there were few serious candidates.

A moment of hope came when, on 9 May 1989, Lincolnshire Police sent a file to the Missing Persons Bureau. It concerned a man named William Mills who had gone missing in the city of Lincoln at around 10.30 a.m. on Wednesday 18 November 1987, the day of the King's Cross fire. Mills's description gave his height as 5'3" and his age as 59, a good match for Body 115, but what really grabbed the police's attention was that Lincoln has a direct rail connection with King's Cross mainline station. It seemed at least possible that Mills had travelled to London that day without telling anyone and had subsequently become caught up in the flashover. Mills's missing persons file was passed straight on to the British Transport Police and the team investigating Body 115.

A follow-up investigation revealed that Mills wore a full set of dentures and that he had a walking stick and walked with a limp. This last comment brought to mind the reports of one of the vagrant types seen asking for money in the underground only moments before the flashover occurred. He had walked using a stick and had even been favourably compared to Richard Neave's facial reconstruction. The same man was also reported to have had a signs of a former head injury. A photograph of William Mills revealed him to be of a similar build to Body 115 and to have some resemblance to Richard Neave's sculpture. This was the strongest match seen for a long while and over the summer of 1989 attempts were made to find Mills's dental and medical records.

In October 1989 the dental records were finally located and, by good fortune, the dentist was able to provide the police with a three-dimensional model of Mills's upper denture. It was given to forensic dentist Bernard Sims who compared the denture with those found with Body 115.

'It bears a reasonable resemblance to our denture,' said Sims, 'as far as the polished surface and the palate of the denture is concerned. The front teeth appear to be consistent or very close to the entire shape but when we look at the sides of the denture there doesn't seem to be that degree of extension in this denture as we have found in the mouth of the deceased. Unfortunately what we don't have is the fitting surface of the denture, we don't have the underlying shape of the mouth that would be the most useful part as that would be the die and counterdie to make a perfect match. I still feel that we have to carry out a few more investigations into this particular model.'[8]

The denture was similar but not identical to that of Body 115 suggesting that, despite a physical similarity between the two men, Mills might not be a candidate after all. A further blow came when it was discovered that the dental technician who had made Mills's denture never initialled his work. Sims remarked that 'this would be rather unusual in the fact that technicians usually like to put their own sort of mark so they don't get the dentures mixed up when they're processing them.'

Shortly afterwards Mills's medical records were traced. They revealed that he had never undergone brain surgery and so he could not possibly have been Body 115; William Mills had been another wild goose chase. Ordinarily the termination of such a promising lead would have been a bitter blow but not on this occasion. At the time that Mills's name was being crossed off their list, the police had another candidate for Body 115 – and this one appeared to be a dead cert.[9]

CHAPTER SIXTEEN

The Itinerant Seaman

During the summer of 1989 a clearout at the unclaimed goods depot in Paddington train station brought to light a suitcase that had lain untouched for over a year. It was large and solidly built but was worn, especially at the corners, and showed signs of having been well travelled. Records attached to the suitcase revealed that it had originally been deposited in a left luggage locker at King's Cross station but that the owner never returned for it. After a while it had been transferred from King's Cross to the central depot in Paddington for permanent storage.

With no obvious address label or other means of identification attached to it, the suitcase was opened to see if it contained any clues as to who its owner had been and how they could be contacted. What the depot staff found puzzled them. The case certainly held papers that identified the man who had owned it, but there was also a large amount of cash, some of it still inside unopened wage packets. This was an unusual situation, to say the least, as few people will deliberately abandon money: it perhaps indicated that the owner had been unable to return for his case, maybe because he had undergone an accident. This prompted the depot manager to call in the British Transport Police.

Sergeant Barney Featherstone was despatched to the scene. His statement reveals what he found: 'The property consisted of a large suitcase, personal property and a large quantity of open wage packets all apparently belonging to a Hubert Leonard Mark

Rose ... Also in the property was a seaman's ID card in the name of Rose and bearing his fingerprint and photograph. Whilst continuing my enquiries and studying the information available my thoughts concentrated on the photograph and the seaman's ID card.'[1]

Featherstone was struck by Hubert Rose's ID card which contained a photograph of the man; his face somehow seemed familiar. Eventually it dawned on Featherstone that Rose's gaunt face reminded him of Richard Neave's facial reconstruction of Body 115. Featherstone says he might have ignored this had he not checked the date that the suitcase had been originally deposited in the left luggage locker: November 1987. Could it be that the owner of the case was somehow connected to the King's Cross fire? Maybe it had even belonged to Body 115?

Chief Inspector Hennigan and his Body 115 investigation team were called in and the suitcase was more formally examined. It held a great many clothes, several wage packets and an assortment of other objects including a first aid kit, a tin of Old Holborn rolling tobacco, a lighter, denture powder, a watch, some scissors, a bunch of keys and an assortment of loose papers. It looked very much as though everything Hubert Rose owned was contained within his suitcase. It would certainly have been difficult for him to have made much headway in life without it. It was presumed that Rose must have deposited the case with the intention of returning to King's Cross to collect it but, for whatever reason, he hadn't done so. A logical deduction was that he had met with an accident which, of course, meant that he could have been a victim of the fire. The police were very interested in Mr Rose; Detective Sergeant Ray Turner and Constable Helen Spears began to search for any evidence that might link him to Body 115. They found it in abundance.

The first similarities were obvious. The suitcase contained a tin of Steradent powder which suggested Rose was a denture wearer; it also contained tobacco and a lighter, suggesting that he was a smoker. His clothes, when measured carefully, revealed his height to have been around 5'5" while his papers showed that he would have been aged 57 in 1987. All these factors matched the few known facts about Body 115.

There was also more circumstantial evidence. In addition to his seaman's card, the suitcase contained a number of papers relating to his employment history since leaving the merchant navy. These revealed that when Hubert Rose and his suitcase had parted company, he was leading a transient lifestyle, working in kitchens and hotels, while staying in temporary accommodation. Again, this matched the idea that Body 115 was not in the best of health and was leading an unhealthy and possibly vagrant-like lifestyle.

From what the police could deduce from his employment history, Rose's transient lifestyle began rather suddenly in 1982. This brought to mind one of Dr Iain West's ideas about Body 115's brain operation having been the trigger of a period of mental instability. Chief Inspector Hennigan also mused on this idea: 'Did Rose have an operation in 1982 or thereabouts, and did he have a mental condition, or did something happen to him, not necessarily a full-blown mental condition, that caused him to change his lifestyle?'

The two final pieces of evidence came from the seaman's identity card which contained a photograph of Rose and, most importantly, a set of fingerprints from his right hand.

The photograph was an old one, having been taken in May 1954, when he was 23 years old. It showed him with a thin, angular face, prominent cheek bones, a narrow nose, a high fore-head and swept-back hair. When viewed next to Richard Neave's sculpture, the photograph of Rose was not an exact match but there was a broad similarity between the two faces. Given the photograph's age and that facial reconstructions can only produce an approximation of a person's face, the police felt that Neave's sculpture could be compared favourably to Hubert Rose.

Rose's fingerprints, which were on the bottom of his ID card, should have been the clincher but the card was old and worn and there were initially problems discerning the print of the crucial middle finger. Eventually a Scotland Yard expert was able to say with reasonable certainty that the fingerprints on the card and those of Body 115 did not match. Ordinarily this would have been reason enough to exclude Hubert Rose from the investigation but the nature of the evidence presented a problem: for the fingerprints on the card to be accepted as evidence, the police had to be certain that they belonged to Rose and not to someone else entirely. Within the merchant navy it was apparently both common and easy for a seaman with a criminal record to circumvent the fingerprint system in order to avoid drawing attention to himself. To do this other seamen would be persuaded or bribed to put their fingerprints on the card in place of the genuine applicant. This meant that unlike a police criminal record, where the person providing a set of prints would be vetted by trained officers, a seaman's ID card was not considered to be an infallible means of establishing identity. Thus the fingerprint mismatch was not considered to be reason enough to exclude Rose as a candidate for Body 115. In fact, the other evidence in Rose's suitcase was so strongly in favour of a match that a new mood of optimism emerged within the investigation team.

Attempts were made to trace records relating to Rose's last known employment as a porter at the *Prince of Wales* Hotel, Bayswater, but the building had been knocked down some time previously. More success came with some of the other papers in the suitcase. His seaman's card contained his merchant naval registration number, which allowed the police to track down his registration papers at the National Archives in south London. Each person wanting to enter the British merchant navy has to register with the Registrar General of Shipping and Seamen in order to obtain a British Seaman's Identity Card and a discharge book. Without these items, a British person cannot legally be employed as a seaman on commercial shipping operating out of the United Kingdom.

The registration process requires, amongst other things, that the candidate give information concerning their background and physical appearance. Within the National Archives, police searched the Central Register of Seamen for Hubert Rose's seaman's pouch, an envelope that would contain his registration papers. It was not difficult to find and gave them the information they required.

According to his papers, Rose had registered to join the merchant navy in 1954 having first had a spell in the army. It revealed him to have been born in 1930 and also provided his measured height which was 5'6". Although short, this was four inches taller than Body 115's height of 5'2" but Iain West, the pathologist who had studied the body, did not believe this to be a problem. From late middle age all men and women begin to lose height as their bones decalcify and their spine compresses; Rose's age and manual profession, when combined with potential errors measuring both his and Body 115's height, meant that a loss of four inches was not inconceivable. These features kept Rose strongly in contention as the true identity of Body 115.

The registration papers also revealed that Rose's eyes were blue, his hair auburn and his complexion 'fresh'. This last point was confirmed by the photograph of him taken in 1954, showing him wearing a suit and with a slightly surprised expression on his face. The only distinguishing mark noted was a scar on his left thumb. Useful as these last few details were, they could be of little use to the police as any trace of hair, eye colour and the skin on the left thumb had been removed from Body 115 by the fire. A comprehensive picture of Rose was slowly beginning to emerge but the itinerant seaman's suitcase contained more documents that would allow the police to track down some of his living relations.[2]

With no obvious fixed address for Rose, the police began searching for evidence of his next of kin or close friends. Rose appeared to have lived a solitary lifestyle but among the mass of papers in the suitcase was a blood donor's card that held an address in East Kilbride, Scotland. Enquiries revealed that a cousin of Rose's lived there and that Rose himself had stayed in East Kilbride some years previously. The cousin had not had any recent contact with Rose and couldn't give them any further details, such as whether he had undergone brain surgery. He did provide the police with the name and address of Hubert Rose's brother Lawrence, who lived in the city of Portsmouth on England's south coast. In the first week of November, Detective Sergeant Turner and Constable Spears took a train from London to Portsmouth with the idea of interviewing Lawrence Rose about his brother Hubert. By then the British Transport Police were so confident that Hubert Rose was Body 115 that they invited a television crew to record the meeting for a documentary.

While on the way to Portsmouth, Turner revealed on camera that Lawrence Rose had not been told about his brother's possible connection to the King's Cross disaster. He said, 'No reference to date has been made about the fire as its rather sensitive and the only thing that I've said so far about it is that his brother is a missing person and I've left it at that.'

He needn't have worried. It turned out that Lawrence Rose had not been close to his brother, whom he called Bertie. In fact, he had not seen him since 1969 when Hubert briefly stayed with Lawrence and his wife Maureen in their high-rise council flat. All Lawrence Rose could offer Turner and Spears were some snatched childhood memories. 'We used to go to school together,' he recalled, 'we used to play together, we had our meals together, we used to have our meals outside in the summer, that's all I seem to remember.'

The only helpful relic that Lawrence could offer the two police officers was a photograph of Hubert taken during the 1969 visit. It showed a balding, smiling man sitting on a sofa smoking a roll-up cigarette. Hubert's face was recognisable as being an older and plumper version of the young man photographed in 1954 for his seaman's ID card. Lawrence could not say whether his brother had ever had a brain operation but he did add that his brother had spoken with a Scottish accent.

With the new photograph in hand, Turner and Spears left Portsmouth and returned to London by train. In their own minds they were hopeful that the mystery of Body 115 was close to being solved. A short time later Turner commented that, 'Since Rose came in we've had a feeling that it could be him, and having seen his brother the other day and the fact that he is a very small person, he fits the bill in every way ... I wouldn't like to say that I'm hoping it's him for his own family, but really if it is him then our enquiries will finish.'[3]

The end of the investigation seemed tantalisingly near but in order to convince themselves (and a coroner) that Rose and Body 115 were the same person, the police needed to find a piece of tangible forensic evidence linking the two. To close the case once and for all, Rose's dental or medical records would need to be traced or a positive fingerprint match found. In the months after the visit to Portsmouth a concerted effort was made to trace these but despite appeals in both Scotland and England, no further information could be found. The inquiry into Rose began to stall but the investigators still believed that the missing seaman was their man, even if the absolute proof eluded them. With resources dwindling and no new evidence forthcoming, the investigation into Body 115 was scaled down with Hubert Rose being considered the likeliest candidate.[4]

In the two years since the King's Cross fire the British Transport Police had devoted over 6000 working hours to the Body 115 investigation. In that time they had investigated a total of 1032 possible names of which 391 had been eliminated on height, age or other physical mismatches, another 486 had been established as being alive with the remaining 154 being probable mismatches, but without enough conclusive information to rule them in or out. Clues had been followed up from across the British Isles and even from such places as Australia and Japan.

Even before the discovery of Hubert Rose's suitcase, the time and financial costs of the Body 115 investigation had begun to worry some senior policemen. In 1989 Superintendent Ian Blair of the Metropolitan Police commented that 'there has to come a stage at which police resources are too expensive, too valuable to go on pursuing the identity of one individual; there are lots of people who are buried in this city who are never identified, this is one of them.'

157

A colleague, Commander David Stockley, appeared to agree with him. He said of the Body 115 investigation: 'The only factor I think which makes this case particularly unusual is the circumstances of the death; the fact that the body is an unidentified disaster victim. As far as unidentified bodies are concerned, he is not unusual. In 1988 we dealt with 240 unidentified bodies and seven of those still remain unidentified.'[5]

Thus in 1990 the Body 115 investigation was wound down. Periodically, the police would still be given possible names. These would be investigated but the conclusions would inevitably be negative; although Hubert Rose remained the prime candidate, Body 115 looked set to be one of those cases that defied resolution. As if to underline the point, as the investigation became dormant, the singer Nick Lowe recorded a song about the unknown victim of the King's Cross fire; he titled it 'Who Was that Man?'. It is not an especially sombre song but the lyrics of the chorus are poignant:

Who was that, who was that man?
Nobody knows him all across this land
Was that an unknown man?
Who was that, who was that man?[6]

CHAPTER SEVENTEEN

The Mystery of Mr Brown

By 2001 James Brown, the Scottish trawlerman who had briefly been a candidate for Body 115, had been listed as a missing person for over seventeen years. Brown's children, especially his daughter Kathleen Wilson, had made a thorough and wide-ranging search for their father. They had made enquiries at hostels, nursing homes, hospitals and shelters in London, Grimsby, Aberdeen and other towns that Brown had frequented earlier in his life. They had even travelled to central London, walking along the streets, subways and Underground stations in the hopes of meeting up with their father. In all that time not one piece of evidence had been found that could shed light on Brown's whereabouts. After so many unsuccessful attempts to find him, it was difficult for the family to know where to turn next. It was at this point that James Brown's daughter Susan had the idea of contacting the National Missing Persons Helpline, to see if they could offer any advice.

The National Missing Persons Helpline (NMPH) is a charity that was established in 1992 to act as a point of contact for those who have gone missing as well as offering advice and support to friends and relations of missing persons.[1] At the time of its founding the only other dedicated unit in the country was the Metropolitan Police's Missing Persons Bureau which, as we have seen, covered only the London area. By 1992 the Bureau was overstretched and underfunded; a report into its activities implied that it was starting to creak at the seams.[2]

Perceived problems with the Missing Persons Bureau and the need for a national computer database of missing persons were the driving factors behind the establishment of the NMPH (which was initially, and confusingly, also called the Missing Persons Bureau). Once up and running, the NMPH collected detailed information about missing persons reported to it by anxious relatives. The information was stored in a central database that, unlike the police's missing persons files, covered the whole of the British Isles. The ability to register and search for missing persons from across the country was instantly popular and not just with concerned relatives – the police and social services also found it useful. Within a short time it was the largest and most active missing persons organisation within Great Britain, with strong links to the police, social workers, hospitals, care homes and foster homes.

Its immediate success prompted the Metropolitan Police to look again at their Missing Persons Bureau. In March 1994, and after much prompting from the Association of Chief Police Officers, the government agreed to provide the funding which would allow the Missing Persons Bureau at Scotland Yard to become a national service. As well as revamping the computer database, the Bureau would receive three full-time staff at a cost of £90,000 a year but before any of this could be implemented an event occurred which highlighted the inadequacies of the current police system and the usefulness of the new NMPH.[3]

In August 1992 Gloucester social services became worried about the treatment of the five children belonging to Fred and Rosemary West and so took them into care. Over the next two years the children were interviewed by police and social services about episodes of physical abuse that had allegedly occurred at the family home at 25 Cromwell Street. In this time the children made several jokes about their sister Heather, who went missing in June 1987, being buried under the patio. These comments were made in jest (a 'family joke') but they were so persistent that in February 1994 a search warrant was obtained and the police made a visit to 25 Cromwell Road, but before they could make a full search, Fred West confessed that he had murdered his daughter Heather and that her remains lay in the garden. On 25 February Heather's skeletal remains were discovered, but when they were examined the pathologist found a third leg bone: clearly there was more than one body buried at the Wests' house. When confronted by this, Fred West confessed to having murdered two other girls, both of whose names he knew, and buried them in the garden. As the police threatened to tear apart his house, West went on to confess to other murders, giving details of their burial places. In total, the remains of twelve women were recovered from three locations and eventually both he and his wife Rosemary were charged with the murders. (Fred West hanged himself in 1995; Rosemary was found guilty on ten counts.) The names of some of the victims, who included Fred's first wife and two of his daughters, were known to the police, but several had been picked up or abducted at random and so remained nameless. Most of the murders occurred in the 1960s and 70s and left the police with few clues to work on other than the pathological information, such as dental records, that could be obtained from the skeletons.

Without names to match to the skeletal remains, identification would be next to impossible but the police were hampered by the lack of a national database of reported missing persons. With the revision and expansion of the Metropolitan Police's database only just underway, Gloucestershire police were forced to request any outstanding missing persons files from national forces. This, together with the publicity generated by the case, led to them receiving hundreds of reports of missing girls. Like the Body 115 investigation, the police had to investigate each of these cases to rule them in or out; given the scale of the task, they asked the NMPH for help.

The police and NMPH worked in co-operation with one another, checking on the status of each missing person and in doing so were able to resolve 110 missing persons cases; they also managed to find matches for all of the Wests' victims. The usefulness of the NMPH was proven and by 1999 the NMPH had persuaded every police force within the United Kingdom and Ireland to assign a designated missing persons liaison officer to the charity, ensuring that there was a smooth and regular flow of information between these organisations. By then the UK Police National Missing Persons Bureau was also operational which, for the first time, collectivised the missing persons reports made to individual police forces.[4]

The NMPH did not exist when James Brown first went missing in 1984 but when his family renewed the search for their father in 2001, it was acknowledged to be a first point of contact for those seeking absent relations. However, James Brown's children did not contact the NMPH with a view to being reunited with their father; after seventeen years without any contact, they had become convinced that he was dead. They were no longer searching for a living person but instead wanted to know the whereabouts of his body.

From early in its history the NMPH recognised that a small percentage of those people who are reported to them each year have not gone missing because they have run away from home, but because they have died and their bodies have never been identified. There can be many reasons for these deaths. Suicide is a common cause, especially among young men, but accidents, crime and murder are also possible. Those whose bodies come to rest in remote or inaccessible locations or whose remains are swept out to sea or are obscured by burial, fire or mutilation may, like Body 115, have few identifying characteristics and thus lie unclaimed for weeks, months or years.

Coroners routinely gather pathological information about such unidentified bodies and pass it on to the police but, until the establishment of the NMPH, matching unidentified remains with their owners was a time-consuming and problematic task. Nowadays running the details of any unidentified bodies through the NMPH missing persons database is a matter of routine. If that fails to find results, then the physical characteristics of the body, and the details surrounding its discovery, can be entered into the NMPH's database of unidentified persons. Unlike the police missing persons database, the information on unidentified bodies held by the NMPH is open to the public so that they can check the details for themselves.

Staff at the NMPH were quickly able to determine that James Brown was not amongst the unidentified bodies on their database. They suggested that Brown could still be alive or that he could have died without his next of kin having been informed. It was also possible that he had been involved in an accident, such as drowning or a house fire, and his body had not been recovered. On hearing this, James Brown's daughter Kathleen was reminded of the visit she had received from the police in 1988, while she was living in Cornwall. She remembered that they had been making enquiries into the King's Cross fire with the possibility that her father could have been a victim. She mentioned the incident to the NMPH.

NMPH staff were well aware of Body 115 and had its details, including Richard Neave's facial reconstruction, on their database of unidentified bodies. They requested a photograph of James Brown to compare with the facial reconstruction but the family could only provide a single picture taken in 1953 when Mr Brown was just 25 years old. Ordinarily this would not have been ideal, but the NMPH staff had a trick up their sleeve: they could take a photograph of somebody in their younger years and then use computer software to age the face by years or even decades. Although not perfect, the results had proven to be effective, making age-progression software an invaluable tool in the search for those who had been missing for several years, especially missing children whose appearance can change markedly in a short time. James Brown's photograph was digitised, aged and compared with the facial reconstruction of Body 115.[5]

What occurred next is a matter of contention. Kathleen Wilson remembers receiving a phone call from a female member of staff at the NMPH with a foreign accent who told her that they were

' ... 82 per cent certain that Body 115 is your father'. Naturally Kathleen's heart leapt, for although this judgement was not based on any firm forensic evidence, it sounded definite enough to suggest that the mystery surrounding her father's disappearance had been resolved. It also meant that her father was dead but with this came the comfort of knowing where and how he had died and, more importantly, the location of her father's body. It was a moment of palpable relief and, flushed with hope, Kathleen contacted the British Transport Police to inform them of the NMPH's judgement.

The lack of definite evidence linking Hubert Rose and Body 115 had led to a period of relative inactivity in the police investigation. The file remained open but with no strong leads to follow and with Hubert Rose remaining the probable candidate, it had become a partial lost cause. Each year the British Transport Police would receive half a dozen enquiries from various police forces and members of the public, including some from abroad, but it had always been possible to discount these names using the forensic evidence. The short height of Body 115, plus its partial fingerprint, excluded the majority of missing people.

John Hennigan, who had been promoted to Superintendent and who remained in charge of the investigation, expressed his frustration at the situation in a letter to a member of the public: 'The search for the identity of 115 has been exhaustive and extensive throughout the world using techniques and technologies in the late 80s and throughout the 90s as these developed. I had a Sergeant working for me almost continuously throughout that period and as the years went on it was safe to say that we received somewhere in the region of five to six enquiries annually. Obviously, as you are aware, because the body is still unidentified all these were proved to be negative as far as we were concerned and we were unable to help the enquirer as they were clearly looking to find a member of the family, friend, etc.'[6]

When she first got in touch with the British Transport Police, Kathleen Wilson must have appeared to be another person who was hopeful that Body 115 could be their missing relation. However, it became apparent that her claim had firmer foundations than most. Not only had her father been of the right age and height to meet the criteria of Body 115, he had also been a heavy smoker, had suffered from cerebral strokes and was thought to have been living a vagrant-like lifestyle in central London during 1987. On paper James Brown would have been an excellent candidate for Body 115 but, as the police were quick to point out, they had already looked into his case in 1988 and excluded him after finding his criminal record, the fingerprints from which did not match that from Body 115.

Kathleen was, however, insistent that the fingerprints on the criminal record found by the British Transport Police, which concerned a James Brown arrested for shoplifting, could not have been from her father. She admits that her father was once arrested but claims that he didn't have a criminal record in England or Scotland. Given how common the name James Brown is, she felt that the police had examined the wrong criminal record and requested that her father's case be re-examined. The request was granted and the task of doing so was handed to Inspector Ian Wilkinson, a long-serving member of the British Transport Police who had a particular interest in Body 115.

Inspector Wilkinson is intimately acquainted with the events surrounding the King's Cross disaster. He had been present on the night of the fire and, together with several other officers, had become trapped in the station. Wilkinson arrived via a Piccadilly Line train just after the flashover had occurred and remained in the lower concourse area for several hours, issuing regular reports on the state of the fire by telephone to the controllers above ground. At one stage he was nearly hit by a two-metre section of burning debris that fell backwards down the escalator shaft and crashed onto the floor where he and a colleague had been standing seconds beforehand. [7]

Inspector Wilkinson was described as a hero by some newspapers but he later received some criticism for an apparent lack of liaison between himself and his colleagues above ground, something that was largely caused by the inability of police radios to work below ground. At Desmond Fennell's public enquiry Wilkinson was on the receiving end of a verbal ear-bashing from both the lawyers and Mr Fennell himself. After a particularly hard grilling, Fennell turned to one of his barristers and said 'I find Mr Wilkinson, in parts, rather unsatisfactory.' Worse was to come as he was berated for not helping the lone firefighter underground to fight the fire. 'I understand that you might not have appreciated that there was a flashover,' said Mr Fennell, 'but what I am bewildered about is you not taking any action in support of the lone fireman.' He was also heard to mutter that 'there is an air of unreality about this so far.'[8]

Given the chaos and uncertainty that reigned during the night of the fire and the inadequacies of the police radios, many considered this attack on Inspector Wilkinson to be unjustly harsh. Nonetheless these criticisms, some of which were repeated in the press, and the memory of the fire itself, greatly affected Inspector Wilkinson. He allied himself to the task of identifying the victims of the fire and, at the first memorial service, was heard to say that he would not rest until every last body had been given a name. The Inspector had been true to his word and as the investigation into Body 115 continued through the years, he stuck with it, acting as a liaison officer between those enquiring about the body as well as doing the necessary legwork into any new leads or names. I have spoken to many people about the King's Cross fire who make it clear that without Inspector Ian Wilkinson the Body 115 case may never have been solved; they have nothing but praise for him. One person told me that 'he did a stunning job; he is a story in himself.'[9]

After Kathleen Wilson's initial contact with the British Transport Police, she found herself in Inspector Wilkinson's hands and he seemed genuinely anxious to help her resolve the issue of her missing father. Wilkinson began a systematic search for any evidence of James Brown's whereabouts in the time before the fire. Given Kathleen's belief that her father had been in

London in 1987, the search initially focused on the capital's homeless hostels. Wilkinson was quickly able to determine that James Brown had been a regular resident at Cedar Lodge, a night shelter in Clapham, south London. Records showed that he had been resident there early in 1987 but that he had left suddenly in February that year. This at least placed James Brown in London in the period of time before the fire occurred.

After obtaining James Brown's National Insurance number, it was possible to check his social security records. These revealed that Brown had claimed unemployment benefit in Clapham up until the time that he had disappeared from Cedar Lodge hostel. After this he had not made any claims at all although the social security had sent a letter to him at Cedar Lodge in May 1988, but because Brown was no longer resident it was returned to them unopened. These were very important clues as James Brown would have been reliant on social security payments to live; he had no other known form of income. This suggested that perhaps he had become ill at around this time and gone into care or that perhaps he had abandoned social security altogether in favour of a vagrant lifestyle. He could also have died. Other lines of enquiry, which included visits to Brown's known haunts in Brighton, came to nothing.

While there was some positive evidence in favour of Mr Brown being Body 115, there was still the issue of his criminal record and the mismatched fingerprints. The British Transport Police were insistent that the records they had traced were for the same man as Kathleen's father; this was not based just on his name but also the photographs and family information that Brown had provided, including his mother's maiden name. All were correct, but to be on the safe side experts at the National Identification Bureau rechecked Brown's fingerprints against those of Body 115 – and the result was demonstrably negative. This, and Inspector Wilkinson's new evidence about the hostel, was submitted to Superintendent John Hennigan for his consideration. His conclusion remained the same and on 6 November 2002 he wrote to tell Kathleen the bad news. After a lengthy explanation of the steps taken to find the identity of Body 115, Hennigan wrote: 'A comparison of your father's fingerprints with those retained for Body 115 was carried out and evidence submitted to me by the senior Identification Officer attached to the National Identification Bureau at New Scotland Yard, to the effect that the fingerprints were not comparable, they were not the same person. As I have already stated, this stage of our inquiry would mean that no further action would be taken with regard to Mr James Brown being a probable identity for Body 115.' [10]

This was a bitter blow for Kathleen and her brothers and sisters, all of whom had come to believe that Body 115 was their father, but the news did not discourage them. They remained convinced that the police had found the wrong set of fingerprints and that it was their father who had died in the fire and who was buried anonymously in a north London cemetery. The one ray of hope offered by Superintendent Hennigan was his agreement to allow Inspector Wilkinson to pursue the matter of James Brown's whereabouts during 1987. During the course of his investigation into James Brown, Inspector Wilkinson had become sympathetic towards Kathleen's plight and was anxious to see if he could find out anything further about her father. Although James Brown was no longer officially a Body 115 candidate, the two kept in touch.

Monday 18 November 2002 marked the fifteenth anniversary of the King's Cross fire. That year, as in all the previous years, Father Jim Kennedy of the Blessed Sacrament Catholic Church, located behind King's Cross station, held a service in memory of the victims. This was usually attended by the relatives of the dead and members of the British Transport Police, including Inspector Wilkinson. That year Kathleen Wilson and her brother also attended the service even though two weeks earlier she had been categorically told that her missing father was not connected with the fire. [11]

The service was a simple one that culminated in the lighting of a candle for each of the fire's victims. As ever, the 31st candle was lit in memory of 'the unknown man'. Afterwards Superintendent Hennigan told a journalist: 'We still have no more idea who he was than when his body was first brought out. I wish I had.' Father Kennedy, who had followed the investigation closely also spoke about Body 115 although he still referred to him as 'Michael', the old nickname. 'At times we have thought the police were close to an identification,' he said, 'but at our service and on the plaque which we are unveiling as a memorial to the dead, he will simply be described as an unknown man.'[12]

In fact, while there was much lamentation at the continued anonymity of Body 115, the memorial service of 2002 was to have a profound effect on the investigation and would indirectly open up a major new lead.

CHAPTER EIGHTEEN

The Perfect Candidate?

The fifteenth anniversary of the King's Cross fire was not a major news story but *The Times* newspaper did carry a small piece about it on one of its inside pages. Rather than concentrating on the commemorative church service, the journalist used much of the article to highlight the continuing mystery of Body 115's identity. The police were happy to publicise the Body 115 issue and gave several quotes to *The Times* which made it clear that the investigation had hit a brick wall.

After so much time and with so much publicity having already been devoted to Body 115, the police could not really having been expecting this brief news item, tucked away on page four, to have made much difference. In fact, the article was to make all the difference in the world when, by chance, it came to the attention of Mary Leishman, a 66-year-old housewife from Stenhousemuir, Scotland, whose father had gone missing many years previously. After reading *The Times* report, she too wondered if his disappearance could be connected with Body 115.

There are some similarities between the life history of Mrs Leishman's father, whose name was Alexander Fallon, and that of the missing trawlerman James Brown. Both men were Scottish in origin, both had a good relationship with their children and yet, following the sudden deaths of their wives, both abandoned a settled domestic existence in favour of living by themselves in London.

Alexander Fallon was born in 1914 in Falkirk, Scotland, and was married just prior to World War II. In 1939 he enlisted with the Royal Artillery and spent the entire war in the army. After being demobilised in 1946, Mr Fallon settled down in Falkirk to lead a normal family life; he fathered four daughters, all of whom had left home by the 1970s. Like James Brown, Mr Fallon's life was to be turned upside down by the death of his wife of ovarian cancer in December 1974. Unable to adjust to his loss, Mr Fallon abandoned the family home in Falkirk, which apparently 'held too many memories', and moved to London where he stayed for a while with his sister.

On 15 September 1980, Alexander Fallon collapsed near Tower Hill in London but for several minutes he was ignored by pedestrians who chose to step over his unconscious body. Eventually an elderly couple came to his aid, an ambulance was summoned and Mr Fallon was taken to the Royal London Hospital in Whitechapel. Doctors diagnosed a brain haemorrhage and performed an emergency operation on him, but for a long time afterwards Mr Fallon was coy with his family about the details of his treatment. 'He just said that he had the surgery; he had a clip inserted in the head and that was it,' said Mrs Leishman. Afterwards Mr Fallon recuperated at his daughter Alexena's house in Falkirk but later returned to London. Here he spent extended periods of time living in shared accommodation, occasionally leaving the city to spend time with his daughters in Scotland.

Although his family were never exactly sure where their father was living, he did keep in contact via telephone calls, letters or, more rarely, personal visits. Mary Leishman received one such brief visit from her father in the summer of 1987 and then, in mid-October, he telephoned her from London. This was the last time that Alexander Fallon got in touch with any of his children; afterwards they heard nothing from him. His absence caused the family great concern, especially as his old brain operation had started to cause him problems and had led to him collapsing a few times. Despite the timing of his last contact, it took the family nearly a decade to connect his disappearance with the terrible fire at King's Cross.

'My three sisters and I often asked each other when we met or spoke, "Have you heard from our father?" ' explained Mrs Leishman in a newspaper interview. 'It was only in 1997, when a cousin we met in church suggested he might have been a victim in the fire, that we really started thinking about it.' [1]

Thus, a decade after the fire had occurred, Mrs Leishman contacted the British Transport Police who agreed to look into the matter. At this time great emphasis was being placed on the height and estimated age of Body 115 so when it was discovered that Alexander Fallon was, at 72 years, twelve years older than their maximum projected age for Body 115 and that, according to Mrs Leishman's estimate, he had been 5'6" in height (around four inches taller than Body 115), the police did not think he was a good match especially in comparison to Hubert Rose who remained their leading candidate. Attempts were made to trace his dental and medical records but neither could be found and so Mr Fallon's case was classified as requiring further information before action could be taken. Having been led to believe that a match with Body 115 was unlikely, Mary Leishman and her family forgot about the King's Cross fire until November 2002 when they read the item about the memorial service in *The Times*. 'That report prompted my wife and her sisters to resume the search for their father,' said Mrs Leishman's husband Andrew. [2]

Mrs Leishman's timing was fortuitous as the passing of the fifteenth anniversary of the fire had prompted the senior investigating officer, Superintendent John Hennigan, to look again at the entire Body 115 investigation. This re-evaluation had been going only a short while when he received Mrs Leishman's request to re-examine the case of Alexander Fallon. For the first time in a long while the Body 115 investigation had no prime suspects; the fate of Hubert Rose having been resolved a short time beforehand. (Rose turned out not to have been involved in the fire but was instead discovered to have assumed a pseudonym under which he had lived until his death, of natural causes, in 2001.) The police were willing to reconsider Mr Fallon's case and the matter was passed on to Inspector Ian Wilkinson who began to liase with Mr Fallon's family. From the outset it was evident that they had a strong claim.

When the known facts of Alexander Fallon's life and physical features were laid out it was evident that he possessed many of the same characteristics as Body 115. Mr Fallon was a smoker, he wore full dentures and, most importantly, he had undergone an operation to the skull that necessitated the insertion of a clip into his brain. Problems still remained with Fallon's height and age, both of which were much greater than those of Body 115 but, in light of the other evidence, these issues were temporarily side-lined. Superintendent Hennigan and Inspector Wilkinson began liaising with Mr and Mrs Leishman in the hope that they might be able to lead them to a positive match via medical, criminal or other records.

'This time we received much more help from the police,' said Andrew Leishman, 'with their assistance we have been able to get information that we were previously denied from the social security benefit agencies.' [3]

Over the years Mrs Leishman had been denied access to her father's social security records on the grounds of data protection. The British Transport Police, who are also subject to the Data Protection Act, were able to persuade the Department for Work and Pensions that Mr Fallon's case was exceptional and that viewing his file was in the man's best interest. The records were released and, as was hoped, they revealed that their father had been receiving benefits in London until the week before the King's Cross fire. In the week of the blaze all the payments stop, with there being no record of Mr Fallon having drawn either his pension or other benefits afterwards. Given that it would have been difficult for him to live without the income from his pension, this was the first piece of independent evidence linking the timing of Mr Fallon's disappearance with the occurrence of the fire.

The social security file also revealed that Mr Fallon had been living in Frognal, an area of north London that at this time was popular with those on lower incomes such as students, casual workers, pensioners and young people. It did not escape the police's notice that Frognal has direct transport links to King's Cross via both the Tube and overland train network.

With each new revelation, the similarities between Mr Fallon and Body 115 grew stronger, so much so that Inspector Wilkinson took the unusual step of inviting Mrs Leishman and her family down to London. The Inspector took the family on a conducted tour to see some of the places associated both with their father and Body 115. The Leishmans were taken to King's Cross Underground Station to see the seat of the fire and the commemorative plaque erected in memory of its victims. From there they went to Finchley to visit the cemetery where Body 115 had been buried. The final stop was to see Father Jim Kennedy whose Catholic church played host to the annual memorial service. He always referred to Body 115 as 'Michael' and, like the police, felt that the unknown man was close to receiving a name. 'I may have to turn "Michael" into "Alex" soon,' he said, optimistically.

Once again the mystery of Body 115 seemed tantalisingly near to a solution but the police still needed a piece of forensic evidence that could unquestionably link Alexander Fallon to Body 115.

At his daughter's house attempts were made to lift fingerprints from objects that Mr Fallon was known to have handled but, after nearly two decades, no trace could be found. The police searched the English and Scottish Criminal Records Office, the Prison Service and military police archives in the hope of finding a set of fingerprints for Mr Fallon. No criminal records relating to Mr Fallon were located which did at least offer a possible explanation as to why Body 115's fingerprint (assuming it was also that of Mr Fallon) had not been found during the initial search of the national police collection in 1988. Concerted attempts were made to find Mr Fallon's dental and medical records in Falkirk but these were also unsuccessful. As with Hubert Rose, and many other missing persons investigated since 1987, Mr Fallon was proving to be something of an enigma.[4]

By the spring of 2003 Mrs Leishman and her family believed that the police investigation was beginning to lose momentum and was possibly even running into trouble; this was a situation that they had already experienced in 1997. They were keen to see the issue of their father's disappearance cleared up as soon as possible, not least because Andrew Leishman was suffering from a progressive illness that was beginning to take a serious toll on his health. With all the traditional forensic avenues exhausted, the Leishmans advocated the use of a new technique that had only recently been introduced into the field of forensic science and that they believed would permit Mr Fallon to be positively identified as Body 115. Importantly, the materials needed to effect this identification were, for once, readily available to the police: the new technique was DNA profiling.

The work of most police forensic scientists centres around finding and utilising characteristics that are so unique to the individual that they can be used to trace a suspect's name, positively link them to a crime scene or, in some cases, exclude them from an enquiry. For decades, fingerprints and dental patterns (both of which are unique to the individual) were the most widely used means of establishing a person's identity. Then, in the late 1980s, the police received a new and extraordinarily powerful forensic technique that has arguably changed the face of policing forever.

It has been known for centuries that all animals inherit biological characteristics from their parents. This is why features such as eye and hair colour can travel from parent to child and why inherited conditions such as colour blindness and haemophilia run in families. Exactly how these biological features could be passed from one generation to the next was not fully understood until the twentieth century when the new science of genetics discovered that at the centre of each cell in our bodies lies DNA (deoxyribonucleic acid), a complex chemical strand that acts as a blueprint for our bodies.

In simple terms, DNA is the body's instruction manual; it tells each and every one of our cells what it should be doing and when it should be doing it. DNA thus co-ordinates the millions of chemical reactions that allow us to eat, move, think and perform other functions. When viewed under a microscope, DNA appears as a collection of small paired strands, arranged in the now familiar and iconic double-helix pattern. These paired DNA strands are known as chromosomes, with each human cell having 46 chromosomes arranged into 23 double-helix pairs. A chromosome is built from millions of smaller chemical units known as 'bases' of which there are four types known as Adenine, Cytosine, Guanine and Thymine. These bases are more commonly referred to by their initials: A, C, G and T. To make up a complete genetic code children inherit half their bases from their mother and half from their father, but because there are millions of bases and because they can combine in different ways, the resulting genetic code is unique to each individual. Even brothers and sisters who share the same parents will have a unique DNA profile. Only identical twins have identical DNA because they result from a fertilised egg that split into two after the mother and father's bases had already combined.

The uniqueness of each person's DNA has been known for decades but until the 1980s there was no quick, cheap and easy means of analysing and comparing genetic codes between people. In 1984 the English scientist Alec Jeffries discovered a technique that permitted sections of our genetic code to be easily analysed and then compared with the genetic code of others. In the same way that each of us can be identified using our fingerprint or dental pattern, Jeffries's technique meant that scientists could identify each person on the planet using their unique genetic code. It is therefore perhaps unsurprising that this discovery became known as 'DNA fingerprinting' although it should more correctly be called DNA profiling. The implication for the police was profound.

Our bodies contain approximately sixty trillion cells, each of which carries a complete copy of our DNA code inside their nucleus. The violent nature of many crime scenes means that criminals, or their victims, often leave behind significant numbers of their cells in the form of blood, semen, saliva, skin, hair or other body parts. Before DNA profiling such samples had only a limited forensic use but the police quickly realised that if they could extract a DNA profile from crime scene samples then at a later date they might be able to match the DNA profile to that of a suspect for the crime. It was hoped that DNA profiling would be able to secure convictions by placing a suspect at the scene of the crime in the same way that a fingerprint can.

DNA profiling proved to be far more successful than anybody could have hoped for, with the first court convictions coming in 1988. The case involved a British man who had raped and murdered two teenage girls and was placed at the scene by the DNA in the semen samples he had left behind. 'Had it not been for genetic fingerprinting, you might still be at liberty,' said the judge as he handed down a life sentence. Just as significant was the case of a second man who had been suspected of the same crime but was cleared when his DNA profile failed to match that from the crime scene.[5]

This was followed by dozens of other prosecutions and led to the establishment of a DNA database into which was placed the genetic profile of anybody arrested in Great Britain, even for minor offences such as drink driving. Genetic profiles obtained from crime scenes are now routinely run through the DNA database in the hope that a match can be found with a known criminal. (The principle is similar to running a fingerprint from a crime scene through the national fingerprint collection.) As the size of the DNA database increased, so it proved its worth. At the time of writing the UK national DNA database holds the genetic profiles of over 3 million people, up from 700,000 in 1997, and in 2005 it was directly used to solve 19,800 crimes, up from 8612 in 2000. It is an extremely powerful tool.[6]

One major discovery is that a DNA profile can be recovered from old evidence such as dried blood, saliva or semen stains as well as from bodies that were buried or discarded years previously. Running DNA evidence from old crime scenes through the DNA database has allowed police to identify and prosecute suspects for incidents that took place decades previously. Scientists have gone a step further than this and have managed to obtain DNA from fossils that are hundreds or even thousands of years old. This ability to recover old DNA had a potential implication for the Body 115 investigation.

At the time of the King's Cross fire, DNA profiling was in its infancy with the patent for the technique only having been granted earlier that year. The first police trials with DNA profiling occurred in early 1988, when Body 115 was still held in St Pancras mortuary, but the technique's potential was not realised until sometime after its burial. Thus the remains were interred without a tissue sample having been taken for DNA analysis. Nowadays the genetic profiling of unidentified bodies is routine; back in 1988 it was not.

A DNA profile is not just useful for tracking down criminals, it has also been extensively used in paternity cases to establish whether or not someone is the biological parent of a child. Because all our genetic material comes from our parents, it is possible to compare a child's DNA profile with that of a man or woman and say with a degree of statistical certainty whether or not they are the mother or father of that child. Hollywood film stars, politicians and others have used this in paternity lawsuits as a means of denying or establishing whether they are the parents of particular children.

It is this ability to establish genetic relationships between a parent and child that caught the attention of the Leishman family. In the absence of any other forensic evidence, they wondered whether it would be possible to obtain a DNA profile from Body 115 and then compare it with profiles taken from Mrs Leishman and her sisters. If Body 115 was Alexander Fallon, as Mrs Leishman and the police strongly suspected, then it should be possible to match his DNA profile to that of his daughters. It seemed to be an easy and effective solution to the problem presented by the lack of any other forensic evidence.

With there being no preserved tissue samples from Body 115, obtaining a genetic profile would require the coffin to be exhumed so that forensic scientists could take a sample of bone from the body. In bringing up the issue of DNA profiling, the Leishmans believed that they had found a reasonable means of matching their father to Body 115 and that, given the circumstances of the case, obtaining an exhumation licence would be a relatively straightforward process. They were wrong on both counts.

The suggestion that Body 115 should be DNA profiled had in fact been suggested before. In 2002 Kathleen Wilson put forward the same idea to the British Transport Police in the belief that the unknown man was her father James Brown. Superintendent Hennigan wrote to her saying: 'I do accept and understand your views with regards to DNA now being an accepted form of identification in criminal and other matters, and that we have not at this point in time obtained a DNA profile from the body ... I had not discounted the probability that at some point in time we would go to the grave and seek an exhumation order from the Coroner in order to be able to take this sample, but this was not something that one should consider likely given the trauma of such an event notwithstanding in the pursuance of right and justice, however in my mind the grounds and justification of such action would have to be fairly strong. For instance, if a fingerprint comparison put forward by an enquirer were very close to or matched the fingerprints that we currently have for 115, I would then resort to DNA at the behest of the coroner to ensure that we had an absolutely 100% comparison and therefore the identification of this body.'[7]

In Kathleen's case the police did not think that there were sufficient grounds to seek an exhumation licence; after all, they had already used fingerprint evidence to discount her father as a candidate. The same could not be said of Mary Leishman whose father fitted the known characteristics of Body 115 in every way possible. In that case DNA profiling looked to be a reasonable option, but the situation was more complicated than it at first appeared.

The reason why the police DNA database has been so effective is because it is tasked with matching two DNA samples taken from the same person (one taken from a crime scene, one on the arrest of a suspect). The odds of two separate people having exactly the same DNA profile is astronomically high, which means that matching two samples from the same person through the DNA database is reasonably secure. However, making a secure identification between a child and its parents (so-called paternity testing) requires the DNA from both the alleged mother and father as well as from their offspring. This is because the child's DNA profile must be seen to be made from a combination of both the father and mother's DNA. Having DNA just from the father and from the child can only produce a statistical likelihood of paternity, because without the mother's profile it is not possible to account for half of the genes that make up the child's DNA profile.

In the cases of both Mary Leishman and Kathleen Wilson, their mothers had died many years previously which meant that their maternal DNA was unobtainable. Even if a DNA profile could be obtained from Body 115, it could only ever be compared with the children's DNA and not that of their mother. Under these circumstances it would be impossible to get a match between Mary Leishman and Body 115 that could say with absolute certainty that the two were related. This degree of uncertainty had already been responsible for errors including the case of Anne Chadwick in Cumbria who, in 2003, was arrested on suspicion of having murdered a six-month-old baby whose remains were uncovered in a garage. The police's chief evidence was Mrs Chadwick's DNA profile which suggested that she could have been the baby's mother. However, the baby turned out to have been murdered at a time when Mrs Chadwick had a cast-iron alibi; further investigation revealed that the dead infant was Mrs Chadwick's sister, whom she had never known and who may have been murdered by her parents (although this was never proved). [8]

A paternity DNA test involving Body 115 and Mrs Leishman could only ever give a statistical likelihood of their genetic relationship, but in order to be certain of identification the police needed an absolute match. It was nonetheless recognised that the exhumation of Body 115 might one day be necessary and so an officer was asked to look at the legal issues surrounding this. It was quickly discovered that the unusual circumstances surrounding Body 115 made any application for its exhumation fraught with difficulty.

The precise legal route to obtaining an exhumation is dependent on several factors. In most circumstances an exhumation can only take place following the issuing of a licence by the Secretary of State for Constitutional Affairs but in the case of a burial on consecrated ground a licence is also needed from the appropriate church authorities. However, there are a number of other minor issues to be taken into consideration such as whether the body has been the subject of a coroner's inquest. If so, and the inquest has been closed, then an exhumation licence will only be granted under the most exceptional of circumstances. Alternatively, it is relatively easy for a coroner to apply for a licence to exhume a body that has yet to be the subject of an inquest. Also, in some circumstances, including exhumation for DNA testing, the next of kin have to agree to allow the body to be disturbed.

Because Body 115 had already been the subject of an inquest, the chances of getting a licence for its exhumation were remote, but it was also not known whether the body lay in consecrated ground. The cemetery in which it was buried is so large that it stretches across the boundaries of several church parishes; this meant that some parts of it were consecrated, while others are not. Thus, on a sweltering hot day, two police officers visited the cemetery in order to find out exactly where the grave was located. It took them quite a while to find the headstone and, on talking to the cemetery's management, they were impressed to find that the burial spot had been carefully selected to ensure that it lay in non-consecrated ground. This decision had been made at the time of the burial so that should an exhumation ever be required, an application could be made to a Secretary of State and not the Church of England authorities.

With Body 115's peculiar circumstances established, the matter of an exhumation was discussed with Dr Andrew Reid, the Inner North London Coroner who had replaced the now retired Dr Chambers. Dr Reid was an efficient and pragmatic man who had worked as a coroner in London for many years and had, in that time, handled many high-profile cases. He offered to liase with the Home Office on the issue but given that the inquest into Body 115's death was closed, he was not hopeful of success. It was therefore not much of a shock when the Home Office wrote back to Dr Reid refusing permission.

'The inquest has already established the cause of death,' wrote the Home Office, 'and an exhumation is not thought necessary in order to establish the man's identity.' They were also concerned that Ralph Humberstone's body was buried in the same grave as Body 115. 'The normal criteria for exhumation or for obtaining DNA material is that permission must be obtained from the relatives of all those who are to be disturbed. If Mr Humberstone has no known relatives, it would seem likely that permission would have to be obtained from Camden Council instead.'[9]

With an exhumation licence all but impossible to obtain, there was going to be no easy means of obtaining a DNA profile from Body 115. It was at this point that Mary Leishman's patience snapped.

Given the high profile of both the King's Cross fire and Body 115, the British Transport Police had always recommended to the Leishmans that they avoid all contact with the media. However, with an exhumation licence having been refused and there being no obvious means of speeding up the investigation, Mary and Andrew Leishman wondered if, by making their case public, it might not persuade the Home Office to grant them an exhumation licence.

In early July 2003 the Leishmans contacted Robin Young, a senior journalist working for *The Times*; they chose him because he had authored the short article concerning the 2002 commemorative church service that had renewed the Leishmans interest in Body 115. Young was already familiar with aspects of the Body 115 story and was intrigued by the possibility that the unknown man might actually be Alexander Fallon. Several telephone interviews were conducted with both Mary and Andrew Leishman and as well as with some of the other people who had been associated with Body 115 over the years. The British Transport Police, however, declined to take part. The result was a lengthy article, published on 14 July, in which Young summarised the fifteen-year investigation into Body 115, gave an outline of Alexander Fallon's life and the reasons why he was considered to be a good match for the unknown fire victim. The story behind the DNA profile and the Home Office's refusal to grant an exhumation licence was also given. The article ended with a quote from Mrs Leishman that perfectly encapsulated the family's feelings: 'I am 66 and I just want to know what happened to my father.'[10]

However, the article made reference to Mr Fallon having been a heavy drinker, an allegation that his children strongly deny and which upset them greatly. Their feelings were further injured after *The Times* article sparked several follow-up pieces in local and national papers that contained the same contentious description of their father. The Leishmans found themselves swamped by requests for newspaper and television interviews; they felt betrayed and a few days afterwards filed a complaint with *The Times* about the original article which, after an internal investigation, was not upheld. The episode left Mrs Leishman feeling upset and led to all of Alexander Fallon's children refusing to have anything further to do with the media.[11]

Despite this run-in with the newspapers, the publicity did catch the attention of Michael Connarty, the Member of Parliament for Falkirk East, the constituency where Alexander Fallon had once lived. He was outraged by the Home Office's inaction over the exhumation and agreed to represent Mr Fallon's family over the matter. He wrote letters to the Home Secretary, David Blunkett, asking for his help in the matter and to Dr Reid, the Inner North London Coroner, requesting that he make efforts to get the body exhumed and DNA profiled.

'The coroner's office has a duty to solve this mystery and the most sensible suggestion would be to exhume the body and use DNA testing,' said Connarty, adding that the family had 'a very strong case that it could be their father and if it is not it closes off that avenue and at least they can get on with their lives.'[12]

This request for help did reveal that in the absence of any next of kin, permission to exhume both Body 115 and Ralph Humberstone lay with Camden Council into whose care the bodies had been delivered in October 1988. A spokesman for Camden Council confirmed that they had yet to receive a request for exhumation. Together the publicity generated by the case and the involvement of the Home Secretary were to give the Body 115 investigation renewed momentum. It also drew the family of James Brown back into the affair.

CHAPTER NINETEEN

Unconventional Detectives

The publicity surrounding the Leishmans' claim to Body 115 did not just spark the interest of the media and government ministers; it also caught the attention of Kathleen Wilson. She was still hopeful that Body 115 would turn out to be her father so the news that Alexander Fallon was a potential match came as something of a shock. She contacted Ian Wilkinson who confirmed that Fallon's case looked very promising. Anxious not to be sidelined, Kathleen made an unorthodox request of Inspector Wilkinson. She asked him if it would be possible to arrange for a clairvoyant to become involved in the Body 115 investigation. 'I had been reading about psychic detectives,' said Kathleen. 'I thought that they could help.' Wilkinson said that he would see what he could do. [1]

For over a century spiritualist mediums (and others claiming paranormal powers) claim to have helped locate murder victims, missing persons and even apprehend suspects. Such people are often referred to as 'psychic detectives' but it is an area that is fraught with controversy.

A classic example of a psychic detective is the Dutchman Gerard Croiset who claimed success in helping to solve a number of important murder cases. Croiset was born in 1909 but it was decades before he discovered that he could gain visual impressions of an object's previous owners simply by holding it (an ability parapsychologists call psychometry). In 1949 he was asked to aid the police in the case of two children who had been murdered some years previously. On handling some bloodstained clothing from the murder scene Croiset is alleged to have had a vision of two children who were cycling along a woodland path when a poacher attacked and strangled them. Croiset is supposed to have said that tinfoil had been found nearby and that he thought the name 'Stevens' was involved. The police confirmed that he had accurately described the murder scene and that they were currently holding a suspect whose name was Stevenson.

In the coming decades Croiset became world famous for his involvement with criminal cases but in most instances it would be anxious relatives or the media that would request his help, not individual police forces. Even so, his services seem to have been in demand and he travelled the world to help solve crimes or disappearances. For example, in 1966 he went to Australia to see if he could locate three missing children but despite massive publicity afforded to his visit, he failed to offer any new evidence in the case.

Exactly how accurate and helpful Croiset's psychic powers actually were is somewhat doubtful. Most of the celebrated cases with which he became involved were not substantially moved forward by his evidence and there were some very high-profile failures, such as his attempt at finding Britain's Yorkshire Ripper in 1979. The description Croiset gave included statements that the Ripper lived in the centre of Sunderland, had a squashed nose and a limp. In the light of Peter Sutcliffe's arrest, all Croiset's information (and that of other psychics) was seriously wrong. This was one of his final predictions for, on 20 July 1980, Croiset died suddenly at the age of 71. Obituaries from around the world gave him credit for helping to solve hundreds of crimes although the exact number remains a matter of debate. [2]

The reliability of psychic detectives notwithstanding, Inspector Wilkinson obtained permission to find a critically acclaimed clairvoyant who might be able to assist Kathleen. To do so he turned to IPM Television, a London-based production company that had made several television documentaries featuring psychic detectives. It was Wilkinson's hope that one or more of the regular psychics used by IPM would be interested in helping with the Body 115 case.[3]

The approach by the British Transport Police was the first of its kind for IPM and the company's managing director, Craig Goldman, admits that prior to this he had never heard of Body 115. He was, however, very interested in the idea of using his psychics to help in the case but he suggested that they should film the proceedings for use in a new documentary. Given the renewed media interest in Body 115 and the sensitive nature of the investigation, this request was more problematic. Most police forces do not like being associated with psychic detectives and there was also the tricky question of confidentiality. Superintendent John Hennigan consulted with the Inner North London Coroner over this issue who agreed that a documentary could go ahead but that neither he nor the British Transport Police would release any information about, or comment on, the current state of the Body 115 investigation. With these boundaries established, IPM began work on the documentary which, it was hoped, could be centred around the two perceived candidates for Body 115: James Brown and Alexander Fallon.[4]

Both men's children were contacted and asked if they wanted to participate. Kathleen Wilson and her brother Jim were willing but Mary Leishman had grown wary of all the media attention and so politely declined to take part. The co-operation of just one of the families was enough to allow the programme to be made and so at the beginning of August 2003, IPM assembled a team that included researchers, mediums, private investigators and various specialist consultants. 'The mediums will provide the leads and we will follow the whole investigation,' said IPM in their proposal for the programme.

Mary Leishman's disinclination to appear on camera and the sensitive nature of the Body 115 investigation meant that the programme had to be restricted to the case of James Brown. At the centre of the programme were three psychics, Lizzie Falconer,

Colin Fry and Tony Stockwell, all of whom agreed to use their alleged paranormal powers to try and find out whether James Brown was Body 115 and, if not, what had become of him.

The clairvoyant trio began their quest by going to the terraced house in Glasgow where James Brown had lived with his family. The house was in a derelict condition and had been scheduled for demolition by the local council. As they wandered from one gutted, rain-soaked room to another, the psychics began to 'sense' aspects of James Brown's personality and life. 'We are dealing with the layers of memory that are embedded in a place,' explained one of the psychics before going on to describe Brown's unhappy childhood and the restlessness of his adult years. 'It is a feeling of a good life gone wrong,' surmised Colin Fry. Kathleen, who was present throughout, agreed with much of what was said. Despite the unorthodoxy of the proceedings, it was a hopeful start. Another meeting was arranged in Kathleen's home town of Edinburgh. Here the mood darkened as the mediums attempted to discern what had happened to her father after his disappearance in 1987. It was not encouraging news.

All three were in agreement that James Brown was dead and, furthermore, that he was not Body 115. Referring to the fire, Tony Stockwell said 'I do feel that within a day or two after that event he passed into the spirit world ... I feel that he may have fallen into water.' As the meeting progressed, the psychics pieced together what they felt was the story of James Brown's last few minutes on earth. They sensed that he had been walking alongside a waterway, possibly a canal, when a young man attacked and hit him on the head. James Brown fell into the water and drowned. The consensus was that the event had taken place in London and that its location was associated with the word 'Turner'.

Some detective work by the production team produced Turner Marina, part of the Regent's Canal waterway system that flows just to the north of King's Cross; all three psychics were taken there to see what, if anything, they could sense from the locale. The result was a dramatic piece of television in which the presenters reconstructed the alleged last moments of James Brown's life. According to them, Kathleen's unfortunate father was pursued along a narrow towpath by a mugger until, exhausted, he was caught. 'I'm too old. I'm too tired and I'm too old to run,' empathised one of the psychics. Trapped beside a large iron bridge, James Brown was said to have been involved in a struggle before being pushed into the canal where he drowned. His attacker then apparently moved the body but not far; dumping it in water again. 'It's like being stuck in the middle of a horrific film,' said Stockwell as he described Brown's violent end. Parts of his body or clothing may remain in a storm drain, he concluded.

With such detailed information, a private investigator was asked to see if any bodies matching Mr Brown had been reclaimed from the area. None had and, on talking to water engineers, it was discovered that the canal did not have any storm drains, nor any current to speak of. Any body dumped in it would have remained in the area for some time but nothing had been recovered, even though the canal had been swept as part of a separate murder inquiry a few years previously. There was, however, a storm drain located in a nearby street. According to the engineer a body dumped there would have gone into the Thames and, if not retrieved by the River Police, would have floated downstream towards the English Channel. With no evidence one way or the other, the mediums' assertions cannot be proved (or disproved).

Kathleen and her brother Jim made a visit to the place on the canal that had been identified with their father's death. For Kathleen it was an emotional moment although her brother seemed less convinced by what he had been told. 'I can't connect with all that,' he said later.

The fate of James Brown was unresolved with his whereabouts still a matter of speculation. There was, however, one thing about which all three psychics were absolutely certain: Body 115 was unquestionably the remains of Alexander Fallon. In the autumn of 2003 they wrote to the British Transport Police to express this opinion. Naturally, evidence obtained by apparently paranormal means is not legally admissible and so the psychics' opinions did not move the investigation into Body 115 forward. For this to happen the police needed something more corporeal, and they were on the verge of getting it. [5]

CHAPTER TWENTY

New Leads

In October 2003, and with the issue of the exhumation and DNA testing of Body 115 still mired down, a decision was taken by the Assistant Chief Constable 'to review the watching brief that had been held by British Transport Police since 1988'. He wanted a complete revision of every aspect of the Body 115 investigation to see what, if anything, could be done to get the case closed.

Reviewing old cases is a commonly used police tactic especially in old and/or stalled investigations. (Indeed, with important cases, such as murder investigations, reviews can be initiated after only a matter of weeks.) In its early years the Body 115 investigation had been subject to more than one review but these, while helpful, had failed to open up significant new lines of inquiry. In the intervening years there had been advances in technology and policing techniques which, it was felt, warranted a re-examination of all the evidence and leads from afresh.

At the heart of the review process is the need to involve new people in an old investigation so that they can look at the accumulated evidence, theories and lines of inquiry with fresh eyes. In the words of one officer, new people 'can bring to light any errors or potential new leads that might have been over-looked by others'. It was up to the Assistant Chief Constable to choose which officers to appoint to the review. After due consideration he gave the job to his Head of CID, Detective Chief Superintendent Nick Bracken, a specialist in forensic science whose qualifications and attention to detail made him ideally suited to the pathological issues associated with the investigation.[1]

191

Bracken wanted a deputy 'to supervise the day to day operation of the investigation, in particular looking at lines of inquiry and the quality of the investigation to ensure that every angle had indeed been researched'. For this task he chose Chief Inspector Philip Trendall, a young, resourceful officer with an academic background in English judicial law, especially its coronial system. The third member of the team was Inspector Ian Wilkinson, a veteran from the original investigation, whose knowledge of the Body 115 case and the people associated with it was unparalleled. In the coming months these officers would use their respective specialities to excellent effect. [2]

Bracken and Chief Inspector Trendall began by reviewing all the paperwork associated with the whole Body 115 investigation. From this it was evident that despite the hundreds of names that had been put forward over the years, there was only one current candidate: Alexander Fallon. Even so, the evidence linking him to Body 115 remained circumstantial which meant that, like so many other promising leads, there was still a possibility that the similarities were coincidental.

Given this, Bracken ordered a review of Mr Fallon's case with the specific aim of finding so-called 'negative evidence' which could be used to exclude Mr Fallon from the Body 115 investigation. Such negative evidence, in the form of fingerprints, had already been used by the police to remove James Brown from the list of candidates. Could similar evidence be found that would exclude Mr Fallon?

The three officers went back across all the lines of enquiry, checking and rechecking the known facts about Mr Fallon with those obtained from Body 115. Only two potential pieces of negative evidence could be found: Mr Fallon's age and height which were mismatches with those for Body 115. The issues of height and age had been problematic to the entire Body 115 investigation, and this was something that concerned Bracken. He decided that the importance of these two factors needed to be re-investigated.

From the outset of the review Detective Chief Superintendent Bracken believed that too much emphasis had been placed on

Body 115's age and height, both of which had been estimated during the original post-mortem examinations. Bracken's extensive knowledge of forensics alerted him to the pitfalls associated with some types of pathological evidence. The issue of a mismatch in age between Mr Fallon and Body 115 was not difficult for him to reconcile. 'It's easy to distinguish a young body from an older one,' says Bracken, 'but much more difficult to differentiate a middle-aged body from that of a pensioner.' This task becomes more problematic when faced with a fire-ravaged body which meant that, in Bracken's opinion, the original age range afforded to Body 115 had been too narrow; instead of stopping at 60, the upper end of the scale could easily be moved to include a 72-year-old man such as Fallon. The apparent age mismatch was therefore no longer the problem that it once was.

Likewise, obtaining an accurate height measurement from a fire-damaged body is also problematic because extreme heat can cause tendons, spinal discs and other parts of the body to tighten or contract, altering the body's profile. Mr Fallon's children had estimated their father to have been approximately 5′6″ tall which placed a gap of four inches between him and Body 115 that, even allowing for pathological considerations, was difficult to reconcile. One possibility remained, that Mr Fallon's height had been incorrectly estimated by his children. This was a distinct possibility given that they hadn't seen him for over fifteen years; Bracken reasoned that the estimate might be unreliable. To prove this an independent means of judging the man's height was needed. Looking at the outline of Mr Fallon's life history, it was noticed that he had spent the duration of World War II serving in the Royal Artillery. Perhaps his army papers could help resolve the issue.

Up to this time Mr Fallon's daughters had not taken any steps towards getting their father declared legally dead; instead he was still officially listed as a missing person which placed many of his records under the Data Protection Act. Ordinarily this would have made it difficult to gain access to his military records, these being generally out of bounds while a serviceman is still considered to be alive. However, the Army Personnel Centre, where all modern military records are held, recognised the exceptional circumstances associated with Mr Fallon's case and gave the police officer permission to examine his service record.

Like many of his generation, Mr Fallon had only been enrolled in the army for the duration of the war years which, in his case, meant that his army file began in 1939 and stopped in 1945, after which he had returned to civilian life. This placed a gap of over forty years between the last entry in Mr Fallon's military file and the King's Cross fire. Even so, his army record did contain useful information most of which came from the medical examinations that Mr Fallon had undergone at various points during his army career. The medicals were rudimentary affairs, designed only to provide an outline of a soldier's general health, but they recorded two key pieces of data.

The first of these was that by 1945, when Mr Fallon would have been 31 years old, he already had a full set of dentures. Unfortunately no description of the dentures was given but the fact that he wore them did tally with Body 115 who was known to have been a long-term denture wearer. The second piece of information was Mr Fallon's height which had been recorded on several occasions but which, perplexingly, placed him between 5'4" and 5'6" tall depending on when the measurement took place. After allowing for the effects of forty years of aging, the lower end of this range placed Fallon within the height range of Body 115. In 1997 Mr Fallon had been sidelined from the Body 115 investigation largely because of his height and age; now the review of the evidence suggested that this was probably a mistake. [3]

With no apparent negative evidence to exclude Mr Fallon, there remained the problem of finding positive evidence that could link him to Body 115. Finding such evidence had proved to be the stumbling block with almost all the other hopeful candidates for Body 115; circumstantial evidence could be found in abundance but the one key piece of evidence that could prove a match would somehow always remain elusive. Detective Chief Superintendent Bracken and Chief Inspector Trendall spent a considerable time thinking about how best they should proceed. It was apparent that techniques such as DNA testing were not going to give them the certainty that the case required. Ideally they needed to find Mr Fallon's medical or dental records but previous searches for these failed and so, while the hunt for these files would not cease, the police officers decided that they needed to find other more obscure methods of matching Mr Fallon to Body 115. In the words of Detective Chief Superintendent Bracken, 'we chose to follow the more laborious deductive route'.

The search began with the police officers contacting Mary Leishman. They asked her to search out any photographs of her father that clearly showed his head and face. Initially she could only find snapshots that were too small or blurred to allow any fine features on Mr Fallon's face to be discernible, but eventually one of Mr Fallon's children tracked down a picture of him taken at a party a couple of years prior to the King's Cross fire. The photograph was not perfectly in focus but it did show a close-up of Mr Fallon looking directly at the camera. The picture showed an ageing man, wearing thick, black-rimmed glasses, whose lips were thin and whose short, dark, receding hair had been combed backwards. On the right hand side of Mr Fallon's forehead was a prominent circular depression which, according to Mrs Leishman, was evidence of the brain operation that he had undergone in 1980; the scar was another compelling link to Body 115. It had been hoped that a clear photograph of Mr Fallon's face would compare favourably to the facial reconstruction made by Richard Neave. However, when the two were placed side by side the similarity was not immediately striking. Perhaps Mr Fallon was not Body 115, after all. To be certain, Mr Fallon's photograph was given to Richard Neave who was able to give a more considered opinion on the matter.

In his studio Neave ignored the apparent visual mismatch, which was considered to be too subjective, and instead chose a more objective means of making a comparison. The clarity of

Mr Fallon's photograph was good enough for Neave to be able to make accurate measurements from his face and use them to create a mathematical map of certain key features on the skull beneath. The same measurements were then made on the facial reconstruction and also on the cast of the skull of Body 115. The sets of measurements were then compared with one another, an act that allowed an independent means of judging the similarity between the sculpture and the missing man. The statistics suggested that the two were very similar indeed.

As a final check, a computer was used to superimpose an image of Mr Fallon's face on top of the facial reconstruction. Features on Mr Fallon's face, such as the position of his eyes, chin and mouth all matched the reconstruction perfectly as did the general outline of his skull. Within a few days Neave was able to tell the British Transport Police that 'there were no anatomical mismatches' between Mr Fallon and his facial reconstruction.

The initial dissimilarity seen by the police had probably been caused by peripheral differences, such as the sculpture's ears which were smaller than Mr Fallon's, but these were the result of Neave having been told that Body 115 was a middle-aged man. Ears are made of cartilage and those of Body 115 did not survive the fire; in the absence of any other information, Neave had given his sculpture the ears of a 50-year-old man, whereas Mr Fallon was in his seventies. [4]

When asked about the facial reconstruction Andrew Leishman said: 'It did not strike me particularly at first but when my brother-in-law in Texas drew the heavy glasses that my father-in-law wore in later life on the police picture, the resemblance was really remarkable.' [5]

From the review's outset Detective Chief Superintendent Bracken had decided that, rather than randomly searching for information about Mr Fallon, the investigation had to focus itself on those areas that were most likely to produce a result and he was quickly able to discern where he and his team should be looking. 'I felt that re-investigating the Sugita clip should be our priority,' he said.

The brain operation performed on Body 115 was one of the few distinguishing features to survive the heat of the fire. This, and the rarity of the Sugita No. 5 aneurysm clip used by the surgeon, had attracted the attention of those involved with the original investigation although attempts at tracing where, when and on whom the operation had been performed had failed. It was the statistics uncovered by the original investigation that grabbed Bracken's attention: a maximum of 300 Sugita No. 5 clips had been imported into the country between 1977 and 1982, and of these around ninety would have been used on the right-hand side of the skull of a male patient. Furthermore, according to the company that imported the clips into Britain from Japan, a maximum of forty hospitals in England and Wales would have used the clip.

Back in 1987 the lack of a probable name for Body 115 meant that all the records from all forty hospitals would have needed to be searched in the hope of stumbling across a medical file containing details of Body 115's surgery. Logistically this was an impossible task. Now, fifteen years later, the investigators had a target name, Alexander Fallon, and an approximate date for the operation, 1980. They also had another vital piece of information: a probable location where the operation had been performed.[6]

When quizzed about her father's medical history, Mary Leishman had not been able to provide much detail. She was aware that he had collapsed in London in 1980 and that he had undergone brain surgery during which a clip was inserted, but Mr Fallon had made light of the incident and had not wanted to talk about it. She did, however, recall that after collapsing he had been taken to the Royal London Hospital in east London. Could this be where the operation had been carried out? Certainly the place where Mr Fallon collapsed, Tower Hill, is within the Royal London's catchment area for emergency patients but, on being contacted, the hospital had some bad news for the investigation team. A spokesman for the Royal London categorically denied that the hospital had carried out operations on cerebral atheroma patients in 1980: they claimed not to have had any surgeons working for them who could have undertaken the surgery. Furthermore, the hospital denied having ever ordered or used the Sugita No. 5 clip; this was borne out by the importer's records which confirmed that the Royal London had not bought any of the aneurysm clips. Mr Fallon could not, said the Royal London, have been a patient of ours.

The Royal London looked to be another failed lead but this did not deter Detective Chief Superintendent Bracken from his belief that the Sugita clip was the key to solving the mystery of Body 115. With the easy routes all exhausted, Bracken took a tough decision; he determined that the best way forward was to search the admittance records of all forty hospitals that were on record as having used the Sugita No. 5 clip. In theory Alexander Fallon's name ought to be found amongst this voluminous archive of information; once it was known which hospital he had used, it should then be possible to find his medical records from within the same institution. The task of searching the records was given to Ian Wilkinson but it was a serious undertaking that would take weeks, if not months, to complete. It began with a request to all of London's major hospitals to check their computerised admission records (which in almost all cases did not go back as far as 1980) to see if they had an Alexander Fallon listed there. It was this that provided the team with their first lucky break.

The Royal Free Hospital is located in Hampstead, at the opposite end of London to Tower Hill where Mr Fallon collapsed in 1980. It is, however, only a short distance from Frognal where Mr Fallon was known to have been living in the months before the fire occurred. Despite this, the team were surprised when the Royal Free rang up to say that they had found the medical file for an Alexander Williamson Fallon who had been admitted to the accident and emergency department after collapsing in the street, not in 1980, but on 9 November 1987. The hospital said they had admitted him overnight for observation and that he had been released the following day. This was only eight days before the King's Cross fire.

There was little doubt that this record referred to the same man who was at the centre of the Body 115 investigation. The medical notes relating to the admission were forwarded to the police and were found to reveal a snapshot of Mr Fallon's general medical health as it had been only a matter of days before the fire. This produced a number of startling similarities between Mr Fallon and some of the pathological information obtained by Dr Iain West from Body 115. For example, the Royal Free noted that Fallon was suffering from 'chronic obstructive airways disease' while West's found that Body 115's lungs showed 'moderate emphysema and bronchiectasis'. This led West to later comment that Body 115 'would have had a chronic cough bringing up sputum, he may have been wheezy, his chest condition would have been noticeable to those who were well acquainted with him'.

The Royal Free also noted that Mr Fallon was suffering from 'high blood pressure' while Dr West noted that Body 115's brain showed 'mild cerebral atheroma', a condition associated with persistent hypertension. It was also suspected by the hospital that Mr Fallon's collapse might have been linked to his earlier brain surgery. This tied in with comments made by Mrs Leishman who recalled that 'the operation had started to give him problems' in the months before he went missing. All this was further tantalising evidence of the similarities between Body 115 and Mr Fallon, and yet despite the growing volume of such evidence, it was still all circumstantial and could be put down to coincidence.[7]

The Royal Free was the only hospital to uncover any records relating to Mr Fallon; the others all drew a blank. Frustrated at this, Bracken turned his attention back to the single clear photograph of Mr Fallon that had been provided by his family. Clearly visible was the circular scar outlining where the section of bone had been removed and then replaced by the surgeon in 1980. In their archives the police held photographs of Body 115's cleaned skull which showed where the surgery had taken place in unmistakable detail. Bracken wondered whether a comparison of the picture of Mr Fallon's surgery scars with the skull of Body 115 would reveal a probable match. This task was offered to, and accepted by, Professor Peter Vanezis, the head of the Forensic Science Service and one of Britain's most experienced forensic scientists.

One of Vanezis's specialities is using computer imaging to aid in the identification of human remains. In its most basic form this means using a computer to enhance images and to then make comparisons of certain key features based on exact measurements and other criteria. The photographs handed to Vanezis included several of Body 115's skull which showed where, during surgery, the circular flap of bone had been removed from the right-hand side of the forehead and then replaced. These were to be compared with the single photograph of Mr Fallon on which the large circular scar on the right-hand side of his forehead was visible. Even to the untrained eye the outlines of the two scars look similar but it was hoped that Professor Vanezis would be able to use scientific methodology to establish whether the two scars were a perfect match.

The photograph of Body 115's skull revealed that at several points around the edge of the bone flap, where it joins to the main part of the skull, the wound had only partially healed. This had left several small holes in the skull with no bone covering at all. The location of these holes appeared to correspond with the positioning of several deep depressions visible on Mr Fallon's forehead but to be certain Professor Vanezis digitised both pictures and then used a computer to scale and match the two photographs. When laid on top of one another, the outline of the two scars appeared to be a perfect match, but to be certain a map was made of six obvious features from Body 115's scar, most of which were the unhealed holes. The map was superimposed onto the image of Mr Fallon, and it could be seen that for each of the six key features on Body 115's skull, there was a corresponding depression on Mr Fallon's forehead. The match was perfect. Professor Vanezis wrote back to the British Transport Police team concluding that the shape, size, contour and depth of the scar on Body 115 was 'totally consistent' with the one seen on Mr Fallon.

News that the two scars matched gave the British Transport Police the one thing that had been missing for nearly sixteen years: a piece of independent medical evidence that could provide a link between a named man and the human remains known as Body 115. The similarities between Fallon and Body 115 were numerous and compelling but Bracken, Trendall and Wilkinson were aware that their evidence had to prove the link 'beyond all reasonable doubt' which meant they could leave no room for error. As it stood, the inability to trace any official records relating to Mr Fallon's brain surgery was still a problem; without proof of where and when this surgery occurred, there was room for doubt. The surgical records had to be found, and fast.

Armed with Professor Vanezis's photographic analysis, Detective Chief Superintendent Bracken re-approached the Royal London hospital. They remained adamant that cranial surgery had not been performed in 1980 and that they had not used Sugita clips but they did agree to allow Inspector Wilkinson to perform a search of their archive in search of any record of Mr Fallon.

Inspector Wilkinson travelled to the Royal London and began by requesting a search of the hospital's computerised admission system. The result was negative but this was not surprising considering that it had only been in place for a relatively short time. Wilkinson enquired about admission records from the early 1980s and was told that these had been computerised but that the computer concerned had long since gone out of service. In fact, the outdated machine was located in a remote part of the hospital where it had lain dormant for several years. At Wilkinson's request the ageing computer was plugged in and, to his relief, still worked. The admission records had been placed on old-fashioned $5\frac{1}{4}''$ floppy discs that, miraculously, had managed to survive being in storage for several years without becoming corrupted. The age of the computer hardware and the primitive nature of the software made searching the records far from straightforward, but once the outdated software had been mastered it did produce a result. There among the jumbled mass of names was Alexander Fallon who, according to the computer records, had been admitted to the hospital's accident and emergency department in the early 1980s. However, the computer database could provide no other information beyond this. It could not say why he had been admitted, what procedures he had undergone or when he had been discharged. Wilkinson was told that this information could only be obtained from Fallon's medical record and, they confessed, there was no ready means of locating this from within their archive. Inspector Wilkinson was led to a large, dusty storeroom piled high with boxes each of which contained several dozen medical files; the Inspector was told that he was welcome to search them for Fallon's file.

It was a Friday afternoon and Inspector Wilkinson was faced with several decades' worth of medical files. The task appeared Herculean but he had spent almost sixteen years pursuing Body 115's identity and so if evidence of Mr Fallon's operation was in that room, he determined that he would find it. The search needed to be methodical and required patience; Wilkinson possessed both these qualities and quietly began to work his way through the dusty boxes of records. It took several hours, but the systematic search eventually paid off; buried within the sea of paperwork was a thin folder labelled 'Alexander Fallon' which, according to the paperwork inside, related to an emergency brain operation that had occurred on 14 September 1980. It was moment of triumph, not just for Inspector Wilkinson, but for the entire Body 115 investigation.

Back at British Transport Police headquarters the file revealed that, contrary to the Royal London Hospital's original denial, Alexander Fallon had undergone surgery for a cerebral atheroma (which was the same operation experienced by Body 115) and that it had been performed in the same part of the skull. Mr Fallon's surgery had also necessitated the insertion of an aneurysm clip but, frustratingly, the medical notes made no mention of its make and type; this was a potential problem given that the Royal London was not one of the hospitals known to have used the Sugita No. 5 clip. Also disappointing was the lack of any X-rays, photographs or other visual evidence of Mr Fallon's surgery that could have been used to match those obtained from Body 115. Fortunately the file did contain one vital piece of information: the details of the surgeon in charge of the operation. His name was David Hardy.

The Royal London was contacted again. They told the officers that David Hardy had been a relatively young man when he joined the hospital but that he had left the institution many years ago. Fortunately Mr Hardy was not a difficult man to trace as he had since risen through the ranks to become Medical Director at the Neurotology and Skull Base Surgery Unit at Addenbrooke's Hospital, near to Cambridge. Detective Chief Superintendent Bracken made contact with Hardy who was somewhat surprised to hear that he could have a connection to Body 115. Bracken quizzed Hardy about his time at the Royal London but he could not remember having performed the operation on Mr Fallon which, after all, had taken place nearly a quarter of a century earlier.

Bracken showed Hardy the picture of Body 115's skull with its prominent circular scar; Hardy confirmed that it was consistent with his style of surgery. He was then shown the photograph of Mr Fallon in which the surgery scar was clearly visible. Hardy was struck by the similarity of two scars but he confessed that he was not expert enough to say for sure whether they were identical; he did confirm that a scar from such an operation would form a unique pattern.

'The point of entry and the shape which it develops is unique,' he said to Bracken, 'and even more so the webbing and repairing makes the [scar] mark unique. In the areas where the skull doesn't web as well, the scar is deeper [and] the contour is deeper.' [8]

Bracken broached the subject of aneurysm clips but before he could ask him any specific questions, Hardy volunteered that at the time of Mr Fallon's operation he preferred to use those manufactured by Sugita. In fact, said Hardy, he liked them so much that he brought a personal supply with him to the Royal London, where Sugita clips were not in use. In a stroke this answered the last outstanding question associated with Mr Fallon's surgery: the

Royal London genuinely hadn't ordered any of the Sugita No. 5 aneurysm clips, it was Hardy who had brought them to the hospital.

By Bracken's estimate, a maximum of ninety Sugita No. 5 clips would have been used on male patients who had undergone surgery on the right-hand side of the forehead. Since 1988 it had been known that Body 115 was one of these ninety men but, thanks to David Hardy's outstanding memory, it could be proved that Mr Fallon was also a member of this select group. To have both Body 115 and Mr Fallon within this same small pool of men was statistically significant but when used in conjunction with their many other similarities, it suggested that the final outstanding mystery from the King's Cross fire had been resolved. As Christmas 2003 approached, the final pieces of the jigsaw had fallen into place but the person who had the final say over whether Body 115 had been correctly identified was not Detective Chief Superintendent Bracken but instead Dr. Andrew Reid, the Inner North London Coroner. However, without dental, fingerprint or DNA evidence, would he agree with the British Transport Police officers' conclusion?

CHAPTER TWENTY-ONE

'Some Sort of Closure'

On 18 November 2003 Kathleen Wilson and her brother made the journey from Edinburgh to London to attend the sixteenth annual commemorative service at Father Jim Kennedy's church, located behind King's Cross station. That year the memorial service was also attended by Mary Leishman and her husband Andrew and so, for the first time, the two families, both of whom believed that their father could be Body 115, met with each other. 'We got on really well with them,' Kathleen said. 'After all, we were in much the same boat, coping with the same difficulties.'

Neither family was at that point aware of the new discoveries being made by the Body 115 investigation team, and they were therefore surprised to hear Detective Chief Superintendent Bracken publicly state that he expected Body 115's identity to be resolved in the very near future.[1]

Two months later, on 12 January 2004, Inspector Ian Wilkinson paid a visit to Mrs Wilson in Edinburgh. He called in on her while travelling to Falkirk in pursuit of Alexander Fallon's dental records. As ever, the two talked about the Body 115 investigation but the complexities associated with the case meant that Inspector Wilkinson could not let her know about the latest evidence relating to Mr Fallon.

Ten days later Kathleen was listening to a national news bulletin that, as its closing item, mentioned that the British Transport Police had identified Body 115 as Alexander Fallon. 'When we heard on the radio that 115 had been identified as Mr Fallon,' said Kathleen, 'it came as a bolt from the blue. It was a painful blow.'[2]

News of the solution to the Body 115 mystery had been released by the British Transport Police on the evening of 21 January. The ITV late-night news was one of the first to make an announcement. They said: 'After more than sixteen years and a worldwide search, investigators from the King's Cross fire have finally got their target. But this was no ordinary police manhunt. Their mission was to put a name to the final victim of the disaster. His identity a mystery, he was given a number – which stayed with him even when he was buried. He's always been known as one one five: until now.'

To accompany the announcement that Body 115 had been identified as Alexander Fallon, a press conference was organised for 22 January. It was here that Detective Chief Superintendent Bracken planned to unveil the new findings about Body 115 that had allowed him and his team to make an identification.

At Detective Chief Superintendent Bracken's insistence, the conference was scheduled to take place in the headquarters of the Worshipful Society of Apothecaries of London where he was an examiner on their Diploma in Forensic Human Identification. Accompanying Bracken at the press conference were Mary Leishman and Ena Logan, two of Mr Fallon's daughters, as well as Chief Inspector Philip Trendall. Watched by a large gathering of press and television journalists, Bracken, Trendall and the two women walked up the steps into the Apothecaries's ornate, wooden-panelled Great Hall to take their seats behind a desk. Bracken opened the proceedings: 'The victim previously referred to as Body 115, because of the mortuary number given to him on the night of the fire, we've identified as being Alexander Williamson Fallon of Falkirk, Scotland.'

Bracken continued, giving the background to the Body 115 investigation and the new evidence that had led the review team to conclude he was Mr Fallon. He was aided by enlarged photographs of Mr Fallon which had been placed next to Richard

Neave's facial reconstruction: the similarity was evident for all to see. A separate photograph showed Body 115's skull, complete with its scar, next to a close up of Mr Fallon's scarred forehead; again the similarity between the two was plain to see. No one present disagreed with the police's conclusions; it was evident that Body 115 had finally been given a name. Afterwards Chief Inspector Trendall read out a short statement by Mary Leishman.

'We have reached some sort of closure now,' he read out. 'We are finding it hard coming to terms with knowing what happened to our father and the tragedy that night. We have lost a loving, protective father and we shall miss his wit and humour for the rest of our lives.'[3]

Extensive media coverage was given to the announcement; television news illustrated it with archive pictures from the night of the fire as well as using more recent footage of Body 115's headstone and the memorial listing him as an 'unknown man'. The coverage was generally positive although many newspapers inaccurately referred to Fallon as a vagrant – something that just isn't true, given that he was known to have had both a job and a permanent address. Because of this misrepresentation, Mr Fallon's children refused to comment publicly about their father or about the Body 115 investigation.

Kathleen Wilson, on the other hand, was upset and perplexed at what to her was an apparent volte-face by the British Transport Police. 'It was a shock,' she said. 'We had become used to the idea that Body 115 was our dad.' She and her family believed that the police had been forced into making a decision by political pressure and that there was still room for error over their identification of Body 115.

'They kept saying the other guy's [Fallon's] age and height didn't match,' said Kathleen. She believed that many of the characteristics of Body 115 used to identify it as Mr Fallon could be applied to James Brown, their father. 'We know my father had a stroke so he could have had this operation after we lost contact and he was a heavy smoker. As for his teeth, they were very bad. Again, he could have been fitted with dentures after we lost contact.'[4]

Kathleen's sentiments were expressed in several newspaper articles in which she and her brother argued strongly that Body 115 should be exhumed and DNA tested, just to be sure. The plea fell on deaf ears, as neither the police nor the coroner's office had any interest in spending additional time and money trying to get an exhumation licence for a body whose identity had already been established. Kathleen's chief worry was that the body would be exhumed by Mr Fallon's children and then cremated. 'If that happens then we'll never be able to sort this out,' she said.[5]

Despite protests from Kathleen and her relatives, the British Transport Police were satisfied that the case was closed although Detective Chief Superintendent Bracken did say that the case of James Brown would not be forgotten. 'We never give up,' he commented.[6]

Following the excitement surrounding the closure of the Body 115 investigation, Bracken, Trendall and Wilkinson had one further task to undertake: to get Body 115's death certificate, which had been issued in 1988, altered so that it bore Alexander Fallon's name. In order to do so, the British Transport Police had first to persuade the Inner North London Coroner that the evidence and reasoning behind their identification was sound. Only then could he petition the Registrar of Births, Marriages and Deaths to amend the death certificate.

On the morning of 3 February 2004 officers from the British Transport Police, plus a few journalists and members of Alexander Fallon's close family, gathered at the St Pancras Coroner's Court, the place where, sixteen years earlier, the original inquest into the victims of the fire had been held under the supervision of Dr Douglas Chambers. Now the same building was to play host to the final chapter in the story of Body 115, and the Coroner was Dr Andrew Reid.

The doors to the court were opened and the press and spectators filed into the public gallery. After giving them time to make themselves comfortable, Dr Reid opened the proceedings by explaining the function of his court.

'Good morning everyone,' he began. 'Let me explain the purpose of the inquiry I'm holding today ... I will hear evidence on oath to assist me in determining matters in relation to the identity of a person who at this time remains an unidentified victim of the King's Cross fire which occurred in 1987. This is not an inquest, it's a matter of determining identity and the process is that I will hear evidence on oath and if I'm satisfied on the evidence [...] that the formerly unidentified body has now been identified, and if I am satisfied that his identity has been ascertained, I will then send a certificate to the Registrar of Births, Death and Marriage, confirming that I am satisfied that the identity has been established.'[7]

With this explanation over, Dr Reid called Mary Leishman as his first witness. In reply to questions, Mrs Leishman confirmed her name and that of her father. Dr Reid went on to establish some facts concerning Mr Fallon's last known whereabouts. Mrs Leishman replied that she had last 'heard from him by telephone round about the middle of October, or something like that and that was the last time I heard from him.'

Dr Reid moved on to talk about his health. 'Did he discuss at any times that he had been to hospital?' asked the Coroner.

'Just after he had the haemorrhage, that was the only time we ever knew him to be hospitalised,' she replied.

'What did he tell you about it?'

'He just said he had collapsed in the street, in a London street. He was told later on that people were passing by him, passing over him and it was an old couple, an old lady and gentleman, who summoned help.'

'And what did he tell you, what did you understand about the surgery he had?' asked Dr Reid.

'He just said he had the surgery, he had a clip inserted in the head and that was it.' said Mrs Leishman. The Coroner asked a few more routine questions concerning Alexander Fallon's medical history and then, after thanking her, asked her to stand down.

The next witness was Inspector Ian Wilkinson. He had the longest experience of anyone involved with Body 115 and was able to outline the early history of the investigation, including the origins of the body's unusual name and the lengths that the police had gone to in order to identify it. Dr Reid's questions then focused on the information obtained by Dr Ian West during the original post-mortem examination, especially concerning the neurosurgery.

As subsequent witnesses were called to give evidence, so Dr Reid began to focus his attention on the neurosurgery that had been performed on Body 115 and in particular on the small aneurysm clip that had been recovered from the skull. Chief Inspector Philip Trendall outlined the early investigations into the aneurysm clip.

'In 1987,' asked Dr Reid, 'investigations in relation to the deceased's neurosurgery appeared to concentrate on the serial number of the clip?'

'Not so much the serial number,' replied Trendall, 'but the range of imports, the imports from a specialist importer of these aneurysm clips and a great deal of work was done at the time in 1987 and early 1988 to ascertain whether the type of aneurysm clip could be traced to a particular location.'

'How did you go about it, that aspect of the investigation, in the re-investigation since autumn last year?'

'The key issue, of course, was the cranial surgery and in respect of Mr Fallon, attempts were made, which were first unsuccessful, to trace the medical records of Mr Fallon to enable us with expert assistance to compare the ante-mortem and post-mortem data. After several attempts, medical records were recovered both from the Royal Free Hospital and from the Royal London Hospital. Those records showed that an operation had been carried out on Mr Fallon in 1980, that enabled us to trace the record of the operation within the hospital notes and to trace the surgeon that carried out that operation.'

The story was continued by the next witness, Christopher Milroy, a professor of Forensic Medicine who had been asked to compare Mr Fallon's medical records with the pathology results of Body 115. Again, the emphasis was on the neurosurgery. [8]

'The autopsy report had revealed the presence of neurosurgery to the right side of the head,' said Professor Milroy, 'and that involves the cutting of the skull and then in this case, because this person had had a ruptured blood vessel, a clip was placed on the blood vessel and that was subsequently recovered. The medical records record that Mr Fallon had undergone neurosurgery on that site and had a clip inserted. It is my understanding that it is highly likely that the Sugita No. 5 clip would have been used, this was a rare clip in that only, I believe, two or three hundred of them were used in neurosurgery.'

Professor Milroy ended by offering his view on the comparison he had made between the medical records for Mr Fallon and those of Body 115. As well as highlighting the remarkable similarity between the medical examination of Mr Fallon made at the Royal Free hospital only days before the fire and Dr West's post-mortem examination notes, Milroy was also able to explain away the apparent mismatch in height. 'Bear in mind that forty years have lapsed since those measurements have taken place,' he said, 'and people do lose height as their disc spaces in the vertebral column collapse down and we also have to bear in mind that there are elements of human error in this. I have to say that as someone who measures bodies quite regularly, that can also be with a margin of error.' Professor Milroy concluded that 'from a medical point of view it is my opinion that Body 115 is that of Mr Fallon.'

Just how useful the Sugita clip had been to the investigation was made clear by the next and final witness, Detective Chief Superintendent Nick Bracken, the man who had overseen the review into Body 115. He explained that 'approximately two-thirds of operations are carried out on the right hand side. So, immediately one third of the [280] clips could be removed and indeed the split between men and women is approximately 50:50 with some suggestion that it may be even slightly higher in females, meaning that the chances of a right-sided clip on a male person would be something like ninety or ninety-three clips of that particular type, a Sugita No. 5. Dr Hardy [the surgeon who performed Fallon's operation], without being informed of the type of clip, actually volunteered that his preferred clip at this time would have been the Sugita. So quite clearly, by now, we were beginning to feel that the probabilities of trying to further this would be becoming quite great in a population of 60 million – down to such discriminatory numbers.'

Detective Chief Superintendent Bracken then answered questions about other similarities between Mr Fallon and Body 115. Especially important in this regard were the findings of Professor Peter Vanezis, who had used computers to match Mr Fallon's surgical scar with the one seen on Body 115. Bracken was able to summarise the similarities between the two men's lifestyles. 'Both were smokers, both were drinkers, both had a full set of dentures and both had no trace on the criminal records system,' said Bracken. When asked about the possibility that Body 115 and Mr Fallon were one and the same person, Bracken replied, 'It is my opinion that it is beyond reasonable doubt.'

With this last statement, Dr Reid was satisfied at what he had heard, and moved to close the hearing. 'That's all the evidence that I intend to call for the inquiry,' he announced to the Court. 'I am now satisfied on all the evidence I have heard on oath today that the unidentified victim of the King's Cross fire, formerly known as Body 115, is in fact Alexander Williamson Fallon. I am therefore going to send a letter certifying that I am satisfied that the details in respect of 115 can be factually corrected and amended to record that this victim was in fact Alexander Fallon.'

Dr Reid paused to thank the British Transport Police and the pathologists for their work in the case. He then offered his and the Court's sympathy to Mrs Leishman for the loss of her father. After that the inquiry into the identity of Body 115, the last unknown victim of the King's Cross fire, was closed.

A few weeks later the Registrar of Births, Marriages and Deaths acted on Dr Reid's advice and amended Body 115's death certificate. By law the original details of the certificate could not be altered and so, rather than change the name at the top, the Registrar placed an addendum at the bottom. This stated that the hitherto unknown man who had died on 18 November 1988 could be identified as Alexander Williamson Fallon.

With the body now having a name, it was possible for Mr Fallon's next of kin to apply for an exhumation licence for the purpose of taking his remains from London back to his native Scotland. The licence was granted and by June 2004 the body that had for so long been a source of anguish to the British Transport Police had been taken north to Falkirk to be buried in a private plot next to his wife. Shortly afterwards the stone memorial to the victims of the fire was amended so that the 'unknown man' could be known by his real name. After sixteen years Alexander Fallon's death can now be mourned alongside those of the other thirty people who were unfortunate enough to be passing through King's Cross Underground Station on the night of 18 November 1987.

Epilogue

In 2004, the plaque erected in remembrance of the King's Cross fire was temporarily removed while the station underwent extensive refurbishment. Two years later it was returned to King's Cross and has been placed in a prominent position at the end of the newly built ticket hall area.

On 25 May 2006 I was privileged to be invited to the rededication ceremony that had been arranged to mark the plaque's return. It was a simple affair, presided over by Father Jim Kennedy and attended by around thirty people that included members of Camden Council, London Underground, the British Transport Police and a few friends and relatives of those who died in the fire. Several short speeches were made and then Father Kennedy said prayers from several religions, taking into account the different faiths of those who had died in 1987. Afterwards Father Kennedy announced that he considered the rededication of the plaque to be an opportune occasion to draw a line underneath many aspects of the King's Cross fire. Lessons had been learned, he said, and while the terrible nature and human cost of the fire should not be forgotten, it was time to move on.

It was not just the passage of time that permitted this decision to be made, but also because the newly installed plaque was different from the one removed in 2004. For years the polished monument had finished with a dedication to 'an unidentified man'. Beneath this it now reads 'later identified as Alexander Williamson Fallon'.

The investigation into the identity of Body 115 took the police sixteen years, two months and fifteen days to accomplish. For much of this time it appeared that the unknown man's real name would forever remain a secret but, thanks to diligent police work, the final mystery from one of the worst accidents ever to occur on the London Underground was solved. This was not just a relief to the British Transport Police, whose investigation into the fire could be closed once and for all, it was also a mercy for Mr Fallon's children who now know how and why their father went missing and, more importantly, where his remains are buried.

It is widely acknowledged that the British Transport Police's investigation into Body 115 went far beyond the normal call of duty. Father Jim Kennedy describes them as having done 'a stunning job'. Others I have spoken to have praised the 'good policing' and the 'excellent relationship' forged by the police (but especially by Inspector Ian Wilkinson) with the many families who came forward in the hope that Body 115 might be a missing relative. The police's pride at having solved the mystery of Body 115 remains evident, as does their continued concern for the feelings of the families associated with the case. As I have delved deeper into this case, so my awe at the scale of their achievement has increased.

The identification of Body 115 may have brought the investigation into the King's Cross fire to an end but it was unable to resolve the whereabouts of James Brown, the father of Kathleen Wilson, who remains a missing person. As part of the research for this book I made several attempts at finding any trace of his whereabouts which, despite considerable help from his family, came to nothing. For me the failure to find any information concerning James Brown's fate is frustrating but for his family, who have been searching for their father for over twenty years, it is upsetting in the extreme. I would ask that anyone who has knowledge of Mr Brown's possible whereabouts after 1984 to contact me through the publisher.

Notes and Sources

CHAPTER 1

1. By 1987 the smoking of cigarettes had been outlawed on the underground but the rule was widely flouted. It was especially common to see people sparking up on the staircases and escalators that led up to the ticket barriers. Most people did this to ensure that their cigarettes would be well and truly alight by the time they hit street level. This is probably what happened on 18 November 1987. See Fennell, D., *Investigation into the King's Cross Underground Fire*, London, HMSO, 1988.

2. King's Cross Tube Station has been described as possessing 'the most confusing maze of passages on the Underground' and was notorious for being a warren of interconnecting and isolated tunnels. These are the result of the station's piecemeal construction as during its 120-year history engineers continually added new platforms, connecting tunnels and exit subways. The main booking hall area into which Philip Squire exited caters for the station's three most popular Tube lines, namely the Northern, Piccadilly and Victoria Lines. All three are so-called 'deep lines' whose platforms lie many metres below the surface of London. The Northern Line is the deepest of the King's Cross platforms, being located some thirty metres below ground level, but the Piccadilly and Victoria Lines are not much shallower than this. A passenger making a journey from any of these platforms to street level would need to use either the Victoria Line escalators, whose three moving staircases were built in 1968 and are made of metal, or one of the three Piccadilly Line escalators which were longer, made of wood and installed in 1939. The Piccadilly Line escalators were amongst the longest in the whole Tube network, descending 18 metres down to the deep Piccadilly Line concourse area. Both the Victoria and Piccadilly Line

escalators exited into the booking hall, a large sub-circular area that is located entirely underground. To get people from the booking hall to the surface there were four main exit tunnels, one of which was over a hundred metres long. These respectively led to the King's Cross mainline train station, to nearby St Pancras train station or to two separate exit points on the traffic-laden Euston Road above. The length and number of corners in these tunnels makes them notoriously difficult to navigate and to this day they are commonly filled with tourists and other people who have become disorientated and confused by the array of exit options. References: TNA: PRO MT 141/126 (TPS 28); MT 141/127 (TPS 127); Fennell, D., *Investigation*, p.49; *Daily Mail*, 20 Nov. 1987.

3. TNA: PRO MT 141/127 (TPS 127)
4. TNA: PRO MT 141/128 (TPS 175)
5. Pushed to the ground: TNA: PRO MT 141/126 (TPS 8)
6. The only other emergency exit was a tunnel that ran from the lower platform area to the Midland train station (now Thameslink), located 250 metres from King's Cross. However, the gates to this exit had been locked earlier in the evening and nobody on duty knew who had the key. To get people out of the station meant either putting them back on stopping trains or herding them out through the booking hall via the Victoria Line escalator. To the police the latter seemed to be the best option.
7. TNA: PRO MT 141/130 (TPS 355). Edited.

CHAPTER 2

1. Witness statement. TNA: PRO MT 141/127 (TPS 133)
2. *Daily Mirror*, 19 Nov., 20 Nov. 1987; *Daily Mail*, 20 Nov. 1987; *Daily Telegraph*, 19 Nov. 1987.
3. Witness statement. TNA: PRO MT 141/127 (TPS 108A)
4. TNA: PRO MT 141/127 (TPS 92)
5. TNA: PRO MT 141/127 (TPS 137)
6. Doctors on scene. TNA: PRO MT 141/129 (TPS 278, TPS 285)
7. Ambulance Service Incident Log
8. TNA: PRO MT 141/127 (TPS 69, TPS 132); Ambulance Service Incident Log.
9. *Daily Telegraph*, 20 Nov. 1988.
10. Firefighters' interviews; TNA: PRO MT 141/129 (TPS 226)

11. Body recovery: TNA: PRO MT 141/129 (TPS 226, TPS 294); Plan of Body Positions.
12. TNA: PRO MT 141/127 (TSP 151)
13. Sign of life in body. TNA: PRO MT 141/129 (TPS 226, TPS 294); Statement given by R. Winch.
14. On the night the Methodist church and the facilities at University College Hospital were referred to as being temporary mortuaries. Technically the term 'temporary mortuary' refers to a facility where post-mortem examinations are carried out on bodies which was not the case in this instance. This means that these facilities should actually be called body holding areas. Mortuary and removal of bodies – TNA: PRO MT 141/128 (TPS 181, TPS 198); Statement by R. Winch. NB: When using their radios the ambulance staff would refer to any bodies as being 'purple plus', a reference to their skin colour.
15. TNA: PRO MT 141/129 (TPS 256, TPS 265, TSP 271, TPS 308)
16. TNA: PRO MT 141/129 (TPS 294)
17. *The Sun*, 20 Nov. 1987
18. TNA: PRO MT 141/129 (TPS 256)
19. TNA: PRO MT 141/129 (TPS 308)
20. TNA: PRO MT 141/129 (TPS 265, TPS 294); Statement by R. Winch.
21. TNA: PRO MT 141/129 (TPS 296)

CHAPTER 3

1. The mainline and Underground stations at King's Cross remain one of the best-known and most heavily used travel centres in Great Britain. The train station has eleven platforms and uses the East Coast mainline railway to service cities and towns in northern and eastern England as well as Scotland; it is the gateway to Leeds, Newcastle, Edinburgh and other major destinations. The Underground is served by the Northern, Victoria, Piccadilly, Metropolitan and Circle lines. The mainline station was opened in 1852 with the first Underground line coming just over a decade later. From then King's Cross Underground Station continued to grow in a rather piecemeal fashion with additional platforms, tunnels, stairs, escalators and ventilation shafts being added as new Underground lines were built. By the time the fifth and final Underground train service was added (the Victoria Line – opened

in 1968) the King's Cross Underground system possessed five subterranean layers, all interconnected: in the view of many the station had become labyrinthine. Statistics: Fennell, *Investigation*, pp.37–40.

2. TNA: PRO MT 141/129 (TPS 232)
3. Ambulance Service Incident Log
4. TNA: PRO MT 141/127 (TPS 134; TNA: PRO MT 141/128 (TPS 178); TNA: PRO MT 141/129 (TPS 294)

CHAPTER 4

1. Role of the modern coroner; C. P. Dorries, *Coroners' Courts: A Guide to Law and Practice*, Oxford, Oxford University Press, 2004; Lane, B., *The Encyclopedia of Forensic Science*, London, Headline, 1992, pp.148–49.
2. To understand the importance of the coroner to the disaster at King's Cross, one has to look back at the history of this institution to see why it came into being and why it occupies such a central and powerful position within English law. The coroner occupies a central role in the English legal system, especially where unexpected or suspicious deaths are concerned. The position is an ancient one that is at least several centuries old but which may have its origins over a thousand years ago in Anglo-Saxon England. The first definite records relating to coroners are found at the end of the twelfth century when, as part of a general legal shake-up, their role was formalised by King Richard the Lionheart. In 1194 the monarch gave an order decreeing that 'in every county of the king's realm shall be elected three knights and one clerk, to keep the pleas of the Crown'.

What King Richard was in effect doing was asking the knights and clerk to make and preserve a written record of the proceedings taking place in his law courts. To reflect this the three knights were given the title of *custos placitorum coronae* (which means 'keeper of the king's pleas'). In time this Latin title was abbreviated to the English word 'crowner' which was itself later transformed into the more modern name of 'coroner'.

The need for coroners arose because in medieval times obtaining justice in the English counties was very difficult. England's central law courts were all in London which placed them many miles and several days' travel from most rural parishes and towns. If people could not get access to the London law courts (and most couldn't) then how could they expect to see justice done against those who committed murder, robbery and other crimes? It was a thorny issue and so, to prevent criminals escaping justice, a system of roving courts called 'eyres' was created. Every few years a judge and several administrators would saddle up and the eyre would begin touring the English countryside on a predetermined circuit. On reaching large towns or other strategic locations, the eyre would stop and set up a temporary court to which local suspected criminals and other wrong-doers would be brought for trial. The judge and a local jury would hear the criminal and civil grievances brought before them and, where necessary, administer justice on behalf of the King. Most punishments came in the form of fines but the eyre courts also had the power to order physical punishments, including the death sentence. The infrequent visits of such courts meant that remembering who had been found guilty and what their punishment should be was problematic. The King was especially concerned that those who had been fined money (which would go straight to his Exchequer) were getting away with not paying because of the poor record-keeping. It was thus chiefly to ensure that that any fines or other money owed to the King made their way back to the Exchequer and not into the pockets of the sheriffs or other embezzling officials that the role of the coroner came into being.

By the thirteenth century the role of the coroner had expanded to include many duties besides just compiling and preserving court records. One additional role demanded that coroners had to seek out and investigate any sudden, accidental or unnatural deaths to have occurred within the court's jurisdiction. Again much of the motivation behind this was financial, with entire villages being threatened with large fines should they fail to report to the coroner a suspected case of murder, manslaughter, suicide, accidental or sudden death within days of its occurrence. The size of such fines led to there being a general wariness about corpses. There are recorded examples of bodies being left by the roadside for days after being deliberately ignored by passers by, none of whom wanted to be dragged into the complex and costly coroner's system. It is even alleged that some dead bodies were surreptitiously dragged across village and parish boundaries so as to move the problem from one region to another.

Once informed about the presence of a body, the coroner had to trace the deceased's relations as well as anybody who might have witnessed the death. He would then make a written report into the circumstances surrounding the manner and cause of death which would be read out at the next eyre court, whose next visit may well have been several years away. In court the coroner's report would be used to allow the jury to give a verdict on the cause of death and thence, in cases of murder or manslaughter, to empower the local authorities to arrest and try any suspected culprits. The coroner's report would also be used to impose fines on anybody who had not followed the correct procedure (e.g. not reporting the body in time or trying to hide it), hence the general distrust of coroners in medieval society. The value of the coroners' rolls to the legal system means that many were carefully preserved and so have survived through to the modern day. They allow us a glimpse of how people lived several centuries ago but, perhaps more importantly, they also tell us something about how they died.

By the sixteenth century the coroners had lost much of their original function to the extent that they were almost exclusively concerned with investigating circumstances of death. Each dead body brought to the coroner's attention would become the subject of an inquest, the aim of which was to provide a cause of death. Although it was up to the coroner to gather the evidence, it was not his job to give a verdict at an inquest; this would be done by a jury of local men (usually landowners or other wealthy types). The jury would be gathered together and either shown the dead body or taken to see it. They would then have to establish the name of the deceased, the cause of death and any additional circumstances associated with it (such as murder suspects or weapons). All this would be written down and presented at the next court's next appearance in the region.

Interestingly, the coroner had no automatic access to medical assistance until the nineteenth century which meant that it was often up to him to perform his own post-mortem examination. This usually amounted to little more than giving a body a quick once-over, looking for obvious wounds, counting them and then trying to work out what might have caused them. Only in 1836 were funds made available for medical post-mortem examinations and only in 1860 did coroners receive a steady salary rather than being paid per inquest (a practice that had hitherto led to much corruption).

The role of the coroner as we know it today stems back to the 1926 Coroners' (Amendment) Act which straightened out the last few medieval quirks remaining in the system. One of these was that hitherto a coroner needed no formal training in law or medicine before taking up the post. After 1926 at least five years' experience as a solicitor, barrister or in some sphere of medicine was needed before anyone could apply to be a coroner. Other important decisions included the ability for the coroner to decide whether or not a jury was required for inquests into deaths that did not involve murder or were not otherwise complicated or suspicious. Since 1976 coroners have not had the power to name the suspect(s) in a crime or to recommend the trial of a suspect. The last person ever to be named as a suspect by a coroner was the notorious Lord Lucan who is believed to have been responsible for the murder of his children's nanny in November 1974. Since that time Lucan has been a fugitive from justice although many believe that he may actually have killed himself a few days after the crime was committed. At the time of writing the government has announced plans for a wholesale review of role and function of the coroner's courts with a view to ridding the system of some of its remaining anomalies. See C. P. Dorries, *Coroners' Courts: A Guide to Law and Practice*, Oxford, Oxford University Press, 2004; R. F. Hunnisett, *The Medieval Coroner*, Cambridge, Cambridge University Press, 1961.

3. It is the duty of a forensic pathologist to make a physical examination of the bodies of the victims of crimes, accidents or suspicious and unusual deaths. Some forensic pathologists may even examine the scenes where these deaths took place although nowadays this is mostly left to crime scene investigators. Forensic pathologists are an integral part of police investigations and can provide the vital pieces of physical or scientific evidence that are ultimately used to bring a case to its conclusion.

4. Stern, C., *Dr Iain West's Casebook*, London, Warner, 1997; *GKT Gazette*, May 2002. Various newspaper obituaries.

5. Stern, *Dr Iain West's Casebook*, p.156

6. Stern, *Dr Iain West's Casebook*, p.156–7

7. Body 115's post-mortem examination report; Stern, *Dr Iain West's Casebook*, p.158–9

CHAPTER 5

1. This figure is given in *The Times*, 20 Nov. 1987, and tallies with information given in TNA: PRO MT 141/127 (TPS 97); TNA: PRO MT 141/128 (TPS 172); TNA: PRO MT 141/129 (TPS 294, TPS 319)

2. A visual inspection of a dead body can be a very unreliable method

of establishing identity, even by those that knew the person in life. Following the Boxing Day 2004 tsunami disaster some people who travelled to south-east Asia in search of missing relations wrongly identified bodies. These mistakes only came to light following later forensic investigations.

3. *The Times*, 20 Nov. 1987
4. TNA: PRO MT 141/127 (TPS 76). Edited to remove names and personal details.
5. Identified twenty-four people; *The Sun*, 21 Nov. 1987; *Daily Mail*, 21 Nov. 1987; *The Times*, 21 Nov. 1987
6. *The Sun*, 21 Nov. 1987; the positions of the family can be deduced from the body location plan.
7. *The Sun*, 21 Nov. 1987; *Daily Mail*, 21 Nov. 1987

CHAPTER 6

1. Because the bodies had undergone a post-mortem examination, they could only be released after the opening of the inquest. This is one reason why the inquest was held so close to the date of the fire.
2. Scenes from the Coroner's court; *The Times*, 25 Nov. 1987; *Daily Telegraph*, 25 Nov. 1987; *The Guardian*, 25 Nov. 1987.
3. *The Times*, 26 Nov. 1987; 7 Dec. 1987.
4. Body 115 autopsy; *The Times*, 26 Nov. 1987; 28 Dec. 1987; post-mortem examination sheet for Body 115; *Neurosurgery Focus*, 11(2), 1–5, 2001.
5. There was a minor fracas in the papers when the father criticised the police for taking so long to identify his son but, given the degree of burning on the body, it was generally agreed that they could not have resolved the issue any quicker.

CHAPTER 7

1. Giving useable names to unidentified bodies has always been a problem for the British authorities. For example, in September 2001 the headless and armless torso of a young African boy was discovered floating in the River Thames. The body was wearing only a pair of orange shorts and evidence from the post-mortem examination suggested to the police that they were dealing with a

ritual killing, possibly even a human sacrifice, of an African boy who had been in England for only a few days. With no head or fingerprints, identifying the boy was clearly going to be a lengthy process and the Metropolitan Police nicknamed the victim 'Adam'. Quite why Adam was chosen is not known; the police explain it was simply 'to give him an identity'. The use of a personal name for the body delighted the media and the 'torso in the Thames' case was followed closely by journalists although, at the time of writing, Adam remains unidentified and no one has been charged with his murder.

The risk in giving an unidentified body an everyday first name such as Adam or Michael is that you begin to impose upon it a personality and culture that may be entirely false. The boy Adam, for example, was almost certainly born and raised in West Africa and is thought likely to have an African name, not a European one. Similarly, had the police continued to refer to the unnamed King's Cross victim as Michael, it would have caused confusion when investigating other named candidates for the body. It could also make life awkward if and when the man's relations were traced. Referring to the unknown man as Body 115 was a sensible and practicable solution.

Body 115; Letter from British Transport Police, 6 Nov. 2002. Adam: see, for example, *Daily Mirror*, 10 Mar. 2003.

2. Ironically, the use of the expressions John Doe and Jane Doe (which can also be used by people who do not want to provide their real names in certain court cases) was borrowed by the Americans from English law. There was never a real individual named John Doe but the name has been cited in English court cases from at least the seventeenth century although some authorities have it going as far back as the fourteenth century. The origins of 'John Doe' are complicated and arise from a now defunct English court procedure called an action of ejectment. As the title suggests, an ejectment suit could be brought by a landowner against a person whom they believed was occupying (or had taken possession of) their property illegally. To do this the court required the creation of fictitious tenants whose imaginary claim to the land would form the basis of the case. It became standard to give the fictitious plaintiff the name of John Doe and the equally unreal defendant the name of Richard Roe. Exactly when this practice began is not known but the *Oxford English Dictionary* records its first use in a 1659 case: 'To prosecute the suit, to witt John Doe And Richard Roe.' It is suspected that there never was a real John Doe (or Richard Roe) and that these

names may have simply been a generic term for the man in the street, a bit like Joe Bloggs is today. Should further names be required for the fictitious tenants then the courts would move onto John Stiles, Richard Miles and John Nokes. This system stopped being used in England in 1852 but continued in North America where it spread from the legal system into the domain of the coroner's office and from there became applied to unidentified bodies. The feminine version, Jane Doe, is a twentieth-century addendum to this system. Source: Staff at *Oxford English Dictionary*, personal communication.

3. 'London Tonight', 10 Nov. 1989. Ian Blair became Commissioner of the Metropolitan Police in 2005 after receiving a knighthood in 2003.

4. Average height: William J. White, 'Skeletal Remains ... ' (1988) cited in Daniell, C., *Death and Burial in Medieval England, 1066–1550*, London: Routledge, 1997, p.135.

5. Herzig, R. *et al.*,'The role of chronic alcohol intake in patients with spontaneous intracranial hemorrhage,' *Cerebrovascular Disease* 2003; Vol., 15, pp.22–8. Body 115 information from post-mortem examination sheet and also *The Times*, 28 Jan. 1988; 'London Tonight', 10 Nov. 1989; *British Dental Journal*, vol. 164, p.160, 1988. Alcoholism and atheroma: *Bulletin of the Academy of National Medicine*, vol. 144, pp.58–62, 1960.

6. Ralph Humberstone; *Horncastle Today*, 23 June, 21 July 2004.

CHAPTER 8

1. *Daily Mirror*, 20 Nov. 1987.
2. Smoulderings: TNA: PRO MT 141/7
3. TNA: PRO 141/26
4. Fennell pp.215–220. Quote: *Daily Mirror*, 20 Nov. 1987.
5. London's Underground network has always been a problematic issue for politicians. The Tube system is vast (the largest in the world), sprawling and has been built in a piecemeal fashion over the last century and a half. By the late 1980s the underground was being used by over 750 million people a year with some key stations, including King's Cross, receiving tens of thousands of passengers in a single hour. Every morning and evening the trains would be filled to capacity with commuters heading to and from work. For this, and many other reasons, London's economy was, and remains, heavily reliant upon its Underground: without the

Tube there is no other means by which so many people can be ferried about the capital.

Given its undoubted importance to Britain's principal city, it is surprising how neglected the system has been. By the 1980s it had been subjected to decades of underfunding while at the same time absorbing an ever-increasing number of passengers. The trouble started in 1948 when, along with the country's railways, the Tube network was nationalised and placed under the direct control of a government-controlled body called the British Transport Commission. From the outset the Tube continually lost out to the more politically important national railway network and was only given small amounts of money. Before spending even modest sums of money the Underground's managers had to seek permission from the British Transport Commission. By the 1970s, when the Tube network was transferred into the hands of the Greater London Council, the underfunding, bureaucracy and mismanagement was beginning to take its toll.

In 1981 Ken Livingstone took over control of the Greater London Council and began subsiding the Tube network but in 1984 control was handed to London Regional Transport, a newly created government body. By 1987 London Underground was in dire straits: the system of funding by the award of an annual government grant was preventing any long-term financial planning and so, year by year, the neglect of the stations, tunnels, track and trains became steadily worse. The situation was not helped by mismanagement at all levels, as James Meek explains: 'It was corrupt at the top – the most senior executives avoided using their own trains by running twenty-six chauffeur-driven limousines at a cost of more than half a million pounds a year – and corrupt at the bottom, with ticket collectors regularly pocketing excess fares at the barriers. In 1982, fewer than half a billion journeys were made, a low point in passenger numbers.'

Sources: *Daily Mirror*, 20 Nov. 1987; *Sunday Telegraph*, 22 Nov. 1987. Tube history from: Wolmar, C., *The Subterranean Railway: How the London Underground Was Built and How It Changed the City For Ever*, Atlantic Books, 2005. D. Fennell, p.25. Quote from *London Review of Books*, Vol. 27(9), 5 May 2005.

6. TNA: PRO EF 7/2413. Edited from the full statement, the bottom part of which reads: 'The evidence will be heard in public. I hope to be able to announce very shortly after discussion with my Right Honourable and learned friend, the Lord Chancellor, the name of the senior lawyer to head the inquiry. The inquiry will be assisted by

a member of the Railway Inspectorate and by an expert in fires and fire prevention. It will be for the inquiry to establish the causes of the disaster and to make recommendations to ensure that all possible lessons are learned. Their report will be published.'

7. Fennell, *Investigation*; *The Times*, 2 Feb. 1988.
8. Letter from British Transport Police; 6 Nov. 2002; Father Jim Kennedy, personal communication.
9. 'London Tonight', 10 Nov. 1989
10. Coroner's inquiry transcript, 3 Feb. 2004
11. Del Maestro, R.F., 'Origin of the Drake Fenestrated Aneurysm Clip', *Journal of Neurosurgery*, vol.92, pp.1056–1064, 2000; Sugita, K., Kobayashi, S., *et al*., 'Characteristics and use of Ultra-Long Aneurysm Clips', *Journal of Neurosurgery*, vol.60, pp.145–150, 1984; Louw, D.F., Asfora, W.T. and Sutherland, G.R., 'A Brief History of Aneurysm Clips', *Neurosurgery Focus*, vol.11(2), pp.1–4, 2001.
12. 'London Tonight', 10 Nov. 1989
13. Statistics from Robin Young, personal communication; Coroner's inquiry transcript, 3 Feb. 2004.
14. 'London Tonight', 10 Nov. 1989

CHAPTER 9

1. Given their physical properties, scientists will sometimes refer to fingerprints as 'friction ridge skin patterns' but in this book I will stick to the more popular term.
2. Grew, N., 'The description and use of the pores in the skin of the hands and feet,' *Philosophical Transactions of the Royal Society*, vol 14 (159), pp. 566–7, 1684.
3. Malpighi, M., *De Externo Tactus Organs in Opera Omnia*. Lyons, France, Petrum Vander Aa, 1686.
4. Cummins, H, and Kennedy, RW, *American Journal of Criminal Law and Criminology*; Vol 31, pp. 343–356, 1940.
5. Quotes from Faulds, H., 'On the Skin Furrows of the Hand,' *Nature*, vol. 22, p.605, 1880. See also Faulds, H., *Dactylography*, Halifax, Milner and Co., 1913.
6. Herschel, W., 'Skin Furrows of the Hand,' *Nature*, 23: p.76, 1880.
7. Herschel, W., 'Skin Furrows ... '; Herschel, W., *The Origin of Finger Printing*, Oxford, Oxford University Press, 1916.
8. Others were not so slow to see the potential usefulness of finger-prints. In 1883 author Mark Twain wrote *Life on the Mississippi*

which includes an unusual tale about a murderer who leaves a bloody handprint at the scene of his crime and as a result is eventually tracked down and arrested. The story is not often considered to be one of his best works but it does show that Twain had picked up on then little-used science of dactylography, the study of fingerprints. In fact, Twain was years ahead of the scientists; it would be almost a decade before fingerprints would be used to actually solve a murder. He was also prescient in his 1894 story entitled *Pudd'nhead Wilson* which concerns an out-of-place lawyer who uses his fascination with people's fingerprints to help unravel a complicated murder mystery. It would be another eleven years before the United States justice system accepted fingerprints as legally admissible evidence. See Twain, M., *Life on the Mississippi*, New York, Dover Publications, 2000, Twain, M., *Pudd'nhead Wilson*, New York, Dover Publications, 1999.

9. Darwin Correspondence Project, Calendar Entries: 12488, Faulds, H. to Darwin, C. R., 16 Feb. 1880; 12565, Darwin, C. R. to Galton, F., 7 Apr. 1880

10. Despite the success of fingerprints in criminology, it is perhaps surprising to learn that the technique of 'lifting' prints from crime scenes was not introduced in Great Britain until 1970; before this prints had to be dusted and photographed *in situ* which made identifying them that much more difficult.

11. History of Fingerprints: Caplan, R.M., 'How Fingerprints came into use for Personal Identification.' *Journal of the American Academy of Dermatology*, vol. 23(1), pp.109–114, 1990; Lane, *Encyclopedia*, pp.275–317; Lyle, *Forensics*, pp.73–84; S.H. James and J.J. Nordby, *Forensic Science: An Introduction to Scientific and Investigative Techniques*, New York, Taylor and Francis, 2005, pp.341–360.

12. Scotland Yard: Fingerprint Centenary press pack. Lane, *Encyclopedia*, pp.275–284, 314–317.

13. Fingerprint information; Letter from British Transport Police, 6 Nov. 2002; London Tonight, 10 Nov. 1989.

CHAPTER 10

1. Prag, J. and Neave, R., *Making Faces*, p.37. The girl's murderer was not identified.

2. Terry, C.S., *Bach: a Biography*, Oxford, Oxford University Press, pp. 279–280, 1932.

3. Iscan, M.Y., and Helmer, R.P., *Forensic Analysis of the Skull*, New York, Wiley-Liss, pp.29–45, 1993. Gerasimov, M.M., *The Face Finder*, London, Hutchinson, 1971. Prag, J., and Neave, R., *Making Faces*, London, British Museum, 1997. Peipert, J.F., and Roberts, C.S., 'Wilhelm His Sr.'s Finding of Johann Sebastian Bach.' *American Journal of Cardiology*, vol. 15(11), p.1002, 1986.

4. Von Eggeling, H., 'Die Leistungsfahigkeit physiognomischer Rekonstruktionsversuche auf Grundlage des Shädels.' *Archiv für Anthropologie*, vol. 12, pp.44–47, 1913.

5. It was alleged that Tamerlane's tomb had a curse attached to it and, so the rumour goes, no sooner had Gerasimov opened it than 4 million German troops poured across the Soviet border. To this day Gerasimov is mostly remembered as the archaeologist who 'began' Russia's Great Patriotic War (World War II). Gerasimov was regarded with suspicion by the authorities who believed him to be a potential troublemaker. One of his colleagues is on record as saying that 'he never worked with the KGB'. His daughter Margarita agrees, 'He wasn't afraid of anything,' she said in a recent interview. 'He risked his own life by always trying to help his friends, even if they were under suspicion.' Indeed, a number of his colleagues and mentors did end up being arrested as suspected subversives; some were later shot.

6. Gerasimov, M.M., *The Face Finder*. Conant, E., 'Man of 1000 Faces,' *Archaeology*, pp. 48–53, July/Aug. 2003.

7. Prag and Neave, *Making Faces*, pp.41–49. Neave, R., 'Reconstruction of the Heads of Three Ancient Egyptian Mummies,' *Journal of Audiovisual Media in Medicine*, vol. 2, pp.156–164, 1979.

8. Reichs, K., *Forensic Osteology*, Springfield, Illinois, Charles C Thomas, 1986. Iscan and Helmer, *Forensic Analysis*. Prag and Neave, *Making Faces*. 'Symposium in Honor of Dr Wilton M Krogman-Held,' *American Association Of Physical Anthropologists*, Vol.38, Jan. 1973.

9. *The Times*, 25 Feb. 1988.

10. Noses are made of cartilage and don't generally get preserved with skeletal remains but the general shape and other features, such as nostril width, can be worked out by measuring key features associated with the skull's nasal bones. As stated earlier in the chapter, Body 115 retained details of its nose which gave Neave a clue as to what its shape would have been in life; this is an advantage that is not often offered to medical artists.

11. Neave's facial reconstruction technique: ITN News, 27 Jan. 1988; Prag and Neave, *Making Faces*, p.20–34.

12. 'ITN News'; 27 Jan. 1988.

13. *The Times*, 28 Jan. 1988; ITN News, 27 Jan. 1988.

14. 'London Tonight', 10 Nov. 1989

CHAPTER 11

1. Quotes from *The Times*, 2 Feb. 1987

2. TNA: PRO MT 141/3

3. TNA: PRO MT 141/4; MT 141/19. This would not be the first time an alternative explanation has been sought in the light of a disaster. The Potter's Bar train crash of May 2002, which killed seven people, was widely believed to have been caused by poorly maintained points. However, one of the companies in charge of track maintenance insisted that sabotage could not be ruled out. See, for example, *Daily Telegraph*, 18 May 2002.

4. TNA: PRO MT 141/7; MT 141/9

5. TNA: PRO MT 141/4; *The Times*, 3 Feb. 1988

6. Figures from Fennell, *Investigation*, p.188

7. This summary of the inquiry comes from Fennell, *Investigation*, pp.15–19. Specific examples from TNA: PRO MT 141/2–93.

8. *The Times*, 30 Mar. 1988

CHAPTER 12

1. 'London Tonight', 10 Nov. 1989; Letter from British Transport Police; 6 Nov. 2002.

2. TNA: PRO MT 141/27, pp.5–6; MT 141/135 (TPS 781); see also MT 141/129 (TPS 223).

3. 'London Tonight', 10 Nov. 1989

4. *The Times*, 30 Jul. 1989; 10 Dec. 1989

5. Vagrant investigation: 'London Tonight', 10 Nov. 1989.

6. Vagrant reports: TNA: PRO MT 141/127 (TPS 148; TPS 149); MT 141/129 (TPS 291).

7. TNA: PRO MT 141/127 (TPS 100).

8. TNA: PRO MT 141/131 (TPS 464).

9. Sightings of vagrants: TNA: PRO MT 141/126 (TPS 18/56); MT 141/127 (TPS 100; TPS 168); MT 141/129 (TPS 251, TPS 290); MT 141/131 (TPS 412, TPS 464); MT 141/7 pg.66.

10. TNA: PRO MT 141/129 (TPS 299).

11. For a discussion on the reliability of eyewitness statements, see Ainsworth, P.B., *Psychology, Law and Eyewitness Testimony*. Chichester, John Wiley and Sons, 1998.
12. TNA: PRO MT 141/129 (TPS 299); MT 141/130 (TPS 362).
13. TNA: PRO MT 141/129 (TPS 223).
14. TNA: PRO MT 141/126 (TPS 11).
15. TNA: PRO MT 141/27, p.104
16. TNA: PRO MT 141/131 (TPS 450).
17. TNA: PRO MT 141/131 (TPS 450).
18. In the light of Body 115's identification I asked the British Transport Police whether they thought the man seen by Balfe and Taylor could have been Body 115. They said that there was not enough evidence to resolve the issue either way.
19. 'London Tonight', 10 Nov. 1989.

CHAPTER 13

1. Harvey, W., *Dental Identification and Forensic Odontology*, London, Henry Kimpton, 1976, p.67.
2. 'London Tonight', 10 Nov. 1989; *The Times*, 28 Jan. 1988; Prag and Neave, *Making Faces*, p.36.
3. Vale, G.L., 'Forensic Odontology,' *Journal of Southern Californian Dentists' Association*, vol. 37, p.248, 1969. Of all the forensic techniques used by pathologists to help identify unknown bodies, the one with the oldest provable track record is dental identification. It is alleged, for example, that in around AD 66 Agrippina, mother of the Roman Emperor Nero, asked her soldiers to decapitate Lollia Paulina, a former wife of Claudius. According to legend Agrippina demanded proof of the death and so the unfortunate Lollia's head was brought to her on a plate. On looking inside the mouth, Agrippina recognised a blackened front tooth and accepted that the soldiers had done their job. Some sources relate this story to the Emperor Nero and his mistress Sabina.
4. Luntz, L. and Luntz, P., *Handbook for Dental Identification*, Philadelphia, Lippincott and Co., 1973.
5. Although most of the techniques for gathering evidence associated with forensic dentistry were standardised by the 1970s, dentists in individual countries continue to have their own means of recording their patients' teeth which makes comparing dental samples internationally difficult.

6. For a brief history of forensic dentistry see James and Nordby, *Forensic Science*, pp.79–98.
7. Cleland, J.B., 'Teeth and Bite-marks in History, Literature, Forensic Medicine and Otherwise.' *Australian Journal of Dentistry*, vol. 48, p.107, 1944; Harvey, *Dental Identification*, p.57.
8. At the time of the King's Cross fire the issue as to whether dentures should be routinely marked with the name of the owner or the dental surgery that had made them had led to a considerable controversy. With over half the adult population wearing dentures, and with the increasing use of dental patterns in pathological work, some forensic dentists pushed for the routine marking of dentures with either the owner's name or that of the dentist who made them. Chief promoter of this idea was Warren Harvey, an experienced odontologist who had become frustrated at the time being wasted trying to identify denture wearers. What turned his frustration into action was the case of a murdered girl found in a Glasgow basement in 1959. She had been raped and then had her face and body mutilated by her attacker. All her possessions were missing, as were the labels from her clothes. Her fingerprints were taken and checked against police records, without success. Like Body 115, there was no obvious means of identifying the girl, leading to frustration amongst the police. However, a forensic dentist was called who recovered her dentures and found, etched onto the upper one, the girl's name and the dental technician's model number. The girl's dentist was contacted and a positive identification made.

During the 1960s and 70s Harvey campaigned for the routine marking of dentures, not just so that bodies could be identified, but also to stop the routine mix-ups that were occurring in hospitals, psychiatric units and nursing homes where several people's dentures would end up in the same bowl, making it difficult to find their original owner. As Harvey himself said at the time: 'This [campaign] is not just a diatribe of the heartbreak felt by many dentists, medical authorities, nursing staff, community workers and police officers – from detectives under training up to Chief Constables – throughout the whole United Kingdom; but also presumably those in at least twenty-one countries. Dentists must realise the contribution they could so easily make to personal identity and forensic science.' Despite emotive statements like this and the backing of the police, medical authorities and others, Harvey's desired marking which, by his own estimate would have cost a few pence per denture to do, did not become compulsory. Of the twenty-one countries in which these campaigns were launched only one, Sweden, adopted the idea and by the mid-1970s the idea was faltering although the lobbying continues through to the current day.

Had Harvey's idea been adopted in the mid-1960s, when campaigning first began, then the dentures belonging to Body 115 would probably have had the man's name and that of his dentist engraved on them, making his identification a much easier process. I base this deduction on the statistic that dentures can be expected to last for twenty years with the average denture wearer owning them for seventeen years. Sources: Melton, A.B., 'Current Trends in Removable Prosthodontics,' *Journal of the American Dental Association*, vol. 131, pp.528–568, 2000. Harvey, *Dental Identification*, p.65; see also *British Dental Journal*, vol. 160, pp.89–91, 1986.

9. In 1987 the proportion of people wearing dentures was greater than it is today. Advances in toothpastes, toothbrushes and dental technique and a greater awareness of the importance of mouth care has led to stronger, healthier teeth, so much so that most children and young adults today can be expected to keep the majority of their teeth into their old age. Even the dreaded childhood fillings are becoming a rarer occurrence, forcing dentists to offer hygienic and cosmetic treatments in place of the more usual tooth repairs.

This was not so in the past where poor diet, inferior toothpastes and ignorance of dental care meant that tooth decay and gum disease were prevalent. Also, there were many dentists who would remove teeth as a matter of course rather than as a last resort, as is the case today. The consequence of this meant that, in 1976, of the 55 million inhabitants in Great Britain, over 21 million were denture wearers. Harvey, *Dental Identification*, p.63. See also Howarth, J.H., 'Post-mortem Identification of a Body by Use of Dental Evidence', *British Dental Journal*, vol. 172(4), p.158, 1992.

10. *British Dental Journal*, Vol. 164, p.160, 1988.

11. 'London Tonight', 10 Nov. 1989.

CHAPTER 14

1. With Desmond Fennell's investigation yet to publish its findings, there was still no agreed consensus as to who, if anyone, might be held responsible for causing the fire although many people, including the media, had already laid the blame at the door of those in charge of managing the Tube network, especially London Regional Transport. To deflect some of the anger being directed at it,

London Regional Transport had agreed to pay compensation to those injured by the fire and to the families of those who were killed by it. They did so, however, without admitting any liability for the cause of the fire or any of the resulting injuries and fatalities. This enraged the relatives of the dead and led to campaigning by some newspapers but only at the coroner's inquest did their anger erupt with full force. In the lead up to the inquest there had been some alarm expressed by the King's Cross families at London Regional Transport's refusal to pay for a solicitor to represent them in court. In inquests that relate to accidents, it is usual for the party paying damages, in this case London Regional Transport, to also pay for the victims' legal representation. However, given that the official investigation into the fire had been held in a separate court, under Desmond Fennell, and that the families had been legally represented there, London Regional Transport felt that they did not also need to be represented at the coroner's inquest. Worried by this, relatives of twenty-seven of the thirty named victims hired a solicitor to voice their disquiet on the first day of the inquest. He said that 'without financial backing the families concerned cannot possibly afford the cost of representation for what looks likely to be a three- or four-week hearing. They therefore face the prospect that this inquest will proceed in their absence, and that their voice will not be heard here.'

Dr Chambers commented that this was an issue over which he had no sway but that any family members wishing to ask questions in court would be welcome to do so. Faced with pressure from the press, and after a request made directly to them by social workers, London Regional Transport eventually agreed to pay for legal representation. *The Times*, 5 Oct. 1988; 7 Oct. 1988.

2. *The Times*, 12 Oct. 1988
3. There were in fact four doctors within this party. The fourth one was there as an observer and at the time was not acting in an official medical role.
4. The doctors were invited into the machine room beneath the fire-damaged Piccadilly Line escalator. At least one of the doctors later remarked at how undamaged it seemed to be. 'The engine room was clean,' he said, 'with absolutely no smell of smoke or burning, with no sign of fire or rubbish. There was a surprisingly small amount of sweet papers, etc., trapped in the mesh collecting tray, and all of these wrapping papers were whole and unsinged.' Personal statement by Peter Davis.
5. Personal statement by Peter Davis.

6. Statement by Robin Winch, 15 Jan. 1988.
7. *Mail on Sunday*, 13 Nov. 1989
8. Ken Hines, personal communication; *Mail on Sunday*, 13 Nov. 1989
9. *Mail on Sunday*, 13 Nov. 1989
10. *Mail on Sunday*, 13 Nov. 1989
11. Foot. See TNA: PRO MT 141/130 (TPS 398). 'I was in St Pancras Road near some Portacabins when a gentleman approached me ... He was not wearing any form of uniform. He said "I just moved some tarpaulin, I think there is a foot there" ... I lifted it up and there was a human foot there. It was burnt and was cut off at the ankle. I picked it up using the tarpaulin and took it to the temporary mortuary.'
12. Reports of the man in overalls were investigated and dismissed by the Fennell inquiry. See Fennell, *Investigation*, pp.222–223.
13. *Mail on Sunday*, 13 Nov. 1989; Chester Stern, personal communication.
14. *Mail on Sunday*, 13 Nov. 1989; Chester Stern, personal communication.; Stern, *Iain West's Casebook*, pp.159–162; Statements to the British Transport Police by Paul Davis (14 Nov. 1988); Robin Winch (14 Nov. 1988) and Peter Ernst (14 Nov. 1988). I have seen an original print of the photograph mentioned by Chester Stern.
15. *Mail on Sunday*, 13 Nov. 1989; Stern, *Iain West's Casebook*, p.160.
16. Statements to the British Transport Police by Paul Davis (14 Nov. 1988); Robin Winch (14 Nov. 1988) and Peter Ernst (14 Nov. 1988).
17. Stern, *Iain West's Casebook*, pp.160–161. Dr West was especially keen to deny that an explosion caused by a bomb or arsonist had taken place at King's Cross. This is because one of the three doctors, Robin Winch, believed that the remains they found might have belonged to a terrorist on the way to the west end of London when he or she accidentally blew himself or herself up in the booking hall area. The other doctors did not support Winch's view and it runs contrary to the wealth of evidence concerning the nature of the flashover.
18. It is difficult to know what to make of these claims. I have spoken to one of the people, a doctor, who witnessed the discovery and recovery of the remains; to this day he remains convinced that what he saw was part of a body. Aside from the three doctors, there were other witnesses to the discovery, including an electrician who was walking past the group of people as they examined the apparent human remains. A few days after the fire, and quite independently

of anyone else, he told the British Transport Police that in the booking hall, 'immediately in front of the [ticket collectors'] boxes, about four feet from the base of the stairs, I saw what I thought it was a piece of a ribcage which was part of a black, burnt lump. This lump was about one foot by two foot in size. I saw members of the emergency services standing round it and discussing and examining it.' (TNA: PRO 141/129 (TPS 265).)

But if we do assume that everything the doctors reported is true, then where are these body parts now? If they could be recovered then establishing whether they are organic or not ought to be a straightforward laboratory procedure. Using various statements given to the British Transport Police and others it is possible to trace the movements of the alleged body parts and to determine what happened to them.

After their discovery, the alleged torso and skull fragment were placed in one evidence bag while the foot was placed in a second bag together with other items of clothing. Both bags were then conveyed by a female police officer to St Pancras Mortuary where they joined the thirty bodies recovered from the scene of the fire. The two bags were given to David Toms, the person who was in charge of mortuary hygiene. He labelled them '15' and '16' and searched them for any sign of human remains but says he could find none. Perplexed, he requested that a medical colleague, Dr Sanjoy Chatterji, be summoned so that he too could search the bags. Chatterji arrived at around 4 a.m. but could also find no sign of human remains in the bags.

'I was shown two disaster bags,' recalled Chatterji in a police statement, 'numbered 15 and 16 by Mr Dave Toms. Bag 15 contained burnt debris including shoes, a bag, beads, keys and a screwdriver. Bag 16 contained burnt and unidentifiable debris of plastic material. No human remains were seen.' (TNA: PRO 141/127 (TPS 64); Statement by David Toms, 11 Dec. 1987)

The two bags were returned to the British Transport Police and logged as property relating to the fire but they were returned to the mortuary on 26 November to be rechecked, again without success. Finally, at an unspecified date after this, and having been examined by Toms, Chatterji and a divisional surgeon, all of whom believed them to contain 'waste materials', the bags were disposed of. (Statement by Brian Forden, 14 Nov. 1988.)

The destruction of the two bags and the controversial objects they contained places the issue of a possible thirty-second victim beyond resolution but the conundrum it leaves us is intriguing. On one side we have three medical doctors (plus one further medical doctor who was present but not officially on duty), all trained and experienced in disaster scenes, plus an electrician, all stating in no uncertain terms that they saw additional human remains (as stated earlier, the fourth doctor was not at the scene in an active medical role but agrees that the object looked like human remains). Opposite this we have the word of two mortuary staff, one of whom is a doctor, who insist that no remains were to be found in the bags. The matter is complicated by the apparent contradiction in Iain West's statements. He allegedly told Chester Stern that he had not examined the remains and appeared to be half-convinced by the photograph he was shown, but then told the inquest that he had seen the controversial object purporting to be a torso and that it was 'a mixture of inanimate debris from the scene'. As one of the foremost forensic pathologists in the world, Dr West's word cannot be dismissed lightly.

Perhaps inevitably there are rumours of a cover-up, designed to save the authorities from the embarrassment of having to admit that they had mistakenly thrown away some human remains. I have certainly heard anecdotal stories of pressure being placed on some of those involved to keep quiet but I have not seen any direct evidence of this. It would thus appear that even with the presence of a photograph of these alleged remains, the matter of the extra body will be irresolvable. Given the difficulties that Body 115 was presenting to the police, the thought of there having been another nameless victim of the fire is quite unsettling.

19. *Horncastle News*, 23 June; 21 July, 2004. In 2003 a researcher working on a television programme related to Body 115 claimed to have found evidence suggesting that Humberstone had been married and fathered two daughters who continued to live in the Horncastle region until at least 1995. No action was taken by the researcher to try and contact the daughters. In 2004 the British Transport Police did manage to trace Mr Humberstone's half-brother who said that he was happy for the body to remain in the Finchley cemetery.
20. *The Times*, 11 Nov. 1988
21. Fennell, *Investigation*, p.183
22. The eyewitness who described seeing the man in blue overalls had his testimony excluded when it became clear that it conflicted with the established facts. 'He was not a reliable witness,' said Fennell. Fennell, *Investigation*, pp.103–104, 221–224.

23. Fennel, *Investigation*, pp.93–114, 166–167; Institute of Mechanical Engineers, *The King's Cross Underground Fire: Fire Dynamics and the Organisation of Safety*, London, Institute of Mechanical Engineers, 1989.

24. It was estimated that in 1988 alone these improvements cost £30 million to implement with the total cost coming in at around £100 million. Together with the compensation and legal expenses, the King's Cross fire had proved to be a costly event but some of the old practices persisted. Until 2003 funding was still allocated in annual amounts making long-term planning impossible. In 1991, for example, the Tube was promised £750 million a year to cover three years' worth of improvements only to have it whipped away again the next year, creating chaos as London Underground tried to work out how it could fund expensive projects that had already begun. The funding system did not change until recently when the network was transferred into a Public Private Partnership (a form of part privatisation) whose potential merits and controversies are far beyond the scope of this book. Wolmar, C., *The Subterranean Railway*.

25. This plaque was in temporary storage at the London Transport Museum, Acton Town, while renovations were carried out at King's Cross Underground. It has since been relocated in the station's new ticket hall area.

CHAPTER 15

1. Missing persons data: 'No Longer at this Address', BBC Radio 4, June 1990. Quote: *The Times*, 30 Apr. 1990.

2. *The Times*, 30 Apr. 1990.

3. *The Times*, 8 Jan. 1986; 17 June 1987.

4. *The Times*, 30 Apr. 1991; 5 Mar. 1992.

5. 'London Tonight', 10 Nov. 1989

6. Sources: K. Wilson, personal communication; Notes from IPM Ltd; *Press and Journal* (Scotland), 29 Mar. 2005; *The Times*, 26 Jan. 2004; *The Observer*, 2 May 2004.

7. K. Wilson, personal communication.

8. 'London Tonight', 10 Nov. 1989

9. William Mills's body was eventually discovered in Skellinthrope Woods, Lincolnshire. A coroner's inquest found that he had died as a result of misadventure.

CHAPTER 16

1. 'London Tonight', 10 Nov. 1989
2. Hubert Rose's seaman's docket; TNA: PRO BT 372/1713
3. *The Times*, 9 Nov. 1989; London Tonight, 10 Nov. 1989
4. The mystery surrounding Hubert Rose was not resolved until recently when it was discovered that not only was he not involved in the fire, but that he had assumed a pseudonym under which he lived until his death (of natural causes) in 2001. British Transport Police, personal communication.
5. 'London Tonight', 10 Nov. 1989
6. Nick Lowe, 'Who Was that Man?', *Party of One*, 1990.

CHAPTER 17

1. Information from NMPH and from 'Lost from View', a report into homelessness by the University of York.
2. In 1992 an internal police report into the Missing Persons Bureau declared that it was 'so inaccurate that it should be started from scratch'. Of a sample of ninety-nine people taken from the computer database, only five were found to still be missing. An intensive ten-day search of criminal and other records accounted for the other ninety-four names. It turned out that forty-five had been arrested, while one was discovered to have been found dead the day after he had gone missing but the file had never been closed. The report questioned the computer database's reliability and recommended a complete revision of all the names on it. However, funds were tight and there were greater demands on the police's time so the reassessment of the Missing Persons Bureau was given a low priority. The Association of Chief Police Officers had been campaigning since 1988 to upgrade the Missing Persons Bureau to a national service but the government had refused to provide the necessary money. *The Times*, 5 Mar. 1992.
3. *The Times*, 15 Nov. 1993; 9 Mar. 1994.
4. *The Cromwell Street Enquiry*, Gloucestershire Police, 1995.
5. Aging software: see *The Times*, 24 Feb. 1993.
6. Letter from British Transport Police; 6 Nov. 2002.
7. TNA: PRO MT141131 (TPS 485)

8. TNA: PRO MT 141/33; *The Times*, 17 Mar. 1988; Father Jim Kennedy, personal communication.
9. Father Jim Kennedy, personal communication. I have yet to meet anyone associated with this investigation that does not have something complimentary to say about Inspector Wilkinson.
10. Letter from British Transport Police, 6 Nov. 2002.
11. Father Kennedy played a crucial role in the aftermath of the fire. As well as campaigning for better safety on the Tube, he also organised, and continues to organise, an annual non-denominational church service for those involved with or affected by the fire. He provided support to a great many of the bereaved families and remains close to many of them. Father Kennedy is highly regarded by the police for the pastoral work that he has provided and because he has been able to become involved with some of the emotional aspects of the fire that they themselves cannot.
12. *The Times*, 19 Nov. 2002.

CHAPTER 18

1. *The Scotsman*, 15 July 2003.
2. *The Times*, 14 July 2003; Robin Young, personal communication.
3. Like so many others searching for missing persons, Mr Leishman is here referring to the problem of obtaining information about their absent relations from government and other bodies. The trouble lies with the Data Protection Act which prevents agencies and commercial companies from releasing details of their clients to anyone other than a select number of organisations. This is mostly to stop data such as people's names, addresses or bank details falling into the hands of criminals or others with evil intent, but it also stops people from finding out whether a missing relation has been drawing social security benefits or pensions, etc. The Data Protection Act also applies to the police who are not routinely allowed to access government data except in exceptional cases or when the person is thought to be in a vulnerable or dangerous situation. *The Times*, 14 July 2003.
4. Coroner's inquiry transcript; 3 Feb. 2004.
5. *The Times*, 8 Mar. 1988.
6. *Daily Telegraph*, 5 Jan. 2006.
7. Letter from British Transport Police, 6 Nov. 2002.

8. *Daily Telegraph*, 29 Jan. 2004; 19 July 2005, *Times and Star* (Cumbria): 22 July 2005; 7 Dec. 2005
9. *The Times*, 14 July 2003.
10. *The Times*, 14 July 2003.
11. Robin Young, personal communication; interview given by Mary Leishman to Monika Kosicka, 4 Aug. 2003.
12. *The Times*, 20 July 2003. Most of the articles written about this affair ignore the unreliability of familial DNA testing and the legal complexities associated with exhumation; they also misunderstand the role of the coroner in exhumations.

CHAPTER 19

1. Mrs Wilson apparently gave an interview to a national Sunday newspaper in July 2003 but if so, I have been unable to trace it.
2. Recent studies of the claims made by psychic detectives does seem to cast doubt on their usefulness in crime solving. A 1994 survey of American police departments found that 72 per cent claimed never to have consulted with psychics over crimes while investigations into the claims made by individual psychics and the media to have solved crimes have revealed an extremely low success rate. It has been suggested that the reason some psychic detectives gain an unjustified reputation for success comes from their having exaggerated their own involvement in police work and the willingness of the media to report these claims. It is also thought that the vagueness of the descriptions given by psychics (e.g. 'the body is near to water', 'there are trees close by') allows so-called 'retrofitting' (i.e. at a later point making the facts of the case fit the psychic's description) to take place should the case ever be solved. Nickell, J., *Psychic Sleuths*, Buffalo, Prometheus Books, 1994; Lyons, A., and Truzzi, M., *The Blue Sense: Psychic Detectives and Crime*, New York, Mysterious Press, 1991.
3. These programmes take various formats but are all centred around a small team of psychics who use their powers to obtain information about members of a studio audience or, in some cases, objects that they own.
4. IPM archives; Craig Goldman, personal communication; Monika Kosicka, personal communication.
5. IPM archive; 'The Mystery of Body 115', first broadcast 2004.

CHAPTER 20

1. Detective Chief Superintendent Bracken is an examiner for a diploma in Forensic Human Identification.
2. Coroner's Inquiry; 3 Feb. 2004. Trendall has since been promoted to Superintendent and now works in counter-terrorism.
3. Following the Boxing Day tsunami disaster of 2004, changes were made to the procedure for declaring a person dead. With so many people missing presumed dead, the time frame for declaring a missing person dead was reduced from seven years to one.
4. Coroner's inquiry transcript, 3 Feb. 2004. British Transport Police, personal communication.
5. *The Times*, 14 July 2003.
6. See Chapter 8 for further details about the Sugita clip.
7. Coroner's inquiry transcript, 3 Feb. 2004.
8. Coroner's inquiry transcript, 3 Feb. 2004, p.12.

CHAPTER 21

1. *The Times*, 26 Jan. 2004. 'The Mystery of Body 115', broadcast 2004. Prior to the service Kathleen Wilson had an unusual encounter whose significance has not been resolved. She met a vagrant woman named Mary who claimed to have known her father and to have hung out with him in the King's Cross area. She was a petite lady in her sixties or seventies who last claimed to have seen him nine years previously (i.e. in 1993). Mary was never traced.
2. *The Times*, 26 Jan. 2004.
3. 'BBC News', 3 Feb. 2004.
4. *The Observer*, 2 May 2004
5. *The Times*, 26 Jan. 2004.
6. James Brown's fate remains unresolved although his family now accepts that he was not Body 115.
7. Coroner's inquiry transcript, 3 Feb. 2004.
8. Professor Christopher Milroy is a consultant pathologist to the Home Office and, with Detective Chief Superintendent Bracken, is an examiner for the Society of Apothecaries's Diploma in Forensic Human Identification. Milroy was used by Bracken during the Body 115 review process to help determine strategies that could move the investigation forwards.

Bibliography

Ainsworth, P.B., *Psychology, Law and Eyewitness Testimony*. Chichester, John Wiley and Sons, 1998.

Anonymous, 'Appeal for Help', *British Dental Journal*, Vol. 164, p.160, 1988.

Appleton, B., *Report of an Inquiry into Health and Safety Aspects of Stoppages caused by Fire and Bomb Alerts on London Underground, British Rail and other Mass Transit Systems*. London, HSE Books, 1992

Atkinson, J.S., *Coroner Service Model Charter*, Lincoln, North Lincolnshire Council, 2005.

Barton, J.A., *Lessons from the King's Cross Disaster*. London, Health and Safety Executive, 1989.

Bettis, R., *Fire at King's Cross Underground Station, 18th November 1987: Part 10; Burner Trials in an Inclined Inverted Channel*. London, Health and Safety Executive, 1988.

Busuttil, A., Jones, J.S.P. and Green, M.A., *Deaths in Major Disasters: The Pathologist's Role*, London: Royal College of Pathologists, 2000.

Caplan, R.M., 'How Fingerprints came into use for Personal Identification,' *Journal of the American Academy of Dermatology*, vol. 23(1), pp.109–114, 1990.

Cleland, J.B., 'Teeth and Bite-marks in History, Literature, Forensic Medicine and Otherwise.' *Australian Journal of Dentistry*, vol. 48, p.107, 1944.

Conant, E., 'Man of 1000 Faces,' *Archaeology*, pp. 48–53, Jul/Aug 2003.

Daniell, C., *Death and Burial in Medieval England, 1066–1550*, London: Routledge, 1997.

Del Maestro, R.F., 'Origin of the Drake Fenestrated Aneurysm Clip', *Journal of Neurosurgery*, vol.92, pp.1056–1064, 2000.

Dorries, C., *Coroners' Courts: A Guide to Law and Practice*, Oxford: Oxford University Press, 2004.

von Eggeling, H., 'Die Leistungsfahigkeit physiognomischer Rekon-struktionsversuche auf Grundlage des Shädels.' *Archiv für Anthropologie*, vol. 12, pp.44–47, 1913.

Faulds, H., 'On the Skin Furrows of the Hand,' *Nature*, vol. 22, p.605, 1880.

Faulds, H., *Dactylography*, Halifax, Milner and Co., 1913.

Fennell, D., *Investigation into the King's Cross Underground Fire*, London, HMSO, 1988.

Gatliff, B.P. and Snow, C.C., 'From Skull to Visage', *Journal of Biocommunications*, vol.6, pp.27–30, 1979.

Gerasimov, M.M., *The Face Finder*, London, Hutchinson, 1971.

Grew, N., 'The description and use of the pores in the skin of the hands and feet,' *Philosophical Transactions of the Royal Society*, vol 14 (159), pp. 566–7, 1684.

Griffiths, J.R., *A Microcomputer-based Data Acquisition System, for use in in-situ Trials at King's Cross Underground Station*. London, Health and Safety Executive, 1988.

Hallén, B. and Kulling, P., *The Fire at the King's Cross Underground Station, November 18, 1987*, Stockholm, Socialstyrelsen, 1990.

Harvey, W., 'Identity by Teeth and the Marking of Dentures,' *British Dental Journal*, vol. 121, p.334, 1966

Harvey, W., *Dental Identification and Forensic Odontology*, London, Henry Kimpton, 1976

Herschel, W., 'Skin Furrows of the Hand,' *Nature*, 23: p.76, 1880.

Herschel, W., *The Origin of Finger Printing*, Oxford, Oxford University Press, 1916.

Howarth, J.H., 'Post-mortem Identification of a Body by Use of Dental Evidence,' *British Dental Journal*, vol. 172(4), p.158, 1992.

Hunnisett, R.F., *The Medieval Coroner*, Cambridge, Cambridge University Press, 1961.

Institute of Mechanical Engineers, *The King's Cross Underground Fire: Fire Dynamics and the Organisation of Safety*, London, Institute of Mechanical Engineers, 1989.

Iscan, M.Y., and Helmer, R.P., *Forensic Analysis of the Skull*, New York, Wiley-Liss, 1993.

Jagger, S.F., *Fire at King's Cross Underground Station, 18th November 1987: Part 9; Fire Growth Calculations*. London, Health and Safety Executive, 1988.

Jagger, S.F., *Fire at King's Cross Underground Station, 18th November 1987: Part 13; A Preliminary Assessment of the Second Fire Growth Test on the Buxton One-third Scale Model Escalator*. London, Health and Safety Executive, 1988.

Jagger, S.F., *Fire at King's Cross Underground Station; 18th November 1987: Part 17; Further One-third Scale Fire Growth Tests*. London, Health and Safety Executive, 1989.

James, S.H., and Nordby, J.J., *Forensic Science: An Introduction to Scientific and Investigative Techniques*, New York, Taylor and Francis, 2005.

Lane, B., *The Encyclopedia of Forensic Science*, London, Headline, 1992.

Louw, D.F., Asfora, W.T. and Sutherland, G.R., 'A Brief History of Aneurysm Clips', *Neurosurgery Focus*, vol.11(2), pp.1–4, 2001.

Luntz, L. and Luntz, P., *Handbook for Dental Identification*, Philadelphia, Lippincott and Co., 1973.

Lyle, D.P., *Forensics for Dummies*, Indianapolis, John Wiley, 2004.

Lyons, A., and Truzzi, M., *The Blue Sense: Psychic Detectives and Crime*, New York, Mysterious Press, 1991

Malpighi, M., *De Externo Tactus Organs in Opera Omnia*, Lyons, Petrum Vander Aa, 1686.

Maltoni, D., Maio, D., Jain, A.K. and Prabhakar, S., *Handbook of Fingerprint Recognition*, New York, Verlag-Springer, 2003.

Melton, A.B., 'Current Trends in Removable Prosthodontics,' *Journal of the American Dental Association*, vol. 131, pp.528–568, 2000.

Moodie, K., *Fire at King's Cross Underground Station, 18th November 1987: Part 1; Damage Assessment*. London, Health and Safety Executive, 1987.

Moodie, K., *Fire at King's Cross Underground Station, 18th November 1987: Part 2; Interim Proposals for Assessment of Fire*. London, Health and Safety Executive, 1987.

Moodie, K., *Fire at King's Cross Underground Station, 18th November 1987: Part 4; Investigation Progress Report*. London, Health and Safety Executive, 1988.

Moodie, K., *Fire at King's Cross Underground Station, 18th November 1987: Part 7; Assessment of Fire Dynamics*. London, Health and Safety Executive, 1988.

Moodie, K., *Fire at King's Cross Underground Station, 18th November 1987: Part 8; Laboratory Fire Growth Tests*. London, Health and Safety Executive, 1988.

Moodie, K., *Fire at King's Cross Underground Station, 18th November 1987: Part 11; Scale Model Fire Growth Tests*. London, Health and Safety Executive, 1988.

Moodie, K., *Fire at King's Cross Underground Station, 18th November 1987: Part 12; Assessment of Fire Dynamics*. London, Health and Safety Executive, 1988.

Moodie, K., *Fire at King's Cross Underground Station, 18th November 1987: Part 14; Further Written Evidence Submitted to the Inquiry (May/July 1988)*. London, Health and Safety Executive, 1988.

Moodie, K., *Fire at King's Cross Underground Station, 18th November 1987: Part 15; 1/3rd Scale Model Tests press handout*. London, Health and Safety Executive, 1988.

Moodie, K., 'The King's Cross Fire: Damage Assessment and Overview of the Technical Investigation', *Fire Safety Journal*, vol. 18, pp.13–33, 1992.

Neave, R., 'Reconstruction of the Heads of Three Ancient Egyptian Mummies', *Journal of Audiovisual Media in Medicine*, vol. 2, pp.156–164, 1979.

Nickell, J., *Psychic Sleuths*, Buffalo, Prometheus Books, 1994.

Peipert, J.F., and Roberts, C.S., 'Wilhelm His Sr.'s Finding of Johann Sebastian Bach', *American Journal of Cardiology*, vol. 15(11), p.1002, 1986.

Phillips, V.M., 'Skeletal Remains Identification by Facial Recognition', *Forensic Science Communications*, vol. 3(1), pp.1–5, 2001.

Prag, J., and Neave, R., *Making Faces*, London, British Museum Press, 1997.

Reichs, K., *Forensic Osteology*, Springfield, Illinois, Charles C Thomas, 1986.

Simcox, S., Wilkes, N.S. and Jones, I.P., 'Computer Simulation of the Flows of Hot Gases from the Fire at King's Cross Underground Station', *Fire Safety Journal*, vol. 18, pp.49–73, 1992.

Stern, C., *Dr. Iain West's Casebook*, London, Warner, 1997.

Sugita, K., Kobayashi, S., *et al.*, 'Characteristics and use of Ultra-Long Aneurysm Clips', *Journal of Neurosurgery*, vol.60, pp.145–150, 1984.

Swift, P.K., *Fire at King's Cross Underground Station, 18th November 1987: Part 6; Temperature Measurements during Laboratory Tests on Escalator Wheels*. London, Health and Safety Executive, 1988.

Terry, C.S., *Bach: a Biography*, Oxford, Oxford University Press, 1932.

Twain, M., *Pudd'nhead Wilson*, New York, Dover Publications, 1999

Twain, M., *Life on the Mississippi*, New York, Dover Publications, 2000.

Vale, G.L., 'Forensic Odontology,' *Journal of Southern Californian Dentists' Association*, vol. 37, p.248, 1969.

Wharton, R.K., *Fire at King's Cross Underground Station, 18th November 1987: Part 3; In-situ Fire Test*. London, Health and Safety Executive, 1988.

Wolmar, C., *The Subterranean Railway: How the London Underground Was Built and How It Changed the City For Ever*, London, Atlantic Books, 2005.

Index

Compiled by Indexing Specialists (UK) Ltd.
Hove, East Sussex